Beyond Colonialism and Nationalism in the Maghrib

Beyond Colonialism and Nationalism in the Maghrib

History, Culture, and Politics

Edited by Ali Abdullatif Ahmida

palgrave

BEYOND COLONIALISM AND NATIONALISM IN THE MAGHRIB

First published 2000 by
PALGRAVE™
175 Fifth Avenue, New York, N.Y. 10010 and
Houndmills, Basingstoke, Hampshire, England RG21 6XS.
Companies and representatives throughout the world.

PALGRAVE™ is the new global publishing imprint of St. Martin's Press LLC Scholarly and Reference Division and Palgrave Publishers Ltd (formerly Macmillan Press Ltd).

ISBN 0-312-22287-4 hardback

Library of Congress Cataloging-in-Publication Data
Beyond colonialism and nationalism in the Maghrib : history, culture, and politics /
edited by Ali Abdullatif Ahmida.
p. cm.
Includes bibliographical references and index.
ISBN 0-312-22287-4 (cloth)
1. Africa, North—History—19th century—Historiography. 2. Egypt—History—19th century—Historiography. 3. Nationalism—Africa, North. 4. Nationalism—Egypt. 5. Group identity—Africa, North. 6. Group identity—Egypt. I. Ahmida, Ali Abdullatif, 1953–
DT193.95.B49 2000
961'.03'072—dc21
00-036904

A catalogue record for this book is available from the British Library.

Design by Letra Libre, Inc.

First edition: October, 2000
10 9 8 7 6 5 4 3 2 1
Printed in the United States of America.

for my parents:
Abdullatif Ahmida
and Mabruka Ali

Contents

Acknowledgments

I wish to thank my contributors for enduring multiple requests for revisions of their chapters despite, in some cases, unpredictable events such as travel and illness, and pleasant events such as marriage. I was fortunate to work with scholars from diverse disciplines who reside on three separate continents. Also, I wish to thank the editors of *The Arab Studies Quarterly* for their permission to reprint revisions of the articles by Burke, Maghraoui, Lazreg, King, and Ahmida 20:2 (Spring 1998).

A few persons have given me support, valuable criticism and suggestions. I am grateful to my St. Martin's Press editor Karen Wolny, who saw potential in my original proposal. I would like to thank Janice Beal, Jamie Hibbard, Denise Gendron, and especially Norman Beaupre for their assistance and support. Thanks to Janet Dinsmore and Rifaat Al Abou El-Haj for their comments on the original proposal and the introduction. Many thanks to Becky Goldfine, who proofread the whole manuscript and made valuable editorial suggestions.

My small family has lived with this book for two years. My wife Beth provided consistent support and encouragement despite her difficult pregnancy and even after the birth of our daughter Haneen. My daughter Haneen with her delightful spirit has been a wonderful reminder that books are not an end but are about real people and the world.

Biddeford, Maine
January 2000

Contributors

ALI ABDULLATIF AHMIDA is an associate professor of political science at the University of New England, Biddeford, Maine. He is the author of *The Making of Modern Libya: State Formation, Colonialization, and Resistance, 1830–1932,* which was a finalist for the Albert Hourani Book Award in 1995. This book was recently translated into Arabic. Currently he is working on a manuscript, "The Nation-State in the Maghrib: Rescuing History from Colonialism and Nationalism, 1879–1962."

ABDERRAHMAN AYOUB is a Fulbright Senior and former professor of Arabic and Folklore at Sorbonnes, Tripoli University, Yarmouk University, University of California Berkeley, University of Washington-Seattle, and University of California Santa Barbara. He served as Researcher at the Institut National du Patrimoine (Tunisia), Professor of Orality at University of Tunis I, and Head of l'Or du Temps publishing house. Abderrahman has written several books and papers on Arab folklore.

EDMUND BURKE III is a professor of history at the University of California at Santa Cruz. The author and editor of numerous books and articles on Middle Eastern and world history, he is currently completing *France and the Sociology of Islam* for Princeton University Press.

ELLIOT COLLA is an assistant professor of comparative literature at Brown University. The present essay comes from the work in his dissertation, "Hooked on Pharaonics."

MONA FAYAD is an associate professor of English and women's studies at Salem State College in Massachusetts. She has recently completed a book on Arab women writers and the problematics of national identity and has written a novel dealing with the Arab-American immigrant experience.

STEPHEN J. KING is an assistant professor of government at Georgetown University. He is currently completing a manuscript on the politics of structural adjustment in Tunisia.

MARNIA LAZREG is a professor of sociology and women's studies at Hunter College and The Graduate School of the City University of New York. She has published in the areas of social theory, social class, cultural movements, development, human rights, and gender.

DRISS MAGHRAOUI is a Ph.D. candidate in history at the University of California at Santa Cruz. He is currently working on his dissertation, "Soldiers without Citizenship: Collective Memory and the Culture of French Colonialism."

DAVID SEDDON is professor of development studies at the University of East Anglia, England. Over the last thirty years, he has undertaken field research and consultancy work in the Maghrib and the Sahara. Joint author of *Free Markets and Food Riots: The Politics of Global Adjustment* (Blackwell, 1994), he recently contributed an essay on the "Unequal Partnership between Europe and the Maghreb" to *Regionalism Across the North-South Divide: State Strategies and Globalization,* edited by Jean Grugal and Wil Hout (Routledge, 1999).

A Note on Transliteration

The proper names of persons and places are spelled according to the Arabic transliteration system followed by the *International Journal of Middle East Studies* with two modifications. First, no diacritical marks are used for the transliteration of the Arabic ayn and hamza. A second modification is the acceptance of French transliteration of common names and places that are widely used, such as *Bourguiba* instead of *Aburaqiba.*

Introduction

> It should be known that the differences of conditions among people are the result of different ways in which they make their living.
>
> —Ibn Khaldun, a Fourteenth Century Historian

> It is now possible for some to combine fundamental social criticism with a defense of non-modern cultures and traditions. It is possible to speak of the plurality of critical traditions and of human rationality. At long last we seem to have recognized that neither is Descartes the last word on reason, nor is Marx that on the critical spirit.
>
> —Ashis Nandy, *The Intimate Enemy: Loss and Recovery of Self under Colonialism*

Why This Book?

I first had the idea for this book in 1996 when a British historian asked me a question that shocked me. "Why are Libyans so paranoid about Italian colonialism?" he said, following a presentation I had given at the London School of Economics on the social origins of Libyan resistance to Italian colonialism. My questioner was a fellow panel member specializing in Libyan colonial history, and I asked him what he meant by "paranoid." Somalians, Ethiopians, and Eritreans had a positive view of Italian colonialism, he claimed. The period of Italian colonialism represented a modernizing stage of Libyan history despite the fact that one half of the Libyan population perished and thousands were displaced and pushed into exile. I answered that the Libyan people, like other humans oppressed by brutal settlers, had every reason to hate colonialism. That encounter combined with my generation's disillusionment with the nationalist regimes in the Maghrib led me to consider a critical examination of colonial and nationalist theories.

This collection of essays focuses on the North African countries of Morocco, Algeria, Tunisia, Libya, and Egypt. Extending from the Atlantic to the Nile Valley and including Mauritania, these countries constitute "the Maghrib," the western portion of the Arab Muslim world. They share a common natural environment, colonial legacy, Maliki Sunni Islam, and a blend of Arab, Berber, African, and European cultures. The book's concerns and scope reach much farther than the Maghrib, however. Its contributors provide a critical, cross-disciplinary examination of mainstream Eurocentric elitist scholarship, offering a range of alternative theoretical approaches to students of history, culture, and politics. Its readers should include all those interested in African, Arab, and European social history, colonialism, nationalism, and gender studies.

The Editor's Background

I was born in Waddan in central Libya but grew up in Sabha, the capital of Fezzan in southern Libya. My grandparents lived through the colonial period, and my parents witnessed its last phase as well as the birth of the Libyan state in 1951. My maternal grandfather Ali fought for ten years in the resistance against Italian colonialism and, after its defeat, lived with my grandmother Aisha as a political refugee in Northern Chad, where she died before I was born. My grandfather and mother told me their history of displacement, anguish and struggle for survival, and I lived through the independent state of the monarchy of the King Idriss al-Sanusi and the revolution of Muammar Qadhdhafi in 1969.

Without the Qadhdhafi government's populist policies, I would not have been able to study in Egypt and the United States. With the revolutionary government's support of rural high school students who competed for university scholarships, I traveled to Cairo with seven other students to study political science. There, I was educated as a political scientist at the Faculty of Economics and Political Science, a small but competitive college within Cairo University. Introduced to a cosmopolitan urban life in Cairo, I undertook a bigger journey, selecting a cosmopolitan city in the United States, Seattle, for my doctoral work in political science. At the University of Washington, where I chose to write about anticolonial resistance, state formation and Libyan social history in the twentieth century, I found myself relying more and more on elements of my family's oral history. I wanted to record their experiences and render them justice by countering racist histories of the colonial state and elitist theories of nationalism after independence.

The Impact of Colonialism and Nationalism on Maghribi Studies

Throughout the nineteenth and twentieth centuries, politics and studies of Maghrib were dominated by colonialism and nationalism, with their own categories and theories of legitimation. The reasons were obvious: Egypt was first invaded by Napoleon Bonaparte in 1789, and then by the British in 1882. France claimed Algeria in 1830, Tunisia in 1881, and Morocco in 1912. Libya fell to the Italians in 1911 and did not gain limited independence until 1951. It was not until the mid-twentieth century that nationalist movements assumed power, producing their own nationalist historiography. While Egypt gained limited independence in 1922, Tunisia and Morocco remained under colonial control until 1956. Algeria was not free of official French control until 1962.

In his survey of scholarship on the Maghrib and the Middle East, British sociologist Bryan Turner decries the poverty of the literature compared with academic studies of other Third World areas. Turner also notes that scholarship typically focuses on the uniqueness of a region, especially the roles of Islam, tribalism, sects, and national character, at the expense of such topics as social class, state formation, and the impact of the world capitalist market through either trade or the colonial state.[1]

One example of a historical-cultural approach is the classic work of H. A. R. Gibb and Harold Bowen, *Islamic Societies of the West,* which argues that Islam was a self-contained, traditional belief system and that eighteenth-century Islamic societies were in decline as a result of their prevailing beliefs. The impact of internal and external socioeconomic factors are completely ignored.[2] Similarly, the rise of "fundamentalist Islam" after the Iranian Revolution of 1979 is explained in the media by orthodox Orientalists and modernization theorists as the resurgence of an idealized, premodern religious social movement. Questions concerning why such fundamentalist movements oppose or support their respective states—i.e., in Iran, Egypt, Tunisia, Syria, and Saudi Arabia—tend to be discussed only in terms of the responses of different classes and ethnic groups in different ecological and historical settings.[3]

Failures of the Dominant Theoretical Approaches

The most influential approach to the Maghrib has been the "segmentary" theory articulated by British social anthropologists E. E. Evans-Pritchard and Ernest Gellner. The segmentary theory assumes the existence of tribal society composed of homogeneous tribal segments. In the absence of state control in precolonial Maghrib, mutually deterring tribal segments maintained order among any clans threatening to disrupt the balance of power. This static view of Maghribi societies fails to acknowledge how "tribal society" reflects other dynamic social institutions and history.[4]

In the 1950s and '60s American social scientists applied structural-functionalist concepts to studies of the Middle East, as well as to scholarship on other Asian, African, and Latin American societies. "Modernization" scholarship tended to perpetuate some of the earlier Orientalist assumptions, including emphasis on traditional religious beliefs and the mosaic of sects, tribes, and ethnic groups. Modernization literature is best characterized by *The Passing of Traditional Society: Modernization in the Middle East* by Daniel Lerner, who describes Maghribi societies as traditional and self-contained, although engaged in the process of transition to modernity. Modernization, for Lerner, is achieved as a consequence of the diffusion of American capital development assistance along with American cultural and political values to be carried out by a Westernized middle class. Lerner dismisses anticolonial nationalist movements as expressions of negative xenophobia hindering rational planning and modernization.[5]

While Lerner and others from the modernization school ignored the socioeconomic and economic impact of colonialism, they simultaneously furthered the foreign policy goals of the United States government—a focus that hampered their ability to explain why modernization did not lead to development, pluralism, and democracy.[6] The shortcomings of modernization literature became clear even to some of its own scholars when in 1976 Leonard Binder admitted that the literature was mainly descriptive and did not explain state-society relations.[7] L. Carol Brown in 1985 explained the historical context of the official American view of the Maghrib since the 1940s as based primarily in geopolitical competition with the Axis powers and the Cold War. Thus, Morocco and Tunisia were viewed as modernizing, "moderate" allies; Algeria as militant; and Libya, after the 1969 military takeover, as a hostile, pariah state.[8]

Marxist scholars such as the French Yves Lacoste and the Egyptian Ahmad Sadiq Saad, who still use the classical "Asiatic mode of production" analysis, are also guilty of Eurocentrism. The Asiatic mode of production assumes existence of a strong state and self-sufficient village communities.[9] Marx, however, not only relied on a sketchy Orientalist image of India for his understanding of Third World countries, but he seemed to abandon his dialectical method when he assumed that change came mainly from outside in the form of European capitalist colonization. Engels, in fact, hailed the French conquest of Algeria in 1830 as a victory of civilization over barbarism.[10]

The dominant scholarship on the Maghrib suffers from two major deficiencies. Eurocentric studies view Maghribi societies as unruly, segmentary, traditional, patrimonial, or Asiatic, assuming a model of sixteenth-century Western Europe is universally applicable. This reasoning ignores the diverse traditions of state formation in the region. The second deficiency, modernization theories, fail to explain social transformation and today's politics in Maghribi societies. It is notable that noncapitalist relations of production such as sharecropping, communal ownership of land, and self-sufficiency in household production persisted as late as the 1970s. Further, instead of the secularization predicted by modernization scholars, social and political Islamic movements emerged as the main oppositional forces in Egypt, Algeria, Tunisia, and, more recently, Libya and Morocco.

Despite "Westernization," contemporary Maghribi societies have not achieved industrialization, development, or a high degree of political participation. Instead, these societies face economic dependency and authoritarian regimes ruled by dynasties and the military. Such characteristics beg for a fresh explanation of the problem. Socioeconomic and historical factors such as modes of production, moral economy, social classes, state formation, and the impact of world economy suggest new avenues of explaining dependency, authoritarian regimes, and social diversity.

Moving Beyond Orthodoxy to Incorporate Socioeconomic Issues

The 1970s witnessed the growth of critiques on the work of culturalist Orientalists and modernization theorists. Authors included young liberal scholars such as Michael Hudson and Dale Eickelman but were primarily neo-Marxists. Two journals were influential in shifting the focus of scholarship: the *Review of Middle East Studies* (1975 -) published in England, and *Middle East Report* (originally *MERIP Reports*), published in the United States from the late 1970s. While the *Review of Middle Eastern Studies* was discontinued after three excellent issues, *Middle East Report* came to resemble the *Bulletin of Concerned Asian Scholars (BCAS),* which emerged in 1969 after the start of the antiwar movement in the United States. Both are independent and critical forums. The publication of Edward Said's *Orientalism* (1978) further pointed to the limits of the Orientalists' epistemology and approach to Maghribi societies.[11]

Despite Said's critique, the study of the Maghrib and the Middle East is still dominated by the Orientalism and modernization theory. Modernization theory is, in fact, resurging under the banners of neoliberalism, especially after the end of the Cold War and the collapse of the Soviet Union in 1989. Said's critique itself ignores the infrastructure and the material production of Orientalist knowledge and provides no alternative, as Sadiq al-Azm, Ijaz Ahmad, and Rifaat Abou El-Haj have pointed out.[12]

Despite the general stagnation of mainstream scholarship on the Middle East, a new trend of studies has begun to recognize socioeconomic forces in the Maghrib. Some of the best examples include Rifaat Abou El-Haj on Ottoman social history; Abdallah Laroui's review of the historiography of the Maghrib; the works of Edmund Burke III and David Seddon dealing with the impact of trade and colonial rule on local governments and rural communities in Morocco; Peter Gran, Abdellah Hammoudi, and Julia Clancy-Smith's studies of Islam, capitalism, and resistance; Marnia Lazreg's and Mahfoud Bennoune's studies of the role of women and the impact of French colonialism on Algerian society; Lucette Valensi on the Tunisian peasantry; Abdal Molla El-Horeir on the social transformation of Barqa (Eastern Libya) under the Sanusiyya; and Roger Owen's and Eric Davis' work on the incorporation of the Egyptian economy in the world capitalist system and the role of the national bourgeoisie.[13]

The contemporary Maghribi state has been going through a crisis of legitimacy and relevance. The food riots and social protests that began in Egypt in 1977 spread to the rest of the region—Morocco in 1981, 1984, and 1990–91; Tunisia in 1984, and finally Algeria in 1988. Each case reflected popular dissatisfaction with the ruling nationalist elites and an end to the era of nationalist euphoria. The challenge is not unique in that established nation states such as the United States and European countries are also facing their own crises of race, citizenship, and identity. Eric Hobsbawm and David Held, among others, point to the historical mythology of nation-state nationalism and the boundaries transcending global capitalism. The crisis of the nation-state in Maghrib suggests that Middle Eastern scholars have taken the claims of the nation-state and Arab nationalism for granted.[14]

Redefining "Nationalism"

A distinction must be made between nationalism as an ideology of resistance and liberation from colonial oppression, and the ideology of state nationalism that emerged in the 1960s and excluded women, Islamists, leftists, liberals, and independent associations. It should also be noted that modern social science developed at a point in history during which Europe dominated the world, including the Maghrib.[15] Thus, it is inevitable that Western social science reflects European choices of subject, categories, and epistemology. A Maghribi nationalist historiography may challenge French, Spanish, Italian, and British colonialism but accept the pattern set by colonial scholars such as definitions of the Maghrib, historical periods, the definition of modernization, the model of the nation-state, and the idea of progress.

The very definition of Maghrib illustrates the pattern set by French colonialists, who redefined the larger Muslim Maghrib to include only former French colonies of Algeria, Tunisia, and Morocco. A careful reassessment of regional unity requires a broader analysis of political traditions—i.e., the Muslim world of Maghrib stretches from Western Egypt to the Atlantic and to the Sahara frontiers of Bilad al-Sudan.[16] In this book, Egypt is included as part of the Maghrib for several reasons: it is located in North Africa; its capital is Cairo, where al-Azhar University was founded by a Maghribi dynasty (the Fatimid); and thousands of Maghribi immigrants settled in Egypt and contributed to its development.[17]

While researching Libyan social history between 1830 and 1932, I discovered two alternative trends to nationalism. The first was the ability of regional tribes and states to oppose the power of the central state in Tripoli derived from both their distance from the central government and their strong socioeconomic ties with regional markets and neighboring tribes in other countries. Prior to the colonial conquest in 1911, strict borders were nonexistent, encouraging local ties to more than one state. The tribes of western Tripolitania and southern Tunisia had strong confederations and were linked with the larger Muslim community of the Maghrib and the Sahara. For example, the state of Awlad Muhammad in Fezzan (1551–1812) was not only linked to the Lake Chad region for trade and the recruitment of soldiers but also formed a strategic refuge from the Ottoman state in time of war. Equally important were strong socioeconomic relationships between the tribes of Barqa and western Egypt. Barqawi tribes viewed western Egyptian cities and desert as sanctuaries from wars and markets for agricultural products. The rise of the Sanusiyya with its pan-Islamic ideology between 1842 and 1932 deepened these ties.

The question of whether there was cooperation among Maghribi nationalist movements is still undetermined. To discover alternative historical possibilities requires looking beyond the contemporary nationalist state and its linear view of the past. One of the most promising approaches is provided by Ibn Khaldun's fourteenth-century interpretation of the role of moral and political economies. This approach calls for analyzing the relationship of ecology, production and the land tenure system to legal, political and social structures. E. P. Thompson's approach in *The Making of the English Working Class* to class as a political and cultural formation provides a useful way of understanding the links between the labor process, culture, and ideology. Thompson's powerful analysis shows how English workers in the nineteenth-century used traditional institutions and culture to resist the pressure of the capitalist market. The larger world political economy in the Wallerstinian sense, especially as revised by Eric Wolf and Janet Abu-Lughod, is important in describing how local forces must be seen as the real agents of change.[18]

Finally, the theories of Benedict Anderson and Eric Hobsbawm's on nationalism are helpful in understanding its formation. Anderson's view of nationalism as imagined political communities is brilliant, but his analysis ignores what Hobsbawm calls the mythologies, contradictions, and conflict associated with producing nationalism. Peasants and tribesmen vigorously resisted efforts to make them nationalist citizens of a nation-state. Further, as Partha Chatterjee points out, Anderson does not define the content of his imagined communities.[19]

The Authors

The contributors to this book explore the ambiguities, failures, and silences of traditional colonial and nationalist scholarship. Together, they provide critical overviews of the dominant academic and nationalist scholarship and writings on colonialism and nationalism, and they present alternative approaches to understanding the history and culture of the Maghrib during the nineteenth and twentieth centuries. They represent a wide range of disciplines and perspectives—political science, history, folklore, anthropology, comparative literature, gender studies, and sociology—but share a common perspective of Maghribi societies, not as footnotes to Europe and capitalism but as states operating within unique dynamics.

Edmund Burke III examines colonial and nationalist historiographies, arguing that colonial historiography reflects the values, culture, and mentality of European colonial society, and hence its goal is to legitimize colonialism. Nationalist historiography, while speaking in the name of the people, has privileged the urban elite perspective, leaving rural populations, women, and ethnic minorities in the shadows.

Abderrahman Ayoub investigates the status of Arab folklore today. Theoretically, he says, the Arab folklorist's field of inquiry covers the entire Arab world, but in practice the folklorist usually works under severe local political restrictions set by nationalist regimes which demand a pro-state interpretation of Arabic traditions and folklore. The past has to be invented to justify the official nationalist-state ideology.

Driss Maghraoui focuses on the Moroccan *goums* soldiers who fought in the French army. He explores through oral memories the voices of these soldiers, who were ignored by nationalist historians or dismissed as collaborators.

Ali Abdullatif Ahmida analyzes the trilogy of the Libyan writer, Ahmad Ibrahim al-Faqih, focusing on the themes of identity, cultural encounter, and alienation. His essay offers a critique of current scholarship on Libya, which is preoccupied with Muammar Qadhdhafi and ignores Libyan society and culture.

Mona Fayad addresses the gender-oriented nationalism of two well-known Maghribi feminists: the Algerian novelist and filmmaker Assia Djabar and Moroccan sociologist Ftima Mernissi, who advocate a postcolonial view of identity that introduces the notion of ambivalence. Both Djabar and Mernissi point out the gaps in traditional narratives and rewrite history to include women, a process of building a postcolonial female subject that embraces the complexities of inescapably hybrid identities.

Elliott Colla brings readers a different focus on history, cinema and the Egyptian nation-state by reinterpreting the famous film *al-Mumiya* by the late brilliant Egyptian film maker Shadi Abd al-Salam. Colla contends the film is usually seen as a simple allegory, the story of national resistance to colonial dispersion of ancient artifacts and an enlightened bureaucracy struggling to cultivate modern values among rural peoples. A closer look reveals a far more ambivalent account. The narration of the triumph of the nation-state is presented in an estranged, melancholy fashion, suggesting the incompleteness of nationalist discourse in the wake of Egypt's 1967 defeat.

Marnia Lazreg challenges the ideology and role of Islamic movement in Algeria's current civil war, arguing that the Islamic movement tries to impose a new hegemony through a mode of cultural recolonization that thrives on nihilism and blatant disregard for human life.

Stephen J. King argues that during the rapid economic liberalization from 1986 until today, Tunisia's hegemonic party abandoned its representation of a broad segment of society and became a vehicle for representing the rural bourgeoisie and urban manufacturers, many of whom had been rural notables. Increased global economy has led to constraints on the state's autonomy and contributed to the emergence of the Tunisian Islamic movement, the strongest organized resistance to the hegemonic party.

David Seddon examines the visions and realities of attempts to build a pan-Maghribi union. He argues that the struggle for national development and continued domination of the political economies by Europe have effectively combined to inhibit a process of integrated regional development in the postcolonial Maghrib. The chapter concentrates on the implications of enforced liberalization for the region and its subordination to the European Community's ambitious program for European hegemony over a Euro-Mediterranean Free Trade Area.

My own research on the social history of colonialism and nationalism in modern Libya has led to three major findings. First, colonialism has had a major impact not only on the Maghrib but on France, England, Italy, and Spain. As Edward Said has pointed out, imperialism connects and shapes the cultures of both colonizers and colonized societies.[20] In addition, history, culture, and politics form part of a process that involves the entire society, not just the ruling institutions.

Second, before the nation-state was established, social groups and tribal peoples in the Maghrib acted in their own self-interest when forming alliances with or resisting the Ottomans, the Alawi states of the Maghrib, or colonial rulers. A nationalist historiography redefined this self-interest to dichotomies of collaboration, treason, or heroism.

Finally, while written records of the colonial and nationalist states are important sources of information, scholars should keep in mind the fact that they reflect the racism of the colonial state and the elitism of the nationalist state. These sources are silent about key events and groups. To gain a comprehensive understanding of a region, scholars must listen to the voices of peasants, tribesmen, minorities, women, and unpopular elites as well as the voices to be found in alternative literature, films, oral traditions, music, songs, and poetry.

Notes

1. Bryan S. Turner, *Marx and the End of Orientalism* (London: George Allen and Unwin, 1978), pp. 6–7.
2. For a classical critique of this type of orientalism, see Edward W. Said, *Orientalism* (New York: Vintage Books, 1979). For a critique of H. A. R. Gibb and Harold Bowen's *Islamic Society and the West,* see Roger Owen, "The Middle East in Eighteenth Century: An Islamic Society in Decline," *Review of Middle East Studies* 1 (1975): 101–112. For a critique of Eurocentrism and the colonial model, see Samir Amin, *Eurocentrism* (New York: Monthly Review Press, 1989); J. M. Blaut, *The Colonizer Model of the World* (New York: The Guilford Press,1993); and Ashis Nandy, *The Intimate Enemy: Loss and Recovery of Self under Colonialism* (New Delhi: Oxford University Press, 1983).
3. See Edward W. Said, *Covering Islam* (London: Routledge and Kegan Paul, 1981); Michael Gilsenan, *Recognizing Islam* (New York: Pantheon Books, 1982); and Sami Zubaida, *Islam, The People and The State* (London: Routledge, 1989). See also an excellent review by the late Egyptian anthropologist Abdul Hamid el-Zien, "Beyond Ideology and Theology: The Search For the Anthropology of Islam," *Annual Review of Anthropology* (1977): 227–254, and Marnia Lazreg's critique of some Western idealist and ethnocentric feminist studies of gender in the Middle East and North Africa, "Feminism and Difference: The Perils of Writing as a Woman on Women in Algeria," *Feminist Studies* 14, 81–107 (Spring 1988).
4. For the classical formulation of the segmentary model, see E. E. Evans-Prichard, *The Sanusi of Cyrenaica* (Oxford: Clarendon Press, 1949), pp. 59–60. The most prominent advocate of this model is the late Ernest Gellner in his *Saints of the Atlas* (Chicago: University of Chicago Press, 1969), pp. 35–70. For the application of this model in political science, see John Waterbury, *The Commander of the Faithful* (New York: Columbia University Press, 1970). For a summary of the major critiques of the segmentary model see David Seddon, "Economic Anthropology or Political Economy: Approaches to the Analysis of Pre-Capitalist Formation in the Maghrib," in

John Calmer, ed., *The New Economic Anthropology* (London: Macmillan Press, 1978). For a critique of the field of anthropology's use of kinship, see David Schneider, *A Critique of the Concept of Kinship* (Ann Arbor: University of Michigan Press, 1984).

5. Daniel Lerner, *The Passing of Traditional Society: Modernizing the Middle East* (New York: Free Press, 1958), pp. 76–101. Also see Manfred Halpern, *The Politics of Social Change in the Middle East and North Africa* (Princeton, NJ: Princeton University Press, 1963), pp. 51–78, and Monroe Berger, "The Middle Class in the Arab World," in *The Middle East in Transition* (New York: Praeger, 1958).
6. For a critique of Lerner's book, see Irene L. Gendzier, "Notes Towards a Reading of the Passing of Traditional Society," *Review of Middle East Studies* 5 (1978): 32–47. On the influence of government policy on some Middle Eastern specialists, see Peter Johnson and Judith Tucker, "Middle East Studies Network in the United States," *MERIP Reports* 5 (1975), and Lisa Hajjar and Steve Niva, "(Re)Made in the USA: Middle East Studies in Global Era," *Middle East Report* (October-December, 1997). See my review, "Colonialism, State Formation and Civil Society in North Africa: Theoretical and Analytical Problems," *International Journal of Islamic and Arabic Studies,* xii (1994).
7. See the essays by Binder and Zartman in Leonard Binder, ed., *The Study of the Middle East* (New York: Wiley Press, 1976).
8. L. Carl Brown, "U.S.-Maghribi Relations: Model or Muddle?" in Halim Barakat, ed., *Contemporary North Africa: Issues of Development and Integration* (Washington, D.C.: Georgetown University Center for Contemporary Arab Studies, 1985), pp. 38–39.
9. Yves Lacoste, "General Characteristics and Fundamental Structure of Medieval North Africa," in *Economy and Society* 3:1 (1974): 10–11, and Ahmad Sadiq Saad, *Tarikh Misr al-Ijtimai wa al-Iqtisadi, fi dawu al Mamat al-Asyawi lil Intaj* [Egypt's Social and Economic History in light of the Asiatic Mode of Production] (Beirut: Dar Ibn Khaldun, 1979).
10. See Karl Marx, "The Future of the British Rule in India," and Friedrich Engels, "Algeria," in Karl Marx and Friedrich Engels, *On Colonialism* (New York: International Publishers, 1972), pp. 81–87, 156–61. See Immanuel Wallerstein, "Eurocentrism and its Avatars: The Dilemma of Social Science," *New Left Review* 226 (November-December, 2–9, 1997) and William A. Green "Periodization in European and World History," *Journal of World History* 3:1 (Spring 1992): 13–53.
11. Michael C. Hidson, *Arab Politics* (New Haven: Yale University Press, 1927); and Dale Eickelman, *The Middle East: An Anthropological Approach* (Englewood Cliffs, NJ: Prentice Hall, 1981). See also a fine collection of essays in Hisham Sharabi, ed., *Theory, Politics, and the Arab World* (New York: Routledge, 1990).
12. Sadiq Jalal al-Azm, "Orientalism and Orientalism in Reverse," *Race and Class* (Autumn 1985); Aijaz Ahmad, *In Theory: Classes, Nations, Literatures*

(New York: Verso, 1992), pp. 183–85; and Rifaat Ali Abou El-Haj, "Preface" to the Arabic translation of Ali Abdullatif Ahmida, *The Making of Modern Libya, State Formation, Colonialization and Resistance, 1830–1932* (Beirut: Center for Arab Unity Studies, 1995), pp. 11–16.

13. Aside from a common critical focus on socioeconomic issues, there are many methodological differences among the following scholars: Rifaat Ali Abou El-Haj, *Formation of the Modern State* (Albany: State University of New York Press, 1991), and "The Social Uses of the Past," *International Journal of Middle East Studies* 14:2 (1982): 185–201; Abdallah Laroui, *The History of the Maghrib* (Princeton, NJ: Princeton University Press, 1977); Edmund Burke III, *Prelude to Protectorate in Morocco: The Pre-Colonial Protest and Resistance 1860–1912* (Kent, England: Dawson, 1981); David Seddon, *Moroccan Peasants: A Century of Change in the Eastern Rif 1879–1970* (Kent, England: Dawson, 1981); Talal Asad, *Genealogies of Religion* (Baltimore, MD: John Hopkins University Press, 1993); Peter Gran, *Islamic Roots of Capitalism* (Austin: Texas University Press, 1977); Abdellah Hammoudi, *The Victim and Its Masks* (Chicago: Chicago University Press, 1993); Julia Clancy-Smith, *Rebel and Saint: Muslim Notables, Populist Protest, Colonial Encounter* (Berkeley: University of California Press,1996); Marnia Lazreg, *The Emergence of Classes in Algeria* (Boulder, CO: Westview Press, 1976); Mahfoud Bennoune, "Socioeconomic-Economic Changes in Rural Algeria: 1983–1945, "A Diachronic Analysis of Peasantry Under Colonialism," *Peasant News Letter* 5 (Jan.-Oct. 1975): 11–117, and "The Origins of the Algerian Proletariat," *Dialectical Anthropology* 1 (May 1976): 201–224; Lucette Valensi, *Tunisian Peasants in the Eighteenth and Nineteenth Centuries* (Cambridge: Cambridge University Press, 1985); Abdalmolla S. El-Horier, "Social and Economic Transformation in the Libyan Hinterlands During the Second Half of the Nineteenth Century: The Role of Sayyid Ahmad al-Sharif al-Sanusi," Ph.D. dissertation, UCLA, 1981; Roger Owen, *The Middle East in the World Economy 1800–1914* (London: Methuen, 1981); and Eric Davis, *Challenging Colonialism: Bank Misr and Egyptian Industrialization, 1921–1941* (Princeton, NJ: Princeton University Press, 1953).
14. Eric Hobsbawm, *Nations and Nationalism Since 1780* (Cambridge: Cambridge University Press, 1990) and David Held, "The Decline of the Nation State" in Geof Eley and Ronald Grigor Suny, eds. *Becoming National: A Reader* (Oxford: Oxford University Press, 1996) p. 407–17.
15. Abdelkader Zghal, "Marxist and Weberian Intellectual Traditions and the Social Structures of the Middle East," *International Review of Modern Sociology* 12 (Jan.-June 1982): 15–38, and Abdelkebir Khatibi "Double Criticism: The Decolonization of Arab Sociology," in Halim Barakat, ibid., 9–19.
16. Maghali Morsy, "Maghribi Unity in the Context of the Nation State: A Historian's Point of View," *Maghrib Review* 8:3–4 (1983): 70–76 and John Dunn ed., *Contemporary Crisis of the Nation State?* (London: Blackwell, 1995).

17. For a broad review of the Maghrib see, Maghali Morsy, *North Africa: From the Nile Valley to the Atlantic* (London: Longman, 1987). The Egyptian historian Abdalrahim Abdulrahman Abdalrahim has published three books of documents on the role of al Magharibah or Maghribi in Egyptian society between the sixteenth and nineteenth centuries. Abdalrahim's documentary evidence shows that Maghribi immigrants were the largest community in Egypt and made one third of the population of the city of Alexandria.
18. See Immanuel Wallerstein, *Historical Capitalism* (London: Verso,1983); Janet Abu-Lughod, *Before European Hegemony* (Oxford: Oxford University Press, 1989); and Eric Wolf, *Europe and the People Without History* (Berkeley: University of California Press, 1982).
19. Benedict Anderson, *Imagined Communities* (London: Verso, 1983); Partha Chatterjee, *Nationalist Thought and the Colonial World* (London: Zed Press, 1986).
20. Edward. W. Said, *Culture and Imperialism* (New York: Vintage Books, 1993), and Immanuel Wallerstein, "Open the Social Sciences," *Items: Social Science Research Council* 50:1 (March 1996): 1–7. Also see Eric Wolf, *Europe and the People Without History.*

Part I

Historiography

Chapter 1

Theorizing the Histories of Colonialism and Nationalism in the Arab Maghrib

Edmund Burke III

The Maghrib and Middle Eastern History

The field of Maghrib studies has always been marginal to the American academy—not quite African, not quite Arab, not quite European, the Maghrib inhabits a space between the essentialisms evoked by each. For Africans (and Africanists), North Africans were slavers and proto-imperialists whose historical experiences diverged from those of sub-Saharan Africa. As constituted in the United States, African studies has tended to see its terrain as Africa south of the Sahara, "black Africa" as opposed to "white Africa" (thereby mindlessly replicating colonial racisms). While Africa specialists are fully aware of the historical links between the two, such as the trans-Saharan gold trade, Islam, and Arabic culture, the field often proceeds as if the North were another world.

Although two thirds of all Arabs live in northern Africa (Egypt and the Arab Maghrib are each one third), Maghribis have long been regarded by American Arabists as "not quite real Arabs," spoiled by colonization and the *mission civilisatrice.* Mashriqi Arabs, confident of their historic primacy and cultural superiority, regard Maghribi Arabic as incomprehensible, Maghribi intellectuals *par trop francisé,* and Maghribi history as inalterably other (forgetting a common Ottoman and Islamic past). Those who study the Mashriq in the United States have tended to absorb these prejudices, often without thinking. As a result, "the Arab world" studied in the United States remains a field seriously out of kilter, shorn of one third of its inhabitants, an essentialized rump of a much larger and more diverse reality.

As a result, a comparative historical approach to the Arab world has been slow to emerge.[1]

Finally, despite 132 years of French colonization (or indeed because of it), French historians see Algeria's history as occurring off-stage rather than as an inalterable part of the history of the French hexagon. Added to this is the way in which the histories of imperial rule have tended to map on to the division of labor of colonial scholarship in Middle East Studies. Eastern Arabs (some of them, anyway) had Britain as their colonial tutor, and thus their colonial records are readily accessible to anglophone scholars. Western Arabs, on the other hand, were ruled by France (as well as Spain and Italy), thereby interposing a further screen over their colonial pasts for the linguistically challenged. British colonialism is a big subject in the United States (itself a former British colonial possession), while French colonialism is not. As a result, serious historians of colonialism in the Maghrib have worked mostly in the shadows, and histories of the colonial Middle East take the British experience as normative while largely ignoring French (and also Spanish and Italian) colonialism.

As a result of its multiple marginality, the Maghrib has been something of an intellectual cul-de-sac in the American Middle East field: professional journals and academic conferences largely ignore it, while books on North Africa go mostly unreviewed.[2] As the history of colonialism and nationalism recedes into the past, however, the marginality of the Maghrib seems increasingly less at issue. For the first time it is possible to imagine North Africa not in terms of what it is not (African, Arab, French), but rather as a site from which to interrogate the dichotomous forms of identity and historical understanding that derive from the history of modernity.

Today, in a different historical moment (that of the "posts-"—colonial, modern, Cold War, Gulf War, structuralist), these "lacks" appear in a different guise as marks of hybridity, alterity, and liminality, and as sites of resistance and contestation. The colonial past of Arab North Africa appears as increasingly fresh and relevant to increasing numbers of scholars from outside of the traditional field of North African studies, a key terrain in which colonial culture can be apprehended.[3] Feminist theory, cultural studies, minority studies, postcolonial studies, the influence of the Subaltern Studies group of Indian historians, and new ways of conceptualizing Europe as a dynamic multicultural arena (rather than a series of hermetically sealed essentialisms) have combined to bring histories of colonialism back onto the academic agenda.[4]

The essay that follows takes the form of a series of reflections on the changing meanings connected to writing colonial and nationalist histories of Arab North Africa, then and now. It also establishes why rethinking colonial histories now may be an urgent task.[5] What did it mean to write colonial history in the time of colonialism? What does it mean now? What did it mean to write nationalist histories in the period of the independence movements? What does it mean now? The arrow of time arcs in the sky, always receding to an ever-distant point of origin, while we in the eternal present continually recalibrate its course as our angle of vision changes.

Colonialism as History

What did colonial histories of the Maghrib mean in their own time? Emanations of a particular moment of time and a particular perspective (European confidence in its own material power and moral superiority as well as its racial arrogance and blindness), colonial histories inscribed the European colonial project: how Europe brought progress to North African societies, rescuing them from the dark night of superstition and ignorance. On this, both Marx and Tocqueville were agreed: the French role in Algeria was to bring civilization and progress. From this angle, Algerian resistance could be painted as futile and indeed antiprogressive, and atrocities (like the massacre of 500 to 1,000 Oulad Riah in 1845) depicted as deplorable but necessary mistakes. Tocqueville cuts through the moralism: "Once we have committed that great *violence* of conquest, I believe we must not shrink from the smaller violences that are absolutely necessary to consolidate it."[6] Inspired by the industrial and democratic revolutions (in unequal proportions, it is true), France saw itself as situated on the crest of the breaking wave of the future, endowed with the capacity to remake nature and reshape societies at will. Through the application of new social and political prophylactics (education, medicine, secular belief in progress), the colonial state would educate and remold local societies in the path of progress (and away from superstition and backwardness).[7] At the same time, guided and encouraged by the colonial state, the opening of the local economy to the market would unleash resources previously frozen by the dead hand of custom, as they had done in Europe itself.

What kind of colonial history of North Africa did this yield in practice? Primarily it led to histories that celebrated the French military conquest and the bringing of French civilization to Algeria, Tunisia and Morocco. In the major volumes of the *Exploration Scientifique de l'Algerie,* Algeria was depicted as culturally retarded, politically corrupt, and economically backward.[8] Above all, its central flaw was seen to be the way in which Islam weighed down upon the society like a leaden mantle, stifling initiative and blocking change. For the most part, the pieties of the colonial vulgate (the composite set of racist stereotypes about colonial North Africa), rather than a more culturally attuned historical judgment, tended to dominate French historical writings. According to the terms of the colonial vulgate, Maghribi society was irremediably backward; its political leaders were despots, and the Ulama were a superstitious bunch of fanatics. (Tocqueville on Islam: "I must say that I emerged convinced that there are in the entire world few religions with such morbid consequences as that of Mohammed. To me it is the primary cause of the now visible decadence of the Islamic world.")[9] The Vulgate came to its fullest development in Morocco, where it divided the Moroccan population into opposites: Arabs and Berbers, nomads and sedentaries, those who accepted the authority of the government (known in Morocco as *makhzan* tribes), and those who opposed it (known as *siba* tribes).[10] Spanish and Italian colonial history were governed by a similar set of stereotypes. In part, colonial history was a product of its sources (which privileged European over Arabic sources), but even more it was the manifestation of a particular time and a particular view of the world. Most French wrote the history of North Africa from a basically liberal and metropolitan-based perspective. (A French Algerian historiography based upon the perspective of the settlers never seems to have developed, unlike the other settler colonies of Ireland, South Africa, and Israel, where it did).[11] While there were French historians critical of aspects of the colonial project in North Africa, their voices were muted. In retrospect, it is striking how historians of the colonial Maghrib as different as Julien, Ageron, Berque, and Montagne all accepted the basic legitimacy of the colonial system, even though they might have opposed certain of its features.

Thus far, we are on the familiar terrain of Edward Said's *Orientalism.*[12] The resulting intellectual division of labor laid out a historiographical landscape marked by a series of binary categories (themselves derivative of the orientalist gaze): colonizer/colonized, European/non-European, male/female, colonialist/nationalist, and collaborator/resister. More recently, theorists of postcoloniality like Nicholas Dirks and Gyan Prakash have taught us to see colonial histories as important not for their truth value but for the insight they afford us into the culture of colonialism.[13] A species of discourse whose premises we cannot share, and whose thought-worlds are no longer fully accessible to us, "the colonial" appears to us (with the advantage of hindsight) as a space saturated with hegemony, Europe's other. As a consequence, these theorists argue, we tend to see colonial histories as taking place in a space that is separate from that in which European history occurs. Accordingly, colonial histories appear as derivative histories rather than shaped by the same world historical processes as modern Europe. In this "sleeping beauty" theory of modern history, agency resides alone with Europe, while the non-West is seen as without history, fatally blocked from change because of its alleged cultural defects (e.g., Islamic obscurantism, oriental despotism, the Asian mode of production) until it is awakened from millennial slumber by the kiss of the West. According to European colonial narratives, it is the dynamism of Europe that alone can bring life to the non-West.[14]

It is here that we touch the heart of colonial history: its sense of itself as invested with a vital progressive mission, and of its adversaries as misguided or perverse. That is to say, colonial historians saw colonialism as a progressive force and therefore one endowed with legitimacy. This is abundantly clear in reading Tocqueville and Marx on Algeria. To raise the question of the legitimacy of colonialism is to invoke the gulf that separates our age from the age of empire. What did it mean to write colonial history under colonialism? The answer is clear (even if we regard it as perverse from our contemporary vantage point). Just as colonialism claimed to bring progress to non-Western societies, so too colonial historians saw themselves as participating in a great progressive enterprise, namely, the introduction of the world's peoples into history (or, more forthrightly, their annexation to the progressive history of an expanding Europe). It is precisely the progressive character of colonialism that is contested by nationalist histories—the struggle between them was first and foremost a discursive one. Eventually, these Manichean colonial histories were canceled by their opposite—nationalist histories, which revalorized as strength what the colonial histories had perceived as lack.[15] Differing on everything else, colonial and nationalist histories resembled each other nonetheless in that they were in effect their own justifications—just-so stories designed to point to a moral.[16]

Writing colonial history has been a politically and intellectually problematic exercise since the emergence of nationalism after World War I. It has been especially so for North Africa, whose colonial legacy is etched in fire and blood in the collective memories of its inhabitants. Perhaps as many as 3 million Algerians and 1 million Libyans (and lesser but still horrifying numbers of Tunisians and Moroccans) perished as a result of the colonial conquest. The violence and cultural hubris of European colonialism called forth its violent negation in the national liberation movements of the 1950s in which many more were killed. Following Algerian independence in 1962, one million Europeans (and virtually all its Jewish population) departed. Not surprisingly, soon thereafter colonial history also went into abeyance. It had no further reason for being.

Before proceeding on to the next section, it may be appropriate at this point to attempt a preliminary verdict. The colonial history of the Maghrib, because it reflected the values, culture, and mentality of European colonial society, provides but a partial introduction to the colonial experience of North Africans. Often willfully ignorant of the realities they comment upon, colonial histories are expressions of the society that created them. It would be pointless to expect them to be anything else. An expression of a particular historical epoch, their principle function was to provide legitimacy for the French colonial venture by inscribing it as invested with a world historic progressive mission. This ideological mission, however, came into crisis following World War I, when with the emergence of nationalism the evident human costs for North Africans began to call into question the colonial venture. Nationalist historiography, to which we turn next, constituted in many ways the antidote to colonial histories. Following a discussion of nationalist historiography, I'll return to the question of whether it is possible to write colonial histories today and, if so, what its importance might be.

Nationalism: Colonialism's Other

After World War I, it became increasingly difficult for France to sustain its hegemony over North Africa. The evident contradictions of the colonial system, in which rights and privileges enjoyed by Europeans were systematically withheld from the subject populations, gradually undermined it. By the 1930s and 1940s, a distinctive nationalist historiography had begun to take shape that challenged the assertions of the colonial vulgate. For their part, European colonial historians viewed the nationalist "writing back" as at best ungrateful, if not traitorous. In the history wars that followed, the stakes (political and intellectual) were high. With the passage of time we can now see that it was the legitimacy of the colonial system that was being challenged. In an attempt to frame the accomplishments, as well as the limits of nationalist history, I ask: what kind of history did nationalists write, and how did it differ from colonial versions of that history?

With the emergence of powerful nationalist movements in the Maghrib in the 1950s and 1960s and the approach of colonial endgame, the history wars intensified. The struggle over the colonial past of North Africa reached a bitter and acrimonious conclusion in the Algerian revolution. Works like Alal al-Fasi's *Independence Movements of Arab North Africa,* Mohamed Lacharef's *Algérie: nation et histoire,* and Habib Bourguiba's *La Tunisie et la France* rejected point for point the assertions of the colonial historians and presented colonialism as seen from the native's point of view.[17] If, for the French colonial writers, France was the bearer of progress and resisters were coded as obscurantist reactionaries, nationalists told the opposite story, in which the French appeared as oppressors and Algerians as noble defenders of their way of life and cultural patrimony. In Alal al-Fasi's classic Moroccan nationalist history, we encounter a Morocco cruelly overwhelmed by a dynamic imperialist West—until the advent of the Istiqlal Party.[18] Al-Fasi provides the rural populations and subaltern classes with only cameo roles, and defines imperialism primarily in political rather than economic terms. Similarly, Mostafa Lacheraf's colonial Algeria is the reversed image of the Algeria of the French colonial historians, with negatives revalorized as positive.[19] (For Mubarak al-Mili, an early Algerian nationalist, the aims of a nationalist history were clear:

"National history is the mirror of the past and the ladder by which one rises to the present. It is the proof of the existence of the people, the book in which their power is written, the place for the resurrection of consciousness, the way to their union, the springboard for their progress."[20] Libyan history works much the same way: compare Enrico de Leone's *La Colonizzatione del Africa del Nord* with its image of a benevolent Italian colonialism whose mission was to bring progress to a benighted Libya, and Ruth First's nationalist version, which serves as an appropriate antidote.[21]

The Algerian war for independence is one of the places in the Third World where these nationalist histories cohered for a time into a self-conscious project: the decolonization of history.[22] This self-consciously nationalist project sought to devise a basis for factoring the colonial presence out of the Algerian past. Fanon's *Wretched of the Earth* underscores the revolutionary vision implicit in much nationalist writing of the period.[23] Elsewhere in the Maghrib, the early independence period saw the development of national historical schools that emphasized the continuities between pre- and postcolonial histories, the better to underscore the extent to which colonialism constituted a disruption. They emphasized the violence of the colonial conquest, the illegitimate appropriation of resources by Europeans, and the impact of the colonial system upon the standard of living of the indigenous population.[24] Despite its considerable achievements in redressing the distorted portrait of Maghribi society, much of this nationalist history was as devoid of complexity as the colonial histories it replaced. Indeed, one could assert, its chief function was to inculcate in the (presumably citizen) reader a sense of veneration for the common past of the people and its struggles: history as civics lesson.

Like the colonial histories they replaced, nationalist histories were progressive narratives; their existence presupposes the sequence precolonial, colonial, postcolonial (and thus the built-in obsolescence of the colonialist narrative). While they claimed to speak in the name of the people, most nationalist histories of the period in fact privileged urban elite perspectives and left the rural populations, women, and ethnic minorities in the shadows. By definition they had no room for the history of European settler populations. Whereas European colonial historians viewed the precolonial past as a time of barbary (in the primary as well as the secondary senses), for nationalists it was an unspoiled Eden to which they longed to return. (Had the imperialists not intervened, some went on to say, they too would have modernized and developed). Both colonial and nationalist histories present a homogenized and essentialized vision of both Self and Other: "Europe" or "the settler" versus "Islam" or "the native."

In order to historicize the transition from colonialism to nationalism more fully, however, we need to situate it against the background of the discursive transformation brought about by the European enlightenment, which undermined the belief that the *ancien regime* order of things was sustained and justified by religion. This "disenchantment of the world" (as Max Weber called it) removed the blinders from men's eyes, permitting them to see for the first time that human beings make their own history according to processes that can be known.[25] Europeans presented themselves to colonial peoples (as they did to their fellow citizens) as the bearers of science, rationality, and progress and the enemies of religion, superstition, and backwardness. The image of colonialism as a progressive project was widely persuasive in its time, not only to the great majority of Europeans but also to many colonial subjects.[26] We can take the metaphor of disenchantment further, however. To believe that Europe was the source of all agency can be seen as itself a form of enchantment, a mystification. What nationalism offered was thus a second "disenchantment," which revealed colonialism for the racist swindle it had always (in part) been.

At this point it is clear that colonial and nationalist histories are greatly imbricated. It remains to be seen how much. In fact both derive from post-Enlightenment thought in which they appear as the successive stages of a world historical narrative—the march of freedom from the French revolution to the present. Already present from the outset, these stages describe the way in which Europeans naturalized the colonial situation. By dividing the world into Europe and the rest, this narrative provided an explanation and justification for non-European "backwardness." History originates in the West and then is brought to the non-West in the form of colonialism. (Even Marx saw the historic role of Britain in India as progressive—the export of the dialectic to India and thus the introduction of change to a hitherto static society).[27] The 1970s dependency narratives of Samir Amin and Andre Gunder Frank, while they moved the terrain from politics to the economy, were based upon the same underlying logic, according to which the non-West existed in a separate and parallel historical space until it was brutally integrated into world history by European imperialism in a subordinate position in the new global division of labor. Dependency theorists, however, wrote from a different historical moment, the 1970s, and sought to explain how and why the fruits of independence failed to appear once colonialism ended.[28]

In the rest of this essay, I'll consider some of the difficulties of the nationalist vulgate, which as we will see is no more satisfactory than the colonial one. One place to begin to explore the inadequacies of nationalist history is in its discussion of precolonial resistance, since what we think of nationalism is shaped in part by our sense of the politics of precolonial society (and it in turn is shaped by how we understand precolonial resistance). Was it, for example, devoid of political meaning, an expression of some traditional cultural essence? Or was it fully political in its own right? Most nationalist histories retrospectively subsume the dissonant voices of precolonial protest into the elite nationalist master narrative and have a hard time admitting the agency of groups other than elites. For most nationalist historians, internal social struggles (as opposed to anticolonial resistance or intra-elite strife) are a scandal.

I first became aware of the ways in which the nationalist narrative shaped an understanding of the precolonial past when I reflected upon a problematic feature in my doctoral dissertation. In it, I had referred to precolonial Moroccan protest movements as "protonationalist." In so doing, I realized later on, I had unwittingly incorporated them into the Moroccan nationalist narrative, which allowed for no voices other than urban elites. Since many of the protest and resistance movements I had examined were directed against these elites as well as against the French, my embrace of the nationalist narrative unwittingly reinforced the existing French colonial stereotypes about supposed Moroccan "anarchy and xenophobia." For example, Alal al-Fasi found movements like those of Abu Himara, the Hafiziya, the mutiny of *makhzan* troops at Fez in 1912, and the millenarian movement of El Hiba to be brave but lacking in all political significance, while Abdallah Laroui's *Origines culturelles et politiques du nationalisme marocain* renders a similar verdict.[29] In my book I recast the story, portraying these movements as politically complex, with social agendas that pitted different groups against others or against the state.[30] They were thus expressions of local social and political conditions, as well as or in addition to being the result of elite political manipulations. Other studies of rural jihads and millenarian protest, like those of Ross E. Dunn, Julia Clancy-Smith, Ali Abdullatif Ahmida, and Hachemi Karaoui, have come to similar conclusions: these supposedly prepolitical movements were in fact eminently political.[31]

What is the relevance of this finding to the way we think about colonialism and nationalism? I think it is considerable. For one thing, it assumes that everyone has politics (rather than politics being the possession of one actor alone: the French or the nationalists). To say that precolonial society had politics means that it was complex and dynamic, not static or frozen in millennial patterns of behavior. It also implies that the colonial conquest was a political process with a specific history and not a Manichean contest between the forces of light and darkness. Groups jockeyed for position vis-à-vis one another, as well as responding to the threat of European hegemony. In particular, the study of precolonial resistance is an important antidote to the belief that rural society was lacking in agency or totally dominated by its tribal leaders. In this new understanding, the resilience and political skills of leaders like the Algerian resistance hero Abd al-Qadir become at least as important as his military prowess or his religious zeal for the jihad.[32]

Of course colonial society also had politics: intertribal and intergroup politics, internal class politics, gender politics, the micropolitics of ordinary life. Nationalist histories have, however, rarely acknowledged that they intervened on behalf of some interests and against others—that is, that they themselves had politics. During the period of the independence struggle, it was easy to accept this justification at face value, along with the idea that the nationalists were selfless servants of the people. Since independence, however, this no longer seems a self-evident proposition. Once in power, nationalist elites turned out to be no less corrupt and brutal than the colonial officials they replaced. Perhaps in memory of colonial divide-and-rule tactics, nationalist histories especially have had a hard time accepting the legitimacy of differing interests and internal conflict within the body politic and have been quick to brand political and ethnic dissidents as enemies.[33]

More recently, an Islamist critique of nationalism has emerged that harshly denounces the secularism of postindependence states and asserts an Islamic moral agenda. Some observers have viewed the emergence of Islamist politics as a retreat from nationalism, if not the upwelling of a primordial religious essence. In a recent essay, I have compared the emergence of nationalism and Islamism in the Middle East, emphasizing the links between the discursive and the political transformations and the ways in which both discourses derive from Enlightenment thought. Ultimately, I suggest that we need to interrogate enlightenment views of religion—positioned as the enemy of progress and development—to understand the ways in which we understand Islamist claims today.[34] What emerges from this line of thought, for me at least, is the crucial importance of the discursive in the successive transformations from colonialist to nationalist to Islamist politics.

Today, our view is shaped by an awareness of multiple agencies and divergent power relations—not just colonial, but also of indigenous elites and subaltern groups, men and women, urban and rural, and interethnic (religious and linguistic) domination and subordination. It is tempting to say that postcolonial histories differ from nationalist and colonial ones in that the latter are homogenous and teleological, whereas ours are aware of multiple causalities and multiple agencies. We are too aware that resisters and nationalists also had political agendas, rivals they sought to deny resources, and scores to settle. In this sense, neither colonialists nor nationalists could live up to their progressive narratives; both were deeply compromised by their own interests. Think of how Abd al-Qadir pursued his rivalry with the Tijaniya, or how the Hafiziya struggle at Fez in 1907–1908 pitted the lower orders of Fasi society against the *ayan* in a contest in which the former's social radicalism warred with the latter's class-based pragmatism. Or finally, think of the politics behind the FLN's role in the liquidation of the "red maquis" in the Soummam Valley in 1956, in which the FLN betrayed a

Communist anticolonial guerrilla unit to the French army.[35] Each of these examples illustrates the problematic character of most nationalist accounts of colonial North African history. The independence struggle seems increasingly inadequately described as a history of resisters and collaborators, and the colonial situation as one of hybridities and marginalities. I will pursue this line of thought in the final section of this essay.

Writing Colonial Histories Today

The foregoing reflections on the relationship between colonial and nationalist histories describe a time in which each was connected to powerful political and discursive forces that, when viewed by their supporters, rendered them self-evidently "natural." The dichotomous formulations of colonial and nationalist histories have cast a large shadow over the ways in which postcolonial history has been written. As a result, we have tended to view independent North Africa through the lens of the colonial freedom struggle, as consisting of parallel histories (colonial and nationalist) equally marked by homogenization and essentialization. On the one hand, colonial historians tended to see the colonial conquest as jump-starting the incorporation of the Maghrib into modern history. Nationalists, on the other hand, while viewing the success of the anticolonial struggle as restoring the wholeness of the national past, also imagined the future of the independent states as linked to the progress-oriented narratives of modernity. What, we may ask, are the implications of these considerations for writing the postcolonial histories of the Maghrib?

To clarify what is at stake, we can look at some recent discussions of the political culture of Morocco, which have emphasized the home-grown Moroccan-ness of Moroccan political culture, and the uniqueness of the gradual accumulation of layers of political legitimation drawing upon sharifism, jihad, and different sufi ideas of charismatic authority. This culturalist understanding has emphasized the continuities of modern Moroccan history with its past, not its discontinuities.[36] Here is a place where Moroccan self-understandings coincide with Western perspectives grounded in modernization theory. For both, the motors of history are internal and cultural. The reasons however are different: Moroccan culturalists stress the specifically Moroccan roots of modern political culture as a way of marking off their history from everyone else's.[37] On the other hand, Western scholars, drawing upon the tradition/modernity dichotomy of modernization theory, see Moroccan politics as rooted in its internal cultural history, the better to position Morocco as a successful case of modernization. While both acknowledge the fact of change (embodied in the sequence precolonial, colonial, postcolonial), what they choose to highlight is cultural continuity: the persistence of segmentation, symbolic systems of legitimation, and/or domination.[38] But the contemporary Moroccan state is not the old *makhzan* writ large. Whereas the latter was puny, the modern Moroccan state can deploy its power throughout the national territory, disciplining and orienting opinion, intervening in depth in the society where it chooses. Seen from this angle, the history of contemporary Morocco is characterized by a radical discontinuity with its precolonial past, and its culture is "modern" and not "traditional." Modern, in the sense that it is the result of a complex layering of heterogeneous cultural practices strongly influenced by the European Enlightenment but shaped also by participation in a global world economy and international system. The selective amnesia of scholars about the colonial auspices under which the Moroccan state made its transition to modernity is especially striking.[39]

The colonial histories of Algeria and Tunisia written in French have also been viewed primarily through the lens of a retrospective nationalism. Thus we have Ageron's liberal indigenophile reconstruction of colonial Algeria, which remains in many ways the high-water mark of this type of historiography, and the half dozen or so French dissertations on the colonial period that were completed in the decade or so after independence.[40] While Algerians are taken seriously as subjects of inquiry, the real subject is liberal handwringing about what went wrong with the dream of biracial harmony in Algeria. In the history of the Tunisian protectorate, with the exception of a notable article by Charles-André Julien that reexamines the politics of the early twentieth century in a remarkably bifocal fashion, there have been few studies of colonial history that rise to the level of the Algerian literature.[41] Libyan colonial history is even more impoverished.[42] In none of these cases is there an attempt to problematize the history of the colonial period or to reimagine the relationship of the colonial past to what preceded and followed it. Simply to reverse the pluses and minuses of the old colonial historiography leaves us stuck in the same old progressive narratives, with no way of rethinking the colonial experience in its complexities and contradictions, apart from its place in the story of modernity. There is so far no work on North African history with the theoretically grounded sweep of Timothy Mitchell's *Colonizing Egypt* or the Indian Subaltern Studies group.[43]

Whose history is colonial history? Is it a shared history? Or is it two tunnel-vision histories that go past each other and never meet? The question goes to the heart of a central weakness of the postcolonial literature theory. If the colonial can only be apprehended as culture, and that culture is only the culture of racism, then the history is impoverished. One way out is through cultural history, especially the history of *mentalités* in which the thought-ways of poor and powerless urban and rural people are taken seriously. There have been a number of preliminary explorations along these lines. Consider, for example, the small miracle of Joelle Bahloul's recent archeological remembering of a Muslim-Jewish household in Setif, Algeria. The Jewish families had long since departed for France; the Muslim families who inhabited the multifamily dwelling continued to reside there. Bahloul's arrival to conduct an oral history let loose a flood of memories and reconnected the families. It also (at least for me) opens an enormous parenthesis in the history of Muslim/Jewish relations, previously thought to be readily understood.[44] Julia Clancy-Smith argues another alternative cultural history. Clancy-Smith's examination of the complex struggle over the headship of the *zawiya* of al-Hamil in nineteenth-century Algeria rather improbably pit the daughter of the deceased *shaykh* against both a male relative and the French colonial authorities. Clancy-Smith's careful unpacking of the ways in which the different claimants sought to utilize the French colonial system to their best advantage takes us far beyond the racial dualisms of colonial discourse.[45]

Driss Maghraoui on the Moroccan goums is another place we can apprehend the shared history of colonialism. Through their oral memories, Maghraoui is able to explore a difficult chapter in Moroccan history. Morocco was, after all, "pacified" by Moroccan colonial troops, not French ones. The majority of "free French" troops to liberate Marseilles in 1944 were Moroccan goumiers, as were most of the "French" troops who surrendered to the Viet Minh at Dien Bien Phu in 1954 (including Mohamed Oufqir). How do we understand these men and their history? Are they collaborators? But then what do we do with the fact that many of them were compelled to enlist after having been militarily defeated by the French? Or the fact that they also provided the nucleus of the "Liberation Army" that emerged in 1955? Accorded only grudging recognition by France and Morocco, the goumiers are a reminder that there is something about colonialism that eludes the dichotomous formulations of colonizer/colonized. The more we look, the stranger the culture of colonialism looks, and the less like the tunnel-vision histories we have come to accept.

The intellectual and political stakes for such an undertaking are enormous. Unless we reimagine colonial history as existing in its own right, apart from the progress-oriented narratives that have operated until now, we will be unable to gain much intellectual understanding of postcolonial histories. If the colonial past is erased from historical memory (as it is in most histories), except as a period of repression and resistance, we are ill-placed to understand the institutions of the modern states of the region or the complex political compromises and bargains with which modernity has been organized and sustained. Most notably this affects the ways in which we understand Islamism and the cultural terrain in which it flourishes. To rehistoricize the colonial period is to face the multirootedness of modernity, including Islamism as a manifestation of it. (From this viewpoint, contemporary Algerian "eradicators" seem the direct descendants of General Bugeaud; their militant secularism a deeply ironic replay of the fiercely secularist nineteenth-century French anti-Islamic *kulturkampf*). It may not be easy to conceive of the task of the historian in this way, but I think it is essential to do so. As a consequence of the postmodern situation, we find ourselves at present confronted with a third disenchantment of the world: after the collapse of religion and the self-evident explanatory power of progress-oriented colonialist narratives, we find ourselves confronting the waning power of nationalist narratives as well.

Notes

1. Such a comparative history would begin by distinguishing the four Arab worlds: Jazirat al-Maghrib, Jazirat al-Arab, Egypt, and the Mashriq (Bilad al-Sham + Iraq).
2. Intriguingly, despite the relative prominence of Morocco in British and American anthropology since the 1970s, this seems to have had little effect upon the history of the Maghrib.
3. See especially David Prochaska, "History as Literature, Literature as History: Cayagous of Algeria," *American Historical Review* (Dec. 1996). Also Herbert Lebovics, *True France: The Wars Over Cultural Identity, 1900–1945* (Ithaca, NY: Cornell University Press, 1992); Kristin Ross, *Fast Cars, Clean Bodies: Decolonization and the Reordering of French Culture* (Cambridge: MIT Press, 1995); Julia Clancy-Smith and Frances Gouda (eds.), *Domesticating the Empire: Race, Gender and Family Life in French and Dutch Colonialism* (Charlottesville: University Press of Virginia, 1998).
4. James Clifford, *The Predicament of Culture* (Cambridge, MA: Harvard University Press, 1988); Nicholas Dirks, Geoff Eley, and Sherry B. Ortner (eds.), *Culture/Power/History: A Reader in Contemporary Social Theory* (Princeton, NJ: Princeton University Press, 1994); Ann L. Stoler and Frederick Cooper (eds.), *Tensions of Empire* (Berkeley: University of California Press, 1997); Ranajit Guha and Gayatri Spivak (eds.), *Selected Subaltern Studies* (Oxford: Oxford University Press, 1988); and Ranajit Guha (ed.), *Subaltern Studies* (Delhi: Oxford University Press, 1982 -), 11 volumes to date.
5. For other surveys, see (among others) L. Carl Brown and Matthew S. Gordon (eds.), *Franco-Arab Encounters* (Beirut: American University of Beirut, 1996); Michel Le Gall and Kenneth Perkins (eds.), *The Maghrib in Question: Essays in History and Historiography* (Austin: University of Texas Press, 1997), Jean-Claude Vatin (ed.), *Connaissances du Maghrib: sciences sociales et colonisation* (Paris: Editions du CNRS, 1984), and G. Wesley Johnson (ed.), *Double Impact: France and Africa in the Age of Imperialism* (Westport, CT: Greenwood Press, 1985).

6. Alexis de Tocqueville, *Oeuvres complètes,* V, 2:217.
7. For a remarkable critique, see Yvonne Turin, *Affrontements culturels dans Algérie colonial: écoles, medecine, religion* (Paris: Maspero, 1971).
8. *Exploration scientifique de l'Algérie pendant les années 1840, 1841, 1842, publiés par l'ordre du gouvernement,* 39 vols. (Paris: Imprimerie nationale, 1844–1867). On it see my *Orientalism Observed: France and the Sociology of Islam* (Princeton, NJ: Princeton University Press, in preparation).
9. Tocqueville to Gobineau, 22 Oct. 1843, in Alexis de Tocqueville, *"The European Revolution" and Correspondence with Gobineau,* ed. and trans. John Lukacs (Westport, CT: Greenwood Press, 1974), 123.
10. On the colonial vulgate, see my "The Image of the Moroccan State in French Ethnological Literature: New Light on the Origins of Lyautey's Berber Policy," in Ernest Gellner and Charles Micaud (eds.), *Arabs and Berbers: From Tribe to Nation in North Africa* (London: Duckworth, 1973), 175–199.
11. The chief exception known to me is Joseph Robin, *L'insurrection de la Grande Kabylie en 1871* (Lavauzelle, 1901).
12. Edward Said, *Orientalism* (New York: Pantheon, 1978), who however makes no reference in this book to Algerian decolonization, arguably the most bitterly contested and radical anticolonial struggle in the Middle Eastern region as a whole in the 1950s and 1960s (or indeed to Frantz Fanon and Jean-Paul Sartre, two of its leading opponents).
13. Nicholas Dirks (ed.), *Colonialism and Culture* (Ann Arbor: Michigan, 1994) and Gyan Prakash (ed.), *After Colonialism: Imperial Histories and Postcolonial Displacements* (Princeton: Princeton University Press, 1995).
14. Partha Chatterjee, *Nationalist Thought in the Colonial World—A Derivative Discourse* (London: Zed Books, 1986).
15. See my "Towards a History of the Maghrib," *Middle East Studies* 11:3 (October 1975): 306–323. Also Wilfrid J. Rollman, "Some Reflections on Recent Trends in the Study of Modern North African History," in Le Gall and Perkins (eds.), *The Maghrib in Question,* 62–79.
16. In an important general summary of the state of colonial history, Kenneth Perkins, "Recent Historiography of the Colonial Period in North Africa: The Copernican Revolution and Beyond," in Michel Le Gall and Kenneth Perkins (eds.), *The Maghrib in Question: Essays in History and Historiography* (Austin: University of Texas Press, 1997), refers (p. 121) to the "Copernican revolution" of decolonization but fails to engage the discursive character of colonial and nationalist histories.
17. Alal al-Fasi, *Harakat al-Istiqlaliyah fi al-maghrib al-Arabi,* English trans. H. Z. Nuseibeh, *Independence Movements in Arab North Africa* (Washington, D.C.: American Council for Learned Societies, 1954), Mohamed Lacharef, *Algérie: nation et histoire* (Paris: Maspero, 1965), and Habib Bourguiba, *La Tunisie et la France* (Paris: Julliard, 1954).
18. Al-Fasi, op. cit.
19. See Mostefa Lacheraf, *Algérie: nation et société* (Paris: Maspero, 1968).

20. Cited by Houari Touati, "Algerian Historiography in the Nineteenth and Early Twentieth Centuries: From Chronicle to History," in Le Gall and Perkins (eds.), *The Maghrib in Question,* 90.
21. Enrico de Leone's *La Colonizzatione del Africa del Nord* (Padua: Cedam, 1960). Ruth First's *Libya* (Harmondsworth: Penguin, 1973) is an early nationalist history in English. See also Umar Ali ibn Ismail, *Inhiyar Hukim al-Usra al-qaramanliyya fi libia, 1790–1835* (Tripoli: Maktabat al-Firjani, 1966) and the critique of Ali Abdullatif Ahmida, *The Making of Modern Libya: State Formation, Colonization and Resistance, 1830–1932* (Albany: State University of New York Press, 1994). For a discussion of modern Libyan historiography, see Michel Le Gall, "Forging the Nation-State: Some Issues in the Historiography of Modern Libya," in Le Gall and Perkins (eds.), *The Maghrib in Question,* 95–108.
22. On the struggle for Algerian history, in addition to Lacharef, *Algérie: nation et société,* see Yves Lacoste, André Noushi, and Jean Prenant's *L'Algérie Passé et Present* (Paris: Editions sociales, 1960), and Mohamed C. Sahli's *Décoloniser l'histoire: introduction a l'histoire du maghreb* (Paris: Maspero, 1965). For a brilliant examination of Algerian nationalist historiography, see Omar Carlier, "Scholars and Politicians: An Examination of the Algerian View of Algerian Nationalism," in Le Gall and Perkins (eds.), *The Maghrib in Question,* 136–169.
23. Frantz Fanon, *The Wretched of the Earth* (New York: Evergreen Books, 1968). The chapter on "The Pitfalls of National Consciousness" stands as a sharp critique of nationalism.
24. For a preliminary verdict, see David C. Gordon, *North Africa's French Legacy, 1954–1962* (Cambridge, Harvard University Press, 1964), and David C. Gordon, *Self-Determination and History in the Third World* (Princeton, NJ: Princeton University Press, 1971).
25. Marcel Gauchet, *Le Désenchantement du monde: Une historie politique de la religion* (Paris: Gallimard, 1985).
26. Yvonne Turin, *Affrontements culturels dans l'Algérie colonial* is the best analysis we have of how this worked for the Algerian case.
27. See Shlomo Avineri (ed.), *Marx on Colonialism and Modernization* (Garden City, NY: Doubleday, 1968).
28. For representative examples, see André Gunder Frank, *Latin America: Underdevelopment or Revolution* (New York: Monthly Review Press, 1970), and Samir Amin, *Imperialism and Unequal Development* (New York: Monthly Review Press, 1977).
29. Abdullah Laroui, *Les origines sociales et culturelles du nationalisme Marocain* (Paris: Maspero, 1977).
30. See my *Prelude to Protectorate in Morocco: Precolonial Protest and Resistance, 1860–1912* (Chicago: University of Chicago Press, 1976).
31. Ross E. Dunn, *Resistance in the Desert: Moroccan Responses to French Imperialism, 1881–1912* (Madison: University of Wisconsin Press, 1978), Julia Clancy-Smith, *Rebel and Saint: Muslim Notables, Populist Protest,*

Colonial Encounters (Algeria and Tunisia, 1800–1904) (Berkeley: University of California Press, 1996), Ali Abdullatif Ahmida, *The Making of Modern Libya* and Hachemi Karoui and Ali Mahjoubi, *Quand Le vent s'est levé à l'ouest: Tunisie 1881—Impérialisme et Résistance* (Tunis: CERES, 1983).

32. See the recent critical discussion by John King, "Abd al-Qadir: Nationalist or Theocrat?" *The Journal of Algerian Studies* 2 (1977): 62–80.
33. The subaltern studies critique of Congress Party nationalism in India is especially suggestive. See Ashis Nandy, *The Illegitimacy of Nationalism* (Delhi: Oxford University Press, 1994) and Partha Chatterjee, *The Nation and Its Fragments* (Princeton, NJ: Princeton University Press, 1993).
34. See my "Orientalism and World History: Representing Middle Eastern Nationalism and Islamism in the Twentieth Century," *Theory and Society* 27:4 (August 1998): 489–507.
35. On these three examples see Raphael Danziger, *Abd al-Qadir and the Algerians* (New York: Holmes & Meier, 1977), chap. 7; my *Prelude to Protectorate in Morocco,* chap. 6, and Emmanuel Sivan, *Communisme et Nationalisme en Algérie 1920–1962* (Paris: Fondation Nationale de Sciences Politiques, 1976), 236–237.
36. See among other works John Waterbury, *Commander of the Faithful* (London: Weidenfeld and Nicolson, 1970), Ernest Gellner, *Saints of the Atlas* (Chicago: University of Chicago Press, 1969); Elaine Combs-Schilling, *Sacred Performances: Islam, Sexuality, and Sacrifice* (New York: Columbia University Press, 1989), and John P. Entelis, *Culture and Counterculture in Moroccan Politics* (Boulder, CO: Westview Press, 1989).
37. For some representative examples, see Abdallah Laroui, *Les origines culturelles du nationalisme marocain* and Abdallah Hammoudi, *Master and Disciple: The Cultural Foundations of Moroccan Authoritarianism* (Chicago: University of Chicago Press, 1997).
38. It is of course also the case that since independence, Morocco has been largely spared the prolonged wars, revolutions, and political turmoil that have disrupted other Middle Eastern societies. In this way, at least, Morocco *is* to a degree unique, at least in the Arab Islamic cultural area.
39. See for example Daniel Rivet's monumental three-volume doctoral thesis, *Lyautey et l'Institution du Protectorat Francais au Maroc, 1912–1925* (Paris: Harmattan, 1988). Rivet, however, makes little effort to explore the impact of the colonial legacy upon the contemporary Moroccan state.
40. Charles Robert Ageron, *Les Algériens Musulmans et la France, 1871–1919* (Paris: Presses Universitaire de France, 1968). See also among others André Nouschi, *Naissance du Nationalisme Algérien* (Paris: Editions Minuit, 1971) and Annie-Rey Goldzeiguer, *Le royaume arabe* (Algiers: SNED, 1977). An important exception is Jean-Claude Vatin's *L'Algérie: Histoire et Politique,* which, while still under the influence of the nationalist moment, makes a brave attempt to critique (and to a degree rethink) the colonial historical literature. See also Carlier, op. cit.

41. Compare Charles-André Julien, "Colons Francais et Jeunes Tunisiens," *Cahiers de Tunisie* (1971), and Béchir Tlili, *Les Rapports Culturels et Ideologiques entre l'Orient et l'Occident, en Tunisie au XIXeme siecle (1830–1880)* (Tunis: Universite de Tunis, 1974).
42. In addition to Ahmida and First, cited above, see Lisa Anderson, *The State and Social Transformation in Tunisia and Libya, 1830–1980* (Princeton, NJ: Princeton University Press, 1986).
43. Timothy Mitchell, *Colonizing Egypt* (Cambridge: Cambridge University Press, 1988). See the recent forum on "Subaltern Studies As Postcolonial Criticism" in the *American Historical Review* (December 1994).
44. Joelle Bahloul, *The Architecture of Memory* (Cambridge: Cambridge University Press, 1997). See also Avram Udovitch and Lucette Valensi, *Juifs en Terre d'Islam: les Communautés de Djerba* (Paris: Editions des archives contemporaines, 1984).
45. Julia Clancy-Smith, "The Shaykh and His Daughter: Coping in Colonial Algeria," in E. Burke III, *Struggle and Survival in the Modern Middle East* (Berkeley: University of California Press, 1993), 145–163.

Part II

Orality, Agency, and Memory

Chapter 2

The Arab Folklorist in a Postcolonial Period

Abderrahman Ayoub

In many Arab countries, both in the Maghrib and the Arab Middle East, some of the disciplines of the social sciences such as sociology, anthropology, and folklore have either been entirely absent in the universities, or only taught superficially (basically as part of the teaching of history). Indeed, they have hardly been encouraged and have even been forbidden subjects of field research. One of the main reasons for the absence or superficial teaching of and official ban on these disciplines has been to some extent simply an official fear of censorship and political persecution. Moreover, the researchers of these disciplines have suffered from double deficiencies: some have been censored by the regimes, and the few who are critically minded have been marginalized or co-opted. In the last two decades, however, the focus on the study of the relationship between the above mentioned fields of research and the "attitudes" of the authorities in power has been a recent development in Academia as a result of human rights activism, the demand of free thought and speech, and the rights of the minorities to free expression and cultural entity.[1] Yet, this research has been hindered by a scarcity of library materials relevant to social sciences and folklore.[2]

When inspecting this current academic situation, it is of interest to consider the following:

1. The factors that lead political authorities to discourage research in some disciplines of the social sciences, and specifically the subject of *collective memory* relevant to Arab folklore.
2. A list of all the specialists in the field in order to determine their research interests and methodologies in their studies of social phenomena. If one

is to evaluate the "pertinence" of studies done up to this time (especially the study of what I call "the official fear"), one must consider the "pertaining" of the majority of these researchers to schools of ethnology, such as the French, the German, and rarely the American. It is important to also consider the researchers' tendencies to "study" their own societies on the basis of methods that hardly focus on specific data (or are related to specific mentalities).

3. The topics that interest or do not interest the researchers.
4. Topics in popular sociology that are promoted or encouraged by the authorities of Arab countries.

In the present study I will attempt to interpret the dichotomy of social sciences and political fear. I will also highlight the social, cultural, economic, and political factors underlying this dichotomy that authorities feel represent a threat to social order and security. Personal inquiries, observations, and field notes collected or conducted during my sojourns and teaching experience in Arab countries—especially in the field of Arab folklore—will form the foundation of this interpretation.

Arab folklore is a vast field. As such it provides the folklorist with various means to touch upon and interpret social, psychological, and historical realities. I use history here as Braudel means it: people's attitudes and world views of the past, present, and future, and specifically for this study, people's views as manifested in popular oral history. Folklore research touches upon sociology, anthropology, and sociolinguistics. Hence, the Arab folklorist studies folklore material that describes Arab social realities—both local and regional—in praxis, in an interactive way, as things of life go, in which the past is always in the present and is shaping, in one way or another, the views of the future. This same folklore material (i.e., folk culture) reflects various aspects of social life that appear on a regional level. That is to say, one may study a phenomena (a reaction toward an event) on a transregional level and find the same folklore material used in oral performances in different Arab countries. But reactions might be totally different toward an event even in the same country within the different social groups. Class, social, and ethnic divisions explain the reasons for such diverse attitudes in Arab folklore in particular and Arab behavior in general. Therefore, the Arab folklorist is led to view the Tunisian social reality as similar to, yet at the same time different from, the regional characters of Jordan, Libya, and Palestine. In any case, these social facts are approached from the folklorist perspective to determine the Arab view of Arab reality, both on global and national levels.

To clarify further let us take the example of a Palestinian oral performance, a lullaby. In its deepest meaning it expresses the collective *hope* aspired to by the mother and her wishes for her own son:

"The dawn will rise tomorrow
and the son will plow the land
and reap its riches"[3]

This song points directly to Palestinian social and emotional reality, and to Palestinian hopes for the liberation and enjoyment of riches. The song is supposed to be sung for children to calm them and to make them sleep, but in reality the mother sings it for herself. This old folkloric song about harvest in a peasant society takes on new meanings referring to the reality of the Palestinians living under occupation. On a political level, it expresses sociopolitical aspirations for the liberation of the Palestinian land and the people. On the historical level, it points to the Israeli occupation. To change this situation, "the young Palestinian" needs to "plow" the land, i.e., transform the Palestinian condition. By using old folkloric songs, the rural Palestinian people call upon their traditions and then adapt these traditions in modern day to assert their political and social hopes.

It is not a coincidence that this song has variants among the same social group (or class) in many Arab countries such as Iraq, Jordan, Lebanon, Syria, Tunisia, Egypt, and Libya. Despite their obviously different circumstances, these countries draw their inspiration from the same pool and the same future vision. All have undergone some degree of colonization. The meaning for this song's variants can be explained by each social, ethnic, historical, and anthropological nature of the regional Arab reality, and undoubtedly by the prevailing political system in each region, which is the product of distinctive historical circumstances, social structure, and, nonetheless, ideological aspirations.

Nationalist Attitude of the Arab Folklorist

For the above reasons, the Arab folklorist will study Arab social phenomena in micro- and macrocomparative perspective. Let me be more specific about the attitudes of this folklorist and define the various conditions under which he is writing. He is an Arab nationalist because he was raised to feel a part of a large ethnic and social community that calls itself Arab. Secondly, he is an Arab because he uses a linguistic mode of communication defined by consensus as the Arabic language despite the diverse regional dialects. Thirdly, this folklorist can hardly not be an Arab because he considers himself involved both emotionally and intellectually in the political and social problems facing the Arab community (e.g., the Palestinian problem, the Six-day War, the death of Nasser, the Gulf War, the 1980 earthquake in Algiers, etc.) and the perception of this community concerning its own future. Therefore, these three elements also allow him the de facto right to consider himself responsible to the microcommunity to which he belongs—Tunisian, Libyan, Egyptian, etc.—and on a larger scale, he is also responsible to the macrocommunity called the Arab nation.

The feeling of intercommunal responsibility, if I may call it so, means that Arab citizens feel Arab citizenship in every Arab country in which they find themselves. A Tunisian can claim himself a Palestinian wherever he is, an Iraqi if he is in Jordan. Thus, the folklorist's feeling of citizenship is a pertinent factor when it concerns the attitude he adopts toward historical and/or current social and political events in the specific Arab country in which he conducts his fieldwork. One may also take into consideration "the Arab feeling of citizenship" as a pertinent factor of an analysis when it comes to evaluate the attitudes of authorities in power toward Arab folklorists in particular and Arab citizens in migration in general.

Since 1967, during the period when Arab nationalism represented a fertile ideological and political current among the Arab masses, every Arab citizen could join and become an active member of any political party in countries not his own. Moreover, he or she was active in this party not as a Tunisian, for example, but as an Arab. Such an opportunity became even more marked when the Palestinian resistance became, first in 1948 and then since 1967, a catalyst, a model and a goal of pan-Arab struggle against Zionist aggression. This was not only a resistance against imperialism but also an expression of Arab struggle against any type of foreign aggression, and it sometimes even took the form of social or political revendications against local authorities. (In 1984, Tunisian masses claimed the liberation of Palestine, but the main goal of their revendications was to protest the increased price of bread.) These authorities were, and probably still are, able to do little against the waves of militant masses manifesting their allegiance to the Palestinian resistance, which has been called "the common struggle of all the Arab peoples."

Nowadays, changes are in the making: Islamism is becoming a mass revendication. Arab regimes are acting to repress pan-Arabism, or any kind of ideology. However, from a cultural perspective, Islamism is not a pertinent or a sufficient tool, at least for folklorists, to understand the "mentality" of masses in the so-called Arab countries. Indeed, Arab authorities have pretended to support the Palestinian resistance, but in fact they have used every sophisticated means at their disposal to dilute, if not to break, the sense of belonging the Arab masses feel toward the Palestinian cause and more recently, toward the Iraqi cause. It seems to me that today, and more precisely since 1973, the Arab citizen is no longer considered by national and political authorities to be part of the Arab macrocommunity. An Arab citizen is an Arab foreigner who must beg for visas to enter an Arabic country other than his own, and therefore no longer has the right to exercise his communal responsibility. The opposite situation was a fact until the 1960s. The Arab folklorist, even more so than other Arab citizens, is chained and governed by these political constraints.

The Arab Folklorist: His Training and Fieldwork

Let me pause here to attempt to delimit the position of the Arab folklorist, his training, and the domain of his fieldwork. In theory, the Arab folklorist's field of inquiry covers all the territory called the Arab world. In practice, rare are the Arab folklorists who have worked in fields other than their own country. For instance, an Egyptian folklorist studies folk culture of Egypt and knows little about Tunisian folklore. Yet, an Arab folklorist truly should belong to no actual territory. As I have emphasized previously, since 1967 and more precisely 1973, Arab regimes share the same attitude toward the Arab folklorists' views on political and social life, especially when these views are considered to have passed the limits imposed by the authorities. They are interpreted as an interference in the internal affairs of the country. Briefly, this means that the folklorist who works in another Arab country and thus becomes part of the large professional immigration to the oil-rich countries and the folklorists who intend to make folklore comparative studies will inevitably find themselves at the edges of interdictions.

In his objective and conscientious contribution, the folklorist must take into account two phenomena: the question of ethnic minorities (such as the Berbers or Kurdics) and the plight of Palestinians. In North Africa, the Berber component represents a solid "background/substrate," which is still being shaped by formal and semiotic references in North African oral literature, even in Arab dialects. As for the Palestinian question, it represents in all Arab countries a political and ideological pole of attraction from which poets and storytellers draw their inspiration and folklore material.[4] Let us define the nature of these political interdictions and their effects on the folklorist and his fieldwork research through a consideration of these two questions.

The Arab Folklorist and "Political Fear/Interdictions"

There are two kinds of Arab folklorists: the "politicized" and the "official." In his native country, the politicized folklorist who attempts to be conscientious and objective in his description, analysis, and argumentation of the social and historical roles in the group's lore he is about to study faces interdictions, though disguised, that are nonetheless a form of political and cultural oppression. On the other hand, this type of interdiction is not a concern for the so-called official folklorist, because his responsibility is already self-limited to purely descriptive studies of material and handicrafts. He is charged with the task of classifying and exhibiting folk material (particularly urban) in museums of "traditional art."[5] This points to the predominance of bourgeois class taste in the classification and selection of what it considers urban and therefore "high." It follows, then, that rural is considered "low." Driven by the political needs of an economy based in tourism, the authorities exhibit the best samples of handicraft and encourage either the imitation of craft work or its mass reproduction.[6]

The state-appointed, official folklorist is also charged with the task of collecting oral literary production that is primarily concerned with panegyrics, or praise, addressed to a head of state, prince, or king. This oral literature deserves to be analyzed from a political point of view in order to show its use by the authorities as a means of brainwashing the population.[7] It can be called fakelore or *folklorismus.*

What I called fakelore is rapidly published (obviously with no critical apparatus), disseminated by the mass media, and is, as one might suppose, propaganda meant to render the political character of the authorities more popular. This type of folklorist, far too numerous in Arab countries, often accompanies chiefs of states engaged in courtesy visits. These social calls provide an opportunity to exhibit and exchange the folklorist's propagandist folk material. In fact, he or she has no training in folklore.

A second type of folklorist belongs to an intermediate category. He is a graduate of a school of fine arts, where he has learned among other things to judge folk material and handicrafts as a beautiful product and thus worthy of being exhibited in a museum. I call this type of folklorist "the archivist" or the "museum folklorist." From the point of view of folklore, the folklorist is a valuable professional contribution, and contrary to the first type of state folklorist, his work deserves, for obvious reasons, full consideration.

Finally, what is the third type of Arab folklorist? He is not very numerous and is defined by the fact that his work has been rejected directly or indirectly by the authorities. He is a researcher who is not content with descriptive studies but goes beyond concrete facts and asks several crucial questions: How have the products of oral and material culture been passed down to us? Why have they come down to us and continued to be transmitted, despite historical circumstances that have tried to eliminate them? I would call this type of folklorist the "politicized folklorist" or the folklorist who is reflective. As for his training, this folklorist has already studied literature and in particular linguistics with an emphasis on dialectology and sociolinguistics. Thus, he is acquainted with the fact that the history of social communities is a determinant factor in the formation and evolution of languages. Languages are the essential material that he has to analyze and define and are the basic structures that make oral literature transmit, generation after generation, the collective memory.

The Arab Folklorist Between Orientalism and "Arabism"

The type of Arab student involved in this field of study will have the opportunity to study in depth the collective behavior of his people, their aspirations, their artistic productions, their emotional link with the past, and the attitudes of their daily reality. The politicized folklorist's discovery of folk studies will only take place when he has migrated to a Western, non-Arab university. The choice to emigrate is limited by the host university's language (usually French, English, Italian, or German) and by what one might call "the model of the colonial image," which is an archetype that becomes an intellectual characteristic of the formerly colonized. In other words, the Arab student is taught that the ideal intellectual models are the French, the Italian, the English, and today the American.

This brings us to say that future Arab folklorists find themselves obliged to become somehow Orientalists because of these choices mentioned above. It must be noted that the French, Italian, German, and English Orientalists were very active collecting folk material during the colonial period and up to 1962 (the year of Algerian independence). Their activities slowed down in the 1960s but continued in certain Arab and European milieus (emigrated workers) with more sophisticated means of field research. We must admit that the material collected by Orientalists constitutes a primary source for the study of the Arab-Muslim cultural patrimony and Arab "mentalities." Yet, the Arab student who emigrates to a Western nation to study is already inoculated with the antibodies against Orientalist studies and cultural imperialism.

These antibodies have several parts:

1. The knowledge on the part of the student that Orientalism is an active colonizing element. During the colonial period (many famous names among Orientalists served in colonizing armies), cultural imperialism actually took the form of francophonia, which was established during the colonial period as the only alternative for the colonized to combat underdevelopment. Through francophonia, the colonized could become "civilized." As a reaction to such an attitude, the student defends the establishment of a national educational system that promotes Arabization in order to rekindle the

national cultural identity. Some reactions would neglect learning other languages, which is another way to rethink interactive cultures.[8]

2. The still lively debate whose central theme is Arab culture versus Western culture and Arab-Western culture.
3. The existence under specific political circumstances in a few Arab countries of ideologies such as Baa'th, Nasserism, Qadhdhafi Third Theory, fundamentalism, etc. that constantly evoke negative images of the colonized.
4. The educational systems of the Arab nations' emphasis on the values of glorious events that mark their national history.

Such antibodies help the student during his training in Western cultures to keep his distance from Orientalist influences. In other words, in a postcolonial situation, Arab folklorists are placed in a conflicted situation, which is fruitful insofar as it enables them to better appreciate problems considered taboo by the authorities of their respective home countries (such as the question of minorities).

The concept of what is taboo deserves attention because it is at the origin of what I called above the "political fear" (from folklorists). The Orientalist tradition, though it frequently presents a disdainful bourgeois attitude, minimizes all folk productions and oral traditions. If Orientalists care about such things at all, it is either to equate the beautiful with the exotic or to give credit to folk production only as evidence with which to strengthen the ethnic diversity theory of the Arab nation.[9] Despite their Orientalist framework, the studies of minorities provide a valuable source. Indeed, it is only within this Orientalist material that the political folklorist finds studies and descriptions of the daily life of the Berbers, Copts, and Kurds. As I mentioned before, these components of the Arab nation cannot be ignored by the folklorist while studying the folk material. For instance, French Orientalism presented its detailed and thorough Berber descriptive studies within a colonial framework. Nonetheless, the Arab folklorist fears to be politically controversial. This fear has affected Berber studies. Indeed, like many other researchers in the field of Maghribi culture, the folklorist realizes its synchronic nature, which the Berbers exemplify. The Arab folklorist tries to define in his fieldwork, for example, the Berber contribution to a lullaby, a craft decorated with symbolical motifs, maraboutism (the cult of saint worship), or a type of a folk agricultural storage system that informs him of the economic system of a given community. In fact, how can one understand the contribution of the storage system of the Berbers in the southeast of Tunisia or the Jabal Niffusa in Libya if he does not conduct fieldwork in their specific geographical areas? The political authorities are suspicious of studies of Berber storage and granary systems, as well as of Berber language, and consequently ban them. Why? Because these studies raise the matter of Berberism, and Berberism is still taboo in North Africa. Why? Because in the French colonial period, differences between Arabs and Berbers were strongly accentuated.[10] This "divisiveness" practiced by the French still resides in the memories of the Tunisian, Algerian, and Libyan authorities, and some groups with similar opinions. These are the same consequences of the colonial period's political divisiveness, namely that the Berbers could think of themselves as a people apart—that is, with a specific cultural background that allows them to be distinguished from other social and cultural groups. As a result, the Arab folklorist is faced with studying Berber folk culture in an Orientalist framework that pits one social group against the other, or he is forced to abandon the study in the name of national unity.

The Arab folklorist returning to his native country finds himself facing the contradictions of this dilemma. Wishing to follow his methodological and folkloristic training, he is confronted with government prohibitions. Nor can he write what he should write. Certain Arab folklorists wishing to study minorities data are forced to "emigrate" again and continue ethnological and folklore studies in the colonialist languages of their earlier host universities. Therefore the outcome is a sort of an "Occidentalist/Orientalist" study. The scarcity of folklore studies in Arabic libraries is the result of these politics. Indeed, government prohibitions prevent the study of topics such as maraboutism, funeral rights, Bedouin customs, the black minority status (called slavery in Arab countries), but not the study of their folk music and dance (both are good merchandise for tourism), or oral literature in a working class milieu. Nowadays, the scarcity of such studies is explained by the lack of training in sociology and anthropology studies. Aren't there other political reasons behind such prohibitions?

An example of the authorities' interdiction can be seen in the Palestinian issue. Collections of Palestinian folklore and related literature are almost nonexistent in the northern part of the Jordan River area despite the increase in the number of Palestinians who are living in precarious conditions. The Arab folklorist who is forbidden entry or residence in the occupied territories will undoubtedly find a wealth of material to study in the Palestinian camps. But the use of tape recorders is not allowed. This is due to the fact that content of the recorded data expresses Palestinian despair in the face of the passivity and lethargy of the Arab authorities towards the continuous Israeli colonization. However, this despair finds an outlet in folk literature: folk poetry and folk tales.[11]

Conclusion

In the postcolonial period, folklore studies that ask the questions why and how are neither appreciated nor approved of by Arab regimes.[12] Yet, during the colonial period, these studies were favored because they documented folk material, attitudes, and behaviors that were used in outlining the colonial political strategy of "divide and rule." It is odd that this kind of study finds itself at a dead end. Yet it was carried out by nationalist researchers after their countries achieved liberation. Therefore, what was a colonial strategy during the colonialist period today is looked upon as a means of disturbing the desired political stability and threatening national security. It is worthwhile to ask if it is possible to write the folklore, the oral history, the collective mentality of a "people," when political decisions establish the critical apparatus that define the limits of what is to be studied.

Notes

1. Although Arab countries are members of the United Nations and UNESCO, one can hardly record before the 1980s a conference that discussed the minorities issue. Also it seems that the first time representatives of American minorities participated at a conference was in 1982, when the argument of this paper was briefly presented orally at the Conference on Cultural Rights: Representation and Misrepresentations, sponsored by the Interdisciplinary Folklore Alliance, University of California at Berkeley, July 23, 1982. It was published later in its Arabic form: "Al-Fulkluri al-Arabi fi Marhalat ma Baad al-Istaamar," in *Dirasat Arabiyya* IV, February 1985, pp. 94–110. The following were some of the themes: the artist as agent for social change; documentation as a means of cultural survival; American researchers in their own backyard; multicultural rights in the urban environment; cultural rights in revolutionary societies; museum collections and cultural rights; ethnic heritage preservation programs.
2. Only few periodicals that incidentally treat of folklore were published since the 1960s. In Egypt, the irregular *Majallat al-Funun al-Shaabiyya;* in Iraq, *Majallat al-Turath al-Shaabi;* in Tunisia, the bilingual *Majallat al-Funun wa al-Taqalid al-Shaabiyya* published by the National Institute of Archeology and Arts. Ethnographic studies may be found in *La Revue Tunisienne* (1902–1956), *Revue des Etudes Economiques et Sociales (1962 -),* and *Revue de l'Institut des Belles Lettres* (IBLA, Tunis); more recently the Qatar *Majalat al-Ma'thurat al-Shaabiyya* (in Arabic). For a listing of periodicals of ethnography and folklore in North Africa and Tunisia, see A. Ayoub, "Notes a propos des revues d'ethnologie en Tunisie et au Maghreb," *Hesiode* 1 (1991): 193–199; A. Louis, *Bibliographie des Etudes de sociologie et d'ethnographie en Tunisie* (Tunis: IBLA, 1965).
3. A. Ayoub, "Al-tahalil fi al-mintaqa al-filahiyya min al-Urdun" ("Lullabies in a rural area of Jordan, a case study"), *Majallat Rabitat al-kuttab al-urduniyyin*

(Amman 1981); "Aspects evolutifs de la geste des Bani Hilal en Jordanie," in *Sirat Bani Hilal* (MTE, Tunis, 1985), pp. 53–112; Susan Slyomovics, *The Merchant of Art: An Egyptian Hilali Oral Epic Poet in Performance,* University of California Publications in Modern Philology, Vol. 120, 1987; A. Khouaja, *Al-Tahawwulat al-Ijtimaiyya min khilal al-Ughniya al-Shaabiyya* (Tunis: Alif, 1998).

4 A. Ayoub, "Hilali Epic, Material and Memory," in *Revue d'Histoire Maghrebine* 34:35 (1985): 189–217; B. Connelly, *Arab Folk Epic and Identity* (Berkeley: University of California Press, 1986).

5. We believe that the main goal for this kind of activity is to serve the tourist demand, but not, as it is often said in Arab political discourse, to confirm the collective identity through the transmission of inherited testimonies of folk-art crafts. Cf. H. Bannour, "Identity as a function of language choice," in *Identity, Culture and Discourse* (Tunis: L'Or du Temps, 1998), pp. 11–30; A. Marchal, "Le muse au service du dialogue culturel euromediterraneen," in M. Hadhri, (ed.), *Dialogue de Civilisations en Mediterranee* (Tunis: L'Or du Temps, 1997), pp. 141–148. See also *Tourism and Identity* (chap. 3), pp. 149–219.

6. R. Lanquar, et al. "Tourisme et environnement en Mediterranee, Enjeux et prospective, Le Plan Bleu," *Economia 8* (Paris, 1996).

7. Official folklorists and official poets used to get regular salaries from the institutions to which they belonged. This is not often the case for the other type of folklorist.

8. Edward Said has largely discussed this theme in his book on Orientalism. The way folk material, customs, and rites were treated by many Orientalists, who belonged to the French army in North Africa, are obviously colonialist. See the works of Quemeneur, mostly published in *Revue Tunisienne, IBLA, Revue des Affaires Indigenes,* Algiers. See also M. Marzouki, *Al-Badwu fi Hillihim wa Tirhalihim* (MTE, Tunis 1984); Al-Hashshayshi, *Al-Adat wa al-Taqalid al-Tunusiyya* (CERES, Tunis, 1997); O. Kaak, *Al-Taqalid al-Saabiyya* (MTE, Tunis, 1975); De Agostini, *Le popolazioni della Tripolitania,* trans. Khalifa al-Tilisi (Beirut, 1975); E. Lane, *An Account of the Manners and Customs of the Modern Egyptians* (London, 1836). Folk literature and folk material are just briefly described and looked at as aspects of a somehow "exotic" underclass culture.

9. Cf. R. Brunchvig, *La Berberie orientale* (Paris, 1947) and *Etudes berberes* of the Group of Berber Studies conducted by L. Galand (Ecole Pratique des Hautes Etudes, Sorbonne IV, Paris).

10. See in *L'Annuaire de l'Afrique du Nord* the various comptes-rendus on "Berber."

11. This theme was largely discussed on the base of cases from Palestinian camps in Jordan, Libya, Iraq, Syria, and Tunisia by A. Ayoub, "Hilali Epic," op. cit., n. 4.

12. Finally a seminar on "orality" within the Department of History (University of Tunis) has been given since 1997. It is financed by UNESCO (Chaire UNESCO d'Archeologie et de Patrimoine).

Chapter 3

The Moroccan Colonial Soldiers

Between Selective Memory and Collective Memory

Driss Maghraoui

Over the last decade, there has been an increasing interest in colonialism as a subject of scholarly inquiry. Whether in the field of anthropology, literary criticism, feminist studies, or cultural studies, there has been a significant amount of "rethinking" about the colonial past and the politics of colonialism and empires. A new set of concepts such as "post-Orientalist," "subaltern," and "postcolonial" that are now in vogue have been more closely associated with the work of the Subaltern Studies Group on colonial India. An interdisciplinary organization of South Asian scholars, the Subaltern Studies Group, focused on the histories of the "subaltern," which Ranajit Guha identifies "as a name for the general attribute of subordination in South Asian society whether this is expressed in terms of class, caste, age, gender, and office or in any other way."[1] For the historian to "rethink" may be understood as to challenge accepted paradigms and engage historical research in new directions by using new methodological tools. This has been very much the goal of the Subaltern Study Group: a challenge not only to the Orientalist discourse but also to the nationalist and Marxist conceptualization of colonial India.[2]

Historians of North Africa have been equally concerned with the impact of colonial expansion on the colonized and its influence on the social and economic organization of indigenous peoples. The colonial history of the Maghrib and the Middle East in general has certainly seen similar challenges and witnessed its own "decolonization" and reevaluation, but not to the same extent and with more theoretical basis and institutional organization than has been the case in India. French colonialism has often been explained in abstract terms and without close analysis of the agency of those who were at the receiving end of colonial rule. My interest in the Moroccan colonial soldiers is partly a modest attempt to look at the history of a "subaltern" group that has been written out of history. The French military was one of the most fundamental forms of colonial control in Morocco. It depended primarily on indigenous soldiers who were at the same time coerced into and instrumental in the implementation of French colonial policies. It is this condition of subalternity within the Moroccan society that I seek to investigate.

In this essay, I will talk about the way Moroccan colonial soldiers, which might include "Goums," "Tirailleurs," and "Spahis," were represented in a colonial discourse that sought to appropriate them, and how they were excluded from a nationalist discourse that chose to silence them. My ultimate goal is to use the oral accounts of some of these soldiers as narratives of contestation, both to nationalist and colonial discourses, in order to legitimate their own place in history. The colonial history of Morocco in its official and codified version stands in contrast to memory in its personal and collective remembrance of the past. Oral history, which is the link between these two versions of history, allows the meaning of prior colonial experiences to be negotiated. To understand fully the histories of the Moroccan colonial soldiers, we must situate them in their local and communal context. In another but related way, this article is about the way the history of these soldiers has been forgotten or selectively remembered. These terms in themselves are clear insinuations to the notion of "memory." Of course memory should not be taken here in its clinical psychological terminology, but in what might be referred to as "historical" and "autobiographical" memories. Historical memory reaches social actors through written records, photographs, commemoration, festive enactment, and films. It is scholarly and theoretically constructed in a certain body of historical knowledge. Historical memory is also about institutionalization and the representation of memory, whether in public museums or in the school curriculum and media for the education of citizens. Finally, historical memory situates itself outside the event and aspires to objectivity by claiming to take a critical approach. Autobiographical memory is the memory of events that living individuals have experienced in the past. It evolves and is heterogeneous because it exists in different social groups such as workers, peasantry, elite, political parties, or armies. The recollection of the past here is possible by reference to different notions and understandings that the people within the same social group can identify with: persons, places, dates, language, and other cultural signs. Autobiographical memory situates itself in the event and becomes part of it; it does not claim any objectivity, but it aspires to some form of recognition.[3] However, both historical memory and autobiographical memory are about remembrance, and they both engage in a process of "selective remembering" and "selective forgetting." I take here the example of Moroccan colonial soldiers as a way of exploring the problematic question of history and memory within the context of both colonial Morocco and France during specific moments of their turbulent histories.

Why the History of Moroccan Colonial Soldiers?

The case of the Moroccan soldiers provides an ideal focal point for addressing three interrelated questions regarding the history of colonial Morocco.

First, the very lack of concern for different social histories within the colonial period in Morocco reveals a general tendency of most historians of colonial Morocco to orient their research toward political, military, and institutional history. Historians of colonial North Africa like Charles Robert Ageron, Augustin Bernard, Jacques Berque, Muhammad Berkaoui, Charles-Andre Julien, Abdallah Laroui, Gilbert Meynier, and Daniel Rivet have been able to show the extent to which colonial soldiers have been used by the French. All of them show how the question of conscription became entangled with the problem of naturalization and the intermittent political conflicts that existed between the metropolitan and colonial interests. Most of them point to the way conscription was seen as part of the overall politics of assimilation, in which "colonial soldiers" were ambiguously perceived as a potential threat. Laroui in particular points to "the extremely cautious, not to say ambiguous, behavior of the Magribis" who fought beside France. He explains that because of the harsh economic conditions of French colonial penetration into the countryside, the dispossessed peasants were forced to work on public works projects or enlist in the army.[4] He puts the phenomenon of indigenous recruitment in the overall socioeconomic dynamics and power relationships associated with French colonialism in Morocco. Because Laroui's book is a work of synthesis in the tradition of grand narratives, the Moroccan colonial soldiers are absent as real human actors in history, and the realities and experiences of these people are formulated in purely abstract terms. In the end, the political and economic establishment of the colonial state, the politics of assimilation, the conflicts between metropolitan and colonial interests, and the resistance and rise of nationalism are still dominant themes in the history of colonial Morocco. From this perspective the historiographies of colonial Morocco focused predominantly on elite politics, colonial administrators, policies, ideas, and institutions.

Secondly, there has been an exclusive interest in resistance and the rise of nationalism but only discrete allusions to other segments of Moroccan society, which had to readapt their livelihood, negotiate their living existence, and in the end respond much differently to the colonial challenge. Because they were "resisters" or "collaborators," the histories of these social groups had to be included in or excluded from the "grand narratives" of a nationalist history. The central modality common to this kind of view is that Moroccan colonial history is the outcome of how a native elite became involved in politics and the subsequent relationship that it created with the colonial authority in order to achieve its political power and economic goals.[5] What is missing in this formulation is the history of the masses and the politics of the people whose responses to the colonial power was not always stimulated by elite politics or charismatic authority.

Thirdly, the history of Moroccan colonial soldiers is one example, among others, that shows France's heavy reliance on the vast reservoir of manpower in its colonial empire. While France was technologically and economically advanced enough to carry out its colonial adventures, it could not count on its population to engage in military campaigns. The recruitment of diverse ethnic and religious groups was a long established tradition in the French army. This phenomenon was for the most part due to a certain amount of pragmatism on the part of the French, but there were also political motivations. The French preferred their "colonial conscripts" instead of their "citizen soldiers" to die for the advancement of colonial expansion. A famous phrase pronounced by Choiseul in 1762 stated that one foreign soldier is the equivalent of three French soldiers: "un enleve a l'ennemi, un gangne pour l'armee francaise, un francais epargne" ("one taken from the enemy, one gained by the French army, and one French spared from death").[6] There is yet a persistent neglect of the fact of the participation of non-French colonial troops in the "French army," especially in its major European wars. Colonial soldiers were extensively used in the defense of France itself during the First and Second World Wars, but they remain absent from its historical memory. As stated very succinctly in a recent documentary film about the Moroccan "goumiers," "They liberated Marseille, but not a single street carries their name."[7] The film produced by Ahmed el-Maanouni deals primarily with the participation of Moroccans during World War II and brings attention to the role that they played during different campaigns in Tunisia, Italy, France, and Germany. It points quite effectively to the "forgotten memory" of the Moroccan troops in France and to the lack of sufficient indemnities provided to them in the present.

For the French, colonial soldiers in general remained present at the level of fiction with the medium of a romanticized language. Most of the French literature that dealt with the subject was written by ex-military officers in commemorative accounts or novels that were careful in portraying an "authentic," "subservient," and brave soldier. Exotism and romanticism were blended with Orientalist notions to represent the character of the Moroccan soldier.[8]

Since the publication of Paul Fussell's seminal book, *The Great War and Modern Memory* in 1975, there has been an important revival of interest in the social and cultural history of the two world wars. His book set the stage for a new scholarship not only on literary questions, but on other aspects of the social history of the war, such as class distinction and gender roles. Margaret Higgonet, Eric Leed, George Mosse, and others associated with European studies at Harvard have argued that there is a need to distinguish among the national, regional, and cultural traditions through which male chauvinism and female subordination have been expressed and justified during the two world wars. While these historians were attentive to important questions of gender, none of them addressed the problem of how the wars perpetuated racial prejudice and the widening gap between those who were fighting as citizens and those who were recruited as "colonial soldiers." None of this literature pays the scantest attention to the considerable numbers of these soldiers in the two world wars. They remained nonexistent in "official history." The point here is not simply to rhetorically recognize the "loyalty" and "heroic" military acts of "nos anciens combattants d'Afrique et d'outre-mere," but more fundamentally to integrate their histories within French/European history and collective memory.

Goums, Tirailleurs, and Spahis

Since the beginning of French colonial expansion in Morocco, the army relied very heavily on the recruitment of indigenous populations for its advancement. What has often been referred to as the "French army" was in large majority made up of Arab and Berber foot soldiers who constituted an important factor of a newly created colonial military institution. Even prior to the signing of the protectorate treaty by Moulay Hafid on March 30, 1912, four major military units were already established and under effective control of French officers (the Goums were created in November 1908, and the Tirailleurs and Spahis in June 1912). From 1908 to 1956, Moroccan colonial troops participated in different military campaigns within and outside of Morocco (Morocco 1908 to 1934, France 1914 to 1918, Tunisia 1942 to 1943, Sicily 1943, Corsica 1943, Italy 1944, France 1944, Germany 1944 to 1945, and Indochina 1948 to 1954). A cursory look at their military history reveals not only the large numbers of Moroccans who were recruited in these units but also the way they were extensively used in different continents.

Goumiers

The name "Goumier" etymologically comes from the Arabic word *khoum,* which is an order to stand up. The history of the Moroccan colonial soldiers known as the Goumiers dates back to the year 1908 with General d'Amade's order for the establishment of the first six Goums.[9] They were recruited predominantly in the Chaouia regions of Sidi Boubaker, Ouled Said, Settat, Kasbeth Ben Ahmed, Dar Bouazza, and Sidi Slimane. Each Goum was made up of about 200 men from different tribes. The mixing of tribal people into military units was conceived for better control and as a precautionary measure against possible insurrections and insubordination. The first six Goums functioned originally as a security force engaging in regular patrol control of newly conquered tribes. Under the control of French officers from the *service de renseignements* known later as the *Services des affaires indigenes,* they also served as scouts and a cover force for regular French troops. But after 1911, their most effective role was not as a police force but as a major fighting force not only in French colonial expansion in Morocco, but also in overseas wars such as World War I, World War II, and Indochina. This new military institution was from the very beginning conceived for fighting. As General d'Amade explicitly stated in 1909, "It is more appropriate to appreciate the conduct of the Goums in the battle field in order to judge the success of this new institution."[10]

Their number increased from 14 Goums to 25 by the end of World War I. Originally they were recruited primarily from different Moroccan tribes of Arab origin. Gradually, however, the Berber element became increasingly significant as the French expansion in the Moroccan hinterland was taking place. Reliance on tribes from remote areas and without local attachment or affinities proved to be a successful strategy for the French military command. By 1934, the year that is generally associated with the decisive military control of Morocco, there were 50 Goums, which was the highest number since 1908. The French control over the countryside in Morocco was more effective as the Goumiers represented not only a reliant fighting and security force but also a very useful mediating element between the Bureau des Affaires Indingenes and various dissident tribes. While there are no definite numbers of casualties, some have estimated that approximately 12,583 died between 1907 and 1922, and others have advanced the figure of 22,000 Goumiers during the period of "pacification" in Morocco (1907–1934).[11]

The rise of Nazi Germany and the escalation of tensions in Europe in the late 1930s would witness one of the most extensive uses of the Goumiers in a European war scene. As a way of preparing for an imminent war with Germany, 91 new auxiliary Goums were created. In September of 1939, 126 active and auxiliary Goums were ready for mobilization. In the early stages of the war, 12 Goums were already mobilized in Tunisia. With the signing of the armistice in June of 1940, France had to limit the number of its army in North Africa to 100,000 men. Faced with the regular inspections of German and Italian military commissions that were imposed on the French after their defeat, General Nogues decided to create "new police troops who were not considered part of the armistice army, but who were capable of engaging in a modern war." These forces were presented instead as part of the *makhzan* army and were under the umbrella of the so called *mehallas cherifiennes.* The period of the "Camouflage des Goums," as it was commonly referred to, made it possible for France to have approximately 19,700 Goumiers ready for mobilization.[12] The German pressure led, however, to a whole process of demilitarization of the *mehallas cherifiennes* that came under the control of the French foreign ministry. The French military officers were integrated in the civil administration. A new period of clandestineness led to an impressive show of support on the part of the Goumiers to conceal weapons and military equipment from German commission. Within the same period, the number of Moroccans under the control of the army increased by 14,300 men serving secretly under various civil organizations, such as the *Travailleurs Auxiliaires* or the *Corps Special Temporaire de Transmissions.* The Goumiers, therefore, had flexible functions that served the colonial administration at two separate levels. First, they were used as a police force at a very critical moment of French presence in Morocco. They were instrumental as a symbol of strength that France desperately needed in order to impress the Berber tribes of the Atlas. In May of 1942, while most of France was under Nazi occupation, General Nogues and Colonel Guillaume were projecting "French" military strength in Khenitra by attending a parade made up of 6,574 Moroccan Goumiers![13] The second function of the Goumiers was their continuous training for modern warfare as a way of preparing them for an imminent war against the Germans. By the time the Allied forces landed in North Africa, the Goumiers were already the first to be used. Armed with U.S. guns, wearing jellabas and British helmets, the Goumiers would fight in Tunisia, Sicily, Corsica, Italy, France, and Germany. Later they were used in Indochina and Algeria. The Goumiers represented a large part of the *Forces Armees Royales* when they were first created in 1956. As a symbol of national independence, the Moroccan army was ironically made up largely out of the residue of colonial troops, such as the goums. (Out of 25,000 soldiers in the *Forces Armees Royales,* 21,000 served under the French and the Spanish.)[14]

Tirailleurs

On June 16, 1912, General Moinier decided to organize the so-called *Troupes Auxiliares Marocaines* (TAM). These units were created from selected soldiers who remained loyal to the French after the Fez mutiny. But the majority came from Arab tribes from the regions of Fez, El Hajeb, Arbaoua, Agourai, and Sefrou.[15] Between 1913 and 1914, their number increased from 4 to 19 companies, which included 6,200 Moroccans all under French military officers. Because of the events in Fez, the TAM were often kept in garrisons outside of the city with regular French troops. By the time World War I was declared, Lyautey decided to send five battalions to the western front. For political reasons, these units were referred to as *Bataillons de Chasseurs Indigenes,* who became part of the Sixth Army on August 20, 1914. Of the 5,000 soldiers who were in the battle of the Marne, only 700 survived. During the whole period of hostilities, new battalions were created. Between 1915 and 1918, seven battalions were formed under the name of *Regiment de Marche de Tirailleurs Marocains* (RMTM). The "Moroccan Poilus" were part of trench warfare in the battles of La Marne and l'Aisne, in Soissons in January 1915, in Verdun in 1916, in the sector of la Main de Massige, in the village of Brueil, on the road from Paris to Soissons, and in Villers-aux-Erables. There is no reliable estimate of the number of Moroccan Tirailleurs who died in the war, but two examples show clearly their sacrifice. In September 1914 alone there were about 3,200 casualties,[16] and in one single day on September 30, 600 Tirailleurs died in the region of la Vesle. By May 1919, all regiments were repatriated to Morocco.[17]

With the end of the war and the process of demobilization, the metropolitan French army had to rely once again on Moroccan troops in the army of occupation in Germany. Between January 1, 1920 and 1925, six new regiments were created. In 1927 the Sixty-fifth and Sixty-sixth regiment were fighting in the Levant.

Between 1919 and 1934, the Moroccan Tirailleurs were used in the "pacification" of Morocco. Their role was less significant in comparison to that played by the Goumiers during the same period. The Tirailleurs were, however, instrumental in the curbing of different rebellions throughout Morocco. In the region of Fez, they were used against the northern tribes of Ouerrha in 1919; in 1920, the mobile guard took over Ouezzane for the control of the Gharb region; and between 1920 and 1921, seven battalions of Tirailleurs confronted the Beni Mestara. In the region of Taza, the Tirailleurs were engaged against the Beni Ouarrain in 1919, the Ait Tserhouchen-Marmoucha in 1922, and the Beni Bou Zert (in the north) in 1923. But the most extensive use of the Tirailleurs within Morocco occurred between 1924 and 1926 against Abd-al-Krim during the Rif rebellion.

As was the case for the Goums, the late 1930s witnessed the most dramatic increase of the Tirailleurs. In 1939 there were 32 battalions of Moroccan Tirailleurs: 18 in Morocco, 12 in France, 1 in Corsica and 1 in the Levant. Some of them joined the French resistance as Moroccan *maquissards.*

In France alone there were 27,500 Tirailleurs out of 90,000 Moroccans surviving in different units.[18] Like the Goumiers, the Tirailleurs participated in all major campaigns during World War II as well as in Indochina.

Spahis

As a colonial institution, the Moroccan Spahis were created in 1911. They first participated in fighting within Morocco in the region of Taza. They were formed in 1914 as the *Regiment de Marche de Chasseurs Indigenes a Cheval* and constituted ten different squadrons. They later became known as *Regiments de Spahis Marocains.* The gradual increase in the number of Spahis, depending on the need of the French army in different conflicts overseas and within Morocco, followed similar trends, as in the case of the Goumiers and Tirailleurs. They were very useful in mountainous areas, whether in the Atlas of Morocco or in Syria. In 1942, the first *Groupe de Spahis Marocains* (GESM) became part of the *Forces Francaises Libres.* There were seven regiments of Spahis involved in the war in Europe, and one in Indochina. They were used to intervene in the uprisings of 1955 preceding the return of the king to Morocco. In comparison with the Goumiers and Tirailleurs, the Spahis had larger numbers of French citizens in their units.

The military colonial institutions that I have outlined above were by no means the only ones. Fewer in numbers but equally important in their use were the *Bataillon du Genie,* the *Bataillon de Sapeurs des Chemins de Fer,* and the *Bataillon des Transmissions.* Of the 4,200 kilometers of roads that were made in the colonial period of Morocco, a large part was made by these troops. The *Sapeurs* were involved in the construction of 1,600 kilometers of rail roads. Most bridges were the work of the *Genie.*[19]

Given the large numbers of colonial soldiers who worked under the auspices of the colonial military administration, and given the "voluntary" aspects of their recruitment, the military history of the Moroccan troops has been largely appropriated by French army officers who found in the success of these colonial institutions a symbol of "attachment and mutual respect" between colonizer and colonized. The colonial discourse on this group of people revealed a clearer aspect of race and power relationships.

Moroccan Troops and the Colonial Discourse

The military history of the Moroccan colonial soldiers has been captured primarily by French army officers. This interest came on the one hand out of a genuine attempt to retrace the general phases of what they considered a "shared history." A certain nostalgia for their experiences in colonial Morocco, *Pays du Soleil Couchant* and *Pays de Lumiere,* was part of this fascination with what they referred to as "nos Goumiers, nos Tirailleurs et nos Spahis." On the other hand, colonial troops represented for a number of French officers a symbol of "loyalism" and success of what they called the "pacification" of Morocco. As Jean Saulay states, the Goumiers "became attached to their French officers in a climate of reciprocal friendship and followed them joyfully to the battlefield."[20]

Early French interest in the Moroccan soldiers came also out of a continuous concern for possible threats of rebellions and mutinies within the army. The protectorate authorities were insistent on having a close knowledge of the soldiers' lives and behaviors. Most of the writing came from army officers who were elements of the *Service des Affaires Indigenes* and who became associated with a governmental institute known as the *Centre des Hautes Etudes d'Administration Musulmane.* This center was created in 1936 under the leadership of Robert Montagne, Sebastien Charlety (rector of the University of Paris), and Pierre Vienot (secretary of state in the French foreign ministry). The center concentrated on the study of various subjects of interest to the colonial administration in the French overseas empire. It contributed to the study of different social and cultural groups, tribal organization, Islam, language, and other institutions. Of major concern was the emergence of the forces of nationalism in the 1930s. The first promotion of the center was made up mostly of army officers and civil servants. They included people like George Spillmann, Paul Dugrais, B. Sanchis, and Leon Roche.

The discourse on colonial troops can be situated within an overall Orientalist discourse common among French imperial administrators. The entire colonial military enterprise in Morocco was a French creation in the sense that they gave it more disciplined and institutional organization. The Moroccan soldier had to be imagined according to the way French colonial officers sought to represent him. He is often referred to as "Moha," a generic name that applies to every single individual within the group. "Existe-t-il un autre moyen de le differencier de tous les autres Moha? Oui, parfois par un sobriquet."[21] The soldier is nameless and has therefore no personal traits or identity. By virtue of being a Goumier, Tirailleur, or Spahi, the soldier seems to have been given his newly acquired identity by the colonial administrator, who speaks for him and represents him in history.

This colonial discourse was also characterized by a tendency to dehumanize the colonial soldier. Images of savagery and an innate inclination to warfare remained part of this representation of the "other." Jacques Berque once wrote that "our Berbers will remain good savages, worthy of our love and respect, but whose ultimate advancement would consist of their promotions in the Goums."[22] The Goumiers were believed to have kept their atavistic qualities of rusticity and endurance because "they did not fear death" and were known for "their ability to walk for a long time, without food, finding on the way wild plants which they ate uncooked."[23] In the most recent book about the Goumiers, Yves Salkin states that the Goumier was "capable of the longest walks in the most difficult trails of mountains, he moved on the ground like a savage beast."[24] It is hard to dissociate the mental framework and symbolism of such representation in the colonial discourse from the fact that the numbers of deaths among the Goumiers were never fully recorded or mentioned in France. Otherwise, the casualties of war, whether in the "pacification" period or overseas, was something that the colonial administration did not have to worry about.

One of the fundamental conceptions that has been perpetuated in this colonial discourse is the notion of "voluntarism." The attractiveness of a career in the Goums or other regiments has often been explained as a result of different forms of social benefits that enhanced a "voluntary" recruitment. As opposed to Algeria, the system of conscription was in fact not put into effect in Morocco. Considered as a French department, Algeria was put in 1912 under the same rules of recruitment that were instituted in the French law of 1872. In Morocco, however, the Tirailleurs could enlist for a period of four years and reenlist again.[25] As I will later show, this discourse of "voluntarism" contrasts sometimes with the oral accounts of some of the Anciens Combatants.

This colonial discourse was generally stereotypical, paternalistic and racist. In 1925, for example, Paul Azan states that "regardless of the selection that soldiers from North Africa are subjected to, they inevitably bring the germs of the most serious diseases to the French population: tuberculosis, syphilis, malaria, without speaking of other physiological miseries."[26] But this identification of the colonial soldier should not be seen only in the context of a military institution. Its meaning should be read in a much broader context in which the difference between French collective identity and that of the "indegenous" as a whole was established. For Paul Azan later states that "we have forgotten an essential factor in the army which is that of a human being. We did not take into consideration the fact that the indigenous is not comparable to the French. He does not have his physical constitution, nor his moral qualities, education, religion, tradition and civilization."[27] Ultimately, the indigenous soldier was perceived not to have the same rights as the French because he was part of the "uncivilized other." As stated by Azan, "L'erreur a deja ete comise par ceux qui ont redige la declaration des droits de l'Homme et du citoyen au lieu de rediger plus modestement la declaration des droits du citoyen Francais" (the error was made by those who wrote the declaration of human and citizenship rights instead of writing more modestly the declaration of French citizen rights).[28] This blatant form of racism from French colonial officers was, however, not unrelated to the overall mood of Orientalist discourse that appeared in the more academic settings. They both fed into each other.

Within the more academic settings, one of the most important conceptions of Moroccan society was the stereotypical distinction that was made between *Bled al-Makhzan* and *Bled al-Siba.* Clearly the distinction is not an academic one, but it was fundamental to the way France sought to portray its mission in Morocco and therefore stigmatize "resistance" as age-old anti-*Makhzan* instincts. Along with this difference emerged the idea that *Bled al-Makhzan* was the region that comprised Arab tribes and *Bled al-Siba* was made up of Berbers. It was also believed that the Berbers were less Islamicized and more apt to be on the side of the French. Colonial ethnographers made a systematic opposition between these two artificial geographical entities in which *Bled al-Siba* was perceived as the region of "anarchy and revolt" against the authority of the sultan, while *Bled al-Makhzan* was the area under the control of the government.[29] With this colonial formulation of the political geography of Morocco, the "Berber policy" was put into effect after 1914. The *Makhzan* lost control of most Berber-speaking regions in Morocco, and Islamic courts were abolished. The officers of the *Affaires Indigenes* were among the first to subscribe to such notions. It was out of this belief in the "Berber Myth" that we can partly explain the heavy reliance on the Goumiers, who were predominantly Berbers. It was very clearly expressed in one of the reports presented to the *Centre des Hautes Etudes d'Administration.* It states that "the non-Arab and less Islamicized circles (such as Kabyles and Berbers) would obviously be more favorable" for recruitment ("certains milieux non-arabes et peut-etre moins islamises (Kabyles, Berbers . . . etc.) seront evidement non defavorables").[30]

The Place of Colonial Soldiers in French History

The history of either the First World War or the Second has been dominated by the perception that they were mainly European wars fought by Europeans in a European land. This Eurocentric view of writing the history of the two world wars has excluded other histories of colonized peoples as major participants in these wars. Indians, West Africans, North Africans, and others fought and died next to Europeans. Yet their memories are today lost or remain still out of memorial festivities and ceremonials that are celebrated each year in Europe. In France, the histories of these "colonial soldiers" remain absent from French "historical memory." Very few high school students learn that there were actually Maghribi among the *maquissards* in World War II, or that there were about 170,000 *Tirailleurs Senegalais* in the trenches of World War I, or that it was the Moroccan Goumiers who liberated Marseilles from Nazi Germany. For the French, the colonial soldiers in general remained present at the level of fiction within the medium of a romanticized language. The colonial soldiers existed, but they do not really exist in the French historical memory. The issue here is not simply a recognition of different heroic military acts, but more fundamentally the integration of these histories within French European history and collective memory. In the present context of the reimagination of the European community, such an issue is an important one. With the current problems of immigration in France and the attempts to create an economically and culturally unified Europe, perhaps such memories may vex the cultural and historical homogeneity that governments are creating to the exclusion of different ethnic minorities. The European past becomes a social construction shaped by the concerns of the present.

The Place of Colonial Soldiers in Moroccan History

The goal of any nationalist discourse, whether in the field of politics, literature or history, is to expose the realities of colonialist oppression. As Frantz Fanon once wrote, "while the politicians situate their action in actual present day events, men of culture take their stand in the field of history." Fanon was very much aware of the violent aspects of colonialism in its different manifestations. "Colonialism is not simply content to impose its rule upon the present and the future of a dominated country. By a kind of perverted logic, it turns to the past of the oppressed people, and distorts, disfigures and destroys it."[31] In this context, the relevant reaction of the nationalist discourse was constrained within its attempt to reaffirm political homogeneity, cultural authenticity, and historical glories. It was what al-Jabiri called a "defense mechanism,"[32] which imposed a retrospective fixation and selective reading of the past. While it may have been a "natural" and legitimate response to a colonialist hegemonic discourse, it has become inadequate from our perspective today. While we should not lose sight of the classic patterns of colonialist economic subjugation and cultural denigration of the colonized, we should open the space for sites of what appears to be a shared history of colonialism that exposes new dimensions of the colonial encounter.

In Morocco the case of the "colonial soldiers" represents such a site. Their histories are similarly absent from the country's "historical memory." Eric Hobsbawm once explained that history has always been the "raw material for nationalist and ethnic fundamentalist ideologies" upon which they base their legitimacy and create their identity.[33] The peculiarity here is that the history of "colonial soldiers" contradicts both the discourse of nationalism (national consciousness) and resistance. Since most national histories and commemorations celebrate the origin and rise of a nation that are perceived to have an effect on its subsequent history, the Moroccan government clearly sees none of these features in the history of the colonial soldiers. I was surprised during a meeting with a high official in the Bureau National des Anciens Resistants, which was much bigger and more organized than the Association Nationale des Anciens Combattants, when he assured me that the "Moroccan colonial soldiers never fought inside the territory of Morocco."[34] His discussion was typical of a nationalist discourse that tends to highlight certain events and periods as representing important moments in the nation's history, while others are seen as disruptive and hence sink into oblivion. Up to World War II, the experiences of these soldiers did not symbolize, at least in the eyes of official history, any national commitment or heroic affirmation of national dignity. The colonial soldier becomes, however, an appropriate and useable national symbol once the sultan Muhammad V gave his *idn* (permission) for the support of the Allied forces in World War II. It is now often said that Moroccans were fighting in Europe for the independence of Morocco. The fact is that the process of "pacification" in Morocco, by the French and with the use of Moroccan colonial soldiers, was done with the consent of the *Makhzan* to control *Bled al-Siba*. A repressed memory like that of the colonial soldiers brings out a broader issue of how historical imagination is possible in Morocco. What are the possibilities of different historical narratives in a country whose historical memory has always been associated with the same symbols and a dominant historical discourse? Since independence, the Moroccan government has controlled how Moroccan historical and cultural imagery has been depicted in the mass media (particularly television). This has effectively displaced alternative models of historical imagination. Control of the educational system also makes possible the persistence of a nationalist/monarchic paradigm for historical representation. Taking the step of defining Moroccan historical identity from the masses would question the convenience of considering as representative the notion of a homogeneous discourse, whose fundamental function is the exercise of authority, not only on the present but also on the past.

Out of an attempt to challenge the colonial discourse about Moroccan society and to show the rational reaction of different social groups to the French conquest, historians of colonial Morocco have concentrated on large scale "resistance movements." They have consequently neglected the large scale "collaboration." The dichotomy between "resisters" and "collaborators" is of course in itself very problematic. Colonial soldiers can not be categorized as either "resisters" or "collaborators." It is known that most of those who became part of the colonial army were originally among the most resisting social groups. About 83 percent of colonial soldiers were peasants who reacted in a rather inconsistent way to the French. The economic aspect of their realities was an important variable that determined their collective response. The uncertainty of economic life, which in many cases was the result of colonial expansion, made different individuals give priority not to political symbols but to the possibilities that guaranteed their human existence. Moroccan colonial troops joined the French army out of rational calculations in which economic considerations were primary. What I would like to insist upon here is the complex and refractory nature of local ordinary experiences and the agency of a group of people who reacted in their ways to colonial advance. Under French colonial pressure, the peasants' response, either as "resisters" or "collaborators," was rational.

The behavior of a large number of Moroccans who became part of the colonial regiments was seen as being "ambiguous" and "contradictory."[35] Was it simply a response to a collaborationist discourse by the elite? While French colonial penetration in Morocco was still in its early stages, Moroccan troops were already fighting next to the French in World War I. There was certainly a kind of "ideological coercion" in which both French officials and the Moroccan elite were implicated. With the support of the Moroccan sultan (commander of the faithful and the holder of religious symbolism), different religious brotherhoods, and the Moroccan urban elite in general, the French were able to "concoct" a propagandist language from within an Islamic field of reference. As a result, a number of fatwas were promulgated for the moral support of the war effort in France. But it would be too simple to accept the notion that colonial troops joined the French army necessarily out of religious conviction in the notion of jihad. French penetration into the countryside affected very drastically the economic structure of peasant society. "These people were losing their land and at the same time continuing to pay heavy taxes."[36] It was these groups of people that constituted the majority of colonial troops, and it is this colonial context that should be taken into consideration. These groups in fact enlisted in a "voluntary" way, but it was out of the coercive economic and military measures that were imposed upon them. To see more closely the reasons of their enlistment, I turn now to an examination of their oral accounts.

Colonial Soldiers: An Oral Account

Let me start by saying that the memories of colonial soldiers are shaped by the past as well as by the present. They are the product of outcomes and consequences which were unknown to them. Their personal accounts of their experiences in the colonial army are in themselves selective, but that they represent their own views and their recollections of the past is clear and tangible. In a sense, these oral accounts reflect the perspectives of those who were at the receiving end of French colonialism in Morocco. Individual remembrances reflect personal experiences, but they coincide simultaneously with the broader social group to which they belong.[37] To read the oral narratives of these soldiers is not simply to emotionalize and glorify their experiences. More importantly these accounts should be read as a way of discerning not only the political and economic context of their colonial past, but also their present-day concerns.

The oral accounts that I will relate here were recorded in the summers of 1995 and 1996. Some of them are taken from a documentary film. I will concentrate here on one main point, which is related to the reasons and motives for their enlistment and the context in which it happened. I tried not to interrupt their oral narratives, so the interviews were not oriented by the interviewer except for occasional clarification. The interviews as a whole served alternately to support and refute previously held views about enlistment in the colonial army. An important value of these narratives is that they provide a tangible and more direct basis for assessing the impact of colonial penetration into the countryside in Morocco and of French recruitment methods. The colonial discourse about recruitment in Morocco, as I mentioned above, tends merely to support the official French assertion that recruitment was, for the most part, dependent upon securing volunteers. Their oral accounts here reveal hidden coercive methods which were used to acquire colonial troops in Morocco.

Hussain Ou Mimun, a Goumier who was in the *Baroud* in Italy and Germany, said: "We defended ourselves with stones and with all that came to our hands. There were a few muskets, but it wasn't enough. You know we were civilians and you know what the situation of civilians is. From the other side, they were well equipped, their tank gun fired from far. They came down and in order to oblige us to surrender, they took all our livelihood, all our livestock. They left us only the minimum. One mule to work with. If you had two mules, the French would take one in order to work for the French. Once we surrendered, they imposed the *corvée* and in addition we were sometimes beaten and those who were with the French beat us. We were in the front with pickaxes, and those with shovels were behind. It was unbearable. Those who refused to do the *corvée* were simply thrown in the river in the middle of the winter; it was very cold, and some of us died. That's it and it was this injustice that pushed me to enlist."

Said Ou Hamu, a Goumier who participated in all the major campaigns in Europe: "The mobile infantry came from all sides. They bombed from all sides, they bombed Ait Serghouchen, they had also planes. There were a lot of deaths. They took all our livestock and left us . . . So why did I enlist in the Goums? Simply because my dad was killed by the French and we were five orphans. In fact the majority of mature men from Ait Serghouchen were killed by the French, and they left a lot of orphans who did not have other choices but to become Goumiers and work for the French."

Sharif al-Madani, Tirailleur: "I was born in 1930. I became part of the army with the French on June 15, 1949. There were special circumstances. I never thought of entering the army. I used to be involved in commerce. I stayed for four years. Between 1948 and 1949, I was involved in the black market. I was with two friends of mine. In the month of June, we were bringing some merchandise from Oujda, and we were caught by the French. The only way out for us was to join the army. We were trained in Taza and taken to Germany, and then to Vietnam."

Hussain Ben Iwish, Tirailleur, was born in 1928. He enlisted in 1943 when he was unemployed. "We were *mahkoumin* [in this context this word means to be under the authority of a foreign ruler], we did not have the possibility to do anything. No job, no nothing. I was in Rabat working as a gardener in Skhirat and I lost my job. I joined the army in 1943. I went to France on the first of January 1946. I became a corporal. We were guarding German prisoners. In 1948 I went back to Morocco. In 1949, I went to Vietnam. In 1953, I went with the Vietnamese army with my gun because I thought that if they exiled Muhammad V, they later would have to imprison the Moroccan soldiers, too. There was a lot of forest, it was dark, and there were a lot of bushes and rain. I ran away by myself. I took with me about 300 bullets and 5 or 6 grenades. The Vietnamese were propagandists. They used to tell us 'go back to your country, the French are colonizing you and us, we are fighting for our country, so you should fight for yours.' They sent tracts and letters in Arabic. They used to tell us to shoot up in the air, and there were a lot of Moroccans who did it and there were a lot of Moroccans who were with the Vietnamese, about a thousand."

What can we make of these statements? My interpretation of these fragments of oral accounts has more to do with the factors that incited each individual to enlist in the army. For Hussein Ou Mimun, who started out as somebody who confronted the French, joining the army was a way of escaping the cycle of what he himself refers to as "injustice." It is quite symbolic that he refers to the *corvée* in the French language. The imposition of the *corvée* on the Moroccan peasantry was a burden that was not financially beneficial. In his narrative, he refers to those who were "in the front with pickaxes and those who were with shovels." The coercive aspect of the *corvée* is also clear in his reference to being thrown in the river if one refused the task. His statement that "it was this injustice that pushed me to enlist" does not carry with it any form of political loyalty.

Said Ou Hamu refers in his own terms to the often forgotten memories of deaths during the conquest of Morocco. Lyautey's most celebrated article, "Du Role Coloniale de l'Officier" would not make sense to Said. His account is revealing in the sense that it brings to light the practice of depriving newly conquered tribes of their livestock. Ou Mimun brings up the same issue about taking away the mules. In the case of Ou Hamu, he himself poses the question of why he joined the Goums. In his reference to the death of his father, he interestingly includes the "majority of mature men from Ait Serghouchen were killed by the French, and they left a lot of orphans who did not have other choices but to become Goumiers and work for the French." Ou Hamu's testimony explains another coercive measure for enlisting in the Goums. It was a matter of survival within an imposed colonial context.

The Moroccan Tirailleur, Sharif al-Amrani, represents a more urban condition for the context of this recruitment. He is literate and speaks French fluently. His recruitment in the Moroccan Tirailleurs was more a matter of coincidence and of being in the wrong place at the wrong time. As he states it, "I never thought of entering the army." Instead, as a way of escaping legal justice for his involvement in the black market, he joined the French army. But this phenomena of enlisting in the army as a way of avoiding a prison sentence was common also among the Goumiers. In other interviews, I came across similar stories. In his book, *La Longue Route des Tabors,* Jacques Augarde states, "In the Goums we find shepherds, peasants, and a good proportion of thieves and bandits."[38]

Finally Hussain Ben Iwish's experience in Indochina reveals the fact that enlistment in the army was a way of escaping unemployment and a means for achieving an improved economic situation. His "loyalty" to the French colonial army was only temporary. He deserted on his own, but he refers to a lot of Moroccans who were with the Vietnamese. Desertions in the colonial army were not something uncommon, but exact data is not yet available. As he himself states, the Vietnamese engaged quite extensively in a continuous propaganda campaign to persuade colonial soldiers to join them in the fight against the French. Moroccans, like others, were also exhausted from the war in Indochina. The idea that the Goumiers "did not fear death," so common in the colonial discourse, is too rhetorical to make any sense. Lucien Bodard states that "nothing is so fantastic as the courage of Moroccans, but nothing is so fantastic as their fear when they break like a stone dropping over a cliff. Their courage is gone . . . Everything is lost in madness save the primeval urge to stay alive."[39] Moroccans like Ben Iwish had to desert. They simply had no political identification with French imperial government and no attachment to the causes for which that war was fought.

Conclusion

In the aftermath of the nationalist movements for independence in the Maghrib, there was a new struggle for recapturing the past and challenging the colonial paradigms that dominated most of the writings about Maghribi history and societies. What often emerged out of the colonial literature was a set of concepts, formulated in a racialized language, that sought to demonstrate the "colonizability" of North African societies and hence give support for the French colonial project. With a few exceptions, colonial histories showed only a partial understanding of the colonial experience and at the same time relegated the conditions of indigenous people to static notions of culture in an unhistorical interpretation of the past. A series of dichotomies were then elaborated ("civilized" and "uncivilized," "modern" and "archaic," "rational" and "irrational") to justify the eminent historical role of the *mission civilisatrice:* to bring reason and progress to people who were perceived as backward.

It is against the colonialist mode of representation that nationalist histories emerged. The "decolonization" of Maghribi history was one of the goals of a kind of revisionist historiography that sought to show the dire effects of French colonial penetration on the socioeconomic structures of societies.[40] The dominant colonialist interpretation of the precolonial Maghribi as anarchic was being challenged by a new vision that emphasized the preexistence of the nation state and the subsequent emergence of resistance movements against colonial rule. Nationalist historians of the postcolonial era concentrated on the political and economic history of the colonial state and on the rise of nationalist movements. In doing so, they remained limited to elite politics and deprived the majority of the people from their agency. A major characteristic of this new historiography was the production of new dichotomies between "colonizer" and "colonized," "resisters" and "collaborators," "colonialism" and "nationalism." The corrective aspect of this conceptual framework was simultaneously a source of its strength and weakness. While it attempted to historicize the social and economic conditions under which colonialism manifested itself, it created a set of homogeneous categories that reproduced a different version of the colonialist discourse itself. What was missing from such conceptual framework was the behavior of a large number of North Africans who reacted in different ways to the colonial enterprise. Our attention should therefore be directed to the ways in which particular groups adapted to, appropriated, or resisted the roles that were imposed on them by the colonizing project. The case of the Moroccan colonial soldiers provides an example of these social categories outside the field of elite nationalist politics. In that sense these soldiers were neither "resisters" nor "collaborators." While their behavior toward colonial rule was ultimately the product of the conditions of exploitation to which they were subjected to as subaltern groups, they had to renegotiate their position and make the best of it. Their reaction to colonial rule was the outcome of local politics and the limited economic options that were available to them. The Moroccan colonial soldiers were coerced into recruitment in the French army, but they became at the same time agents of colonization.

At least one way of rewriting the history of colonial Maghrib is to look at the histories of subaltern groups from the perspective of oral history and popular memory. As Frederick Cooper and Ann Stoler aptly wrote, "We need to confront the more elusive methodological problem of connecting what was written to what was said and to what was done, of exploring the relationship of the language of the written documents to the language of the people who were the objects of bureaucracy but the subjects of their own life."[41] In the case of the Moroccan colonial soldiers, oral accounts not only enrich our understanding of the diverse motives that stimulated enlistment in the colonial army but also give more direct testimonies of the broader historical consequences resulting from French colonial penetration in Morocco. Historians can no longer rely solely on the archives in order to do colonial history of the Maghrib. More conceptual and methodological tools will be required to broaden our understanding of the political, social and cultural dynamics of colonial rule in the Maghrib. I think it is also time to shake off any lingering hold of colonialism in the Maghribi collective consciousness and to unmask the illusive realities of nationalism.

For the past three decades, the idea that nations are created has become more widely accepted. Scholars such as Benedict Anderson, Eric Hobsbawm, and Terence Ranger have shown how nations are imaginary constructs even though they remain legitimate political entities.[42] Historians of the Maghrib should start asking similar questions about how the "nation" was imagined and to what extent this whole process was implicated in the colonial project. Because it emerged more strongly in the colonial context of nationalist struggle for independence, the "nation" in North Africa is still perceived as a totality without being problematized. This conceptual/political stance was fundamental for its existence in the aftermath of the independence movements. But is it still legitimate today to concentrate historical research around the category of nation? Can we speak of "other histories" that do not take nation-forming as the central theme of their narratives?

Notes

A different version of this paper was originally presented at the thirtieth annual meeting of the Middle East Studies Association in Providence, Rhode Island. I would like to thank Edmund Burke III, Ali Abdullatif Ahmida, Moshe Gershovich, and Tyler Stovall for their suggestions and comments on this paper. Part of the research for this paper was supported with grants from the American Institute for Maghrib Studies and the History Department at the University of California at Santa Cruz. The author wishes to thank both institutions for their support.

1. Ranjit Guha and Gayatri Chakravorty Spivak (eds.), *Selected Subaltern Studies* (New York: Oxford University Press, 1988), p. 35.
2. On the debate about the Subaltern studies group, see Ranajit Guha and Gayatri Chakravorty Spivak (eds.), *Selected Subaltern Studies.* See also Gyan Prakash, "Writing Post-Orientalist Histories of the Third World: Perspectives from Indian Historiography," *Comparative Study of Society and History* 32:2 (1990).
3. This distinction between "autobiographical memory" and "historical memory" is borrowed from Maurice Halbwach's *La Memoire Collective* (Paris: P.U.F., 1950). More recent studies of memory are to be found in Maurice Crubelier's *La Memoire des Francais: recherche d'Histoire Culturelle* (Paris: Henry Veyrier, 1991); Henry Rousso, *Le Syndrome de Vichy* (Paris: Seuil, 1990); and Pierre Nora, *Les Lieux de Memoire* (Paris: Gallimard, 1986).
4. Abdallah Laroui, *The History of the Maghrib* (Princeton, NJ: Princeton University Press, 1977), pp. 351–354.
5. Most historians of colonial North Africa deal with the colonial troops within the overall political conflicts between metropolitan and colonial interests. Colonial soldiers are not dealt with as real human actors in history.
6. Quoted in Andre-Paul Comor, *La Legion Etrangere* (Paris: P.U.F., 1992), p. 12.
7. "La Memoire Oubliee des Goums Marocains," Serie d'Alain de Sedouy et realisation de Ahmed el-Maanouni, 1992.
8. Examples of this literature include, among others, Louis Berteil, *Baroud Pour Rome Italie 44* (Paris: Flammarion, 1966); Henry Bordeaux, *Henry de Bournazel* (Paris: Plon, 1935); Jacques Weygand, *Goumier de L'Atlas* (Paris: Flammarion, 1954).
9. Commonly known as "l'ordre 100 du premier November 1908," it called for a more institutionalized and disciplined military formation.
10. Quoted in Jean Saulay, *Histoire des Goums Marocains* (Paris: La Koumia, 1985), p. 34.
11. The number of 22,000 is presented in Commandant Coudry's article, "L'Armee et la Mise en Valeur du Maroc," *Revue Historique de l'Armee* 2 (June 1952): 79. The figure of 12,583 is estimated in Daniel Rivet, *Lyautey et L'Institution du Protectorat Francais au Maroc, 1912–1925* (Paris: L'Harmattan, 1988), vol. 2, p. 68.
12. Colonel Yves Jouin, "Le Camouflage des Goums Marocains Pendant la Periode d'Armistice," *Revue Historique de L'Armee,* Vol. 2, 1972, p. 107.
13. Ibid., p. 116.
14. Jean Naudou, "Le Maroc en 1963," C.H.E.A.M. no. 3771, p. 5.
15. See Lt. Col. Lugand, "Historique des Tirailleurs Marocains," *Revue Historique de l'Armee* 2 (June 1952).
16. Muhammad Berkaoui, *Le Maroc et la Premiere Guerre Mondiale,* unpublished doctoral thesis, Universite de Provence, 1987, p. 193.

17. Lugand, p. 47
18. Ibid., p. 32.
19. Coudry, p. 80.
20. Jean Saulay, *Histoire des Goums Marocains* (Paris: La Koumia,1985), vol. 1, p. 15.
21. Yves Salkin, *Histoire des Goums Marocains* (Paris: La Koumia, 1989), vol. 2, p. 23.
22. Quoted in Charles-Andre Julien, *Le Maroc Face Aux Imperialismes* (Paris: Editions J. A., 1978), p. 99.
23. Spillmann, "Les Goums Mixtes Morocains," *Revue Historique de l'Armee* 2 (June 1952): 139–140.
24. Yves Salkin, *Histoire des Goums Marocains* (Paris: La Koumia, 1989), p. 22.
25. Paul Ducray, "Les Tirailleurs Marocains, Leur Recrutement," C.H.E.A.M., no. 1143, 1947, p. 5.
26. Colonel Paul Azan, *L'Armee Indigene Nord-Africaine* (Paris: Charles-Lavauzelle, 1925), p. 32.
27. Ibid., p. 38.
28. Ibid., p. 39.
29. Robert Montagne, *Les Berberes et le Makhzen Dans le Sud du Maroc* (Paris, 1930), p. 4.
30. P. Rondot, "Remarques Sur la Selection des Contingents Nord-Africains," C.H.E.A.M. no. 1007.
31. Frantz Fanon, *The Wretched of the Earth* (New York: Grove Weidenfeld,1991), pp. 209–210.
32. Muhammad Abid Al-Jabiri, *Nahnu wa al-turath* (Beirut, 1980).
33. Eric Hobsbawm, "The New Threat to History," *New York Review of Books* 15 (December 1993).
34. From an interview conducted in the summer of 1995.
35. Abdallah Laroui, *The History of the Maghrib* (Princeton, NJ: Princeton University Press, 1977), pp. 352–354
36. Ibid., p. 352.
37. See Maurice Halbwach, *La Memoire Collective* (Paris: P.U.F., 1950).
38. Jacques Augarde, *La Longue Route des Tabors* (Paris: Editions France-Empire, 1983), p. 44.
39. Lucien Bodard, *The Quicksand War: Prelude to Vietnam* (Boston: Little, Brown, 1967), pp. 300–308.
40. Muhammad Sahli's title was quite revealing as to the purpose of this kind of nationalist literature: *Decoloniser l'Histoire: Introduction a L'Histoire du Maghreb* (Paris: 1965).
41. Frederick Cooper and Ann Stoler, "Tensions of Empire: Colonial Control and Visions of Rule," *American Ethnologist* 16:4 (1989).
42. Benedict Anderson, *Imagined Communities: Reflections on the Origin and Spread of Nationalism* (London: Verso, 1980); Eric Hobsbawm and Terence Ranger (eds.), *The Invention of Tradition* (Cambridge: Cambridge University Press, 1983).

Part III

Identity Formation, Gender, and Culture

Chapter 4

Identity and Alienation in Postcolonial Libyan Literature

The Trilogy of Ahmad Ibrahim al-Faqih

Ali Abdullatif Ahmida

Literature, films, and oral traditions are important but often neglected resources for the study of social and political life in Middle East studies. These nonconventional resources provide a counter view to official state history.[1] Furthermore, writers in Third World societies play a different role from that of their counterparts in Western societies. Like Latin American writers, Arab poets and novelists have been active in political and social challenges of postcolonial societies and are taken very seriously by the public. One can think of Taha Hussain, Abbas Mahmud al-'Akkad, Tawfiq al-Hakim, Naguib Mahfouz, Badr Shakir al-Sayyab, Abdulwahhab al-Bayati, Ahmad Fu'ad Najam, Mudhafar al-Nawab, and Nizar Qabani, to mention only a few influential Arab writers. These writers play a public role similar to the role played by American public intellectuals such as W. E. B. Du Bois, Noam Chomsky, Cornel West, and Edward Said.

The need for cultural and social sources is even more urgent in the case of Libyan studies in the United States, where most of the journalistic and scholarly writings on Libya are characterized by a fixation on a state-centered perspective, especially the persona of Col. Muammar Qadhdhafi and terrorism. Yet no state exists without a society, and unless one assumes that political leaders—like Qadhdhafi—are above society, then taking society seriously is an essential prerequisite for understanding any culture.[2] Extending a study to include Libyan society and analyzing its diverse voices by exploring its literature will shed new light on understanding where Qadhdhafi originated and how Libyan society has reacted to state policies. As a political scientist deeply involved with literature, one of my objectives is to recapture some neglected aspects of Libyan politics and culture. This essay attempts to introduce the magnum opus of the leading Libyan writer Ahmad Ibrahim al-Faqih and to analyze how he interprets questions of identity, cultural encounter, and social alienation in contemporary Libya.

The focus of this chapter is the most recent work of al-Faqih, his trilogy *Sa Ahbiqa Madinatu Ukhra, Hadhihi Tukhum Mamlakati,* and *Nafaq Tudiuhu Imra Wahida (I Shall Present You with Another City, These Are the Borders of My Kingdom,* and *A Tunnel Lit by a Woman),* which won the award for best novel in Beirut's book exhibition of 1992. Al-Faqih narrates the story of his childhood in the village of Mizda and in the city of Tripoli. The narrative reflects his perception of Libyan culture and politics under two regimes: the monarchy from 1951–1969 and the republic/jamahiriyya after 1969. I shall be focusing on the novelist's responses to the social and cultural transformation and upheavals following the creation of the Libyan state, the discovery of oil, and the military revolution of 1969. I shall argue that these changes put tremendous pressures on Libyan writers to find new forms to articulate their experiences and the new social realities that they encountered. A review of Libyan literature since the 1960s is important to place al-Faqih's trilogy in a larger social and cultural context.

Al-Faqih is a middle-class modernist writer who belongs to what is called in Libya the "1960s generation." This group includes prominent Libyan fiction writers such as Al-Sadiq al-Naihum, Yusif al-Sharif, Ali al-Rgaii, Muhammad al-Shaltami, and Ibrahim al-Kuni. These writers began to publish poetry and short stories in the early 1960s.[3] Recently, al-Faqih and al-Kuni have gained acclaim in the Arab world, and some of their works have been translated into other languages, including Russian, German, Chinese, and English.[4] Al-Faqih received critical acclaim as one of the most talented short-story writers in Libya. In 1965, his first collection of short stories, *Al-Bahr La ma Fih* (There Is No Water in the Sea), appeared in 1965 and won the highest award sponsored by the Royal Commission of Fine Arts in Libya.

Al-Faqih's work reflects themes of tension and conflict between patriarchal, rural village life and individualistic, urban values. This is not surprising, as Libyan society had just begun to experience a deep process of urbanization and social change due to the impact of the new oil economy in the early 1960s.[5] Most Libyan writers of that period focused on the genre of the short story, and only when urban life became more complex in the late 1980s did the novel appear in Libyan literature. If the novel is the product of bourgeois capitalist society, then the emergence of the novel as a new genre in Libyan literature is a clear sign that a bourgeois middle class developed in Libyan society.

The most prolific writer of his generation, al-Faqih has published eighteen books, ranging from plays and short stories to novels and essays.[6] The trilogy is not only the culmination of his creative work and productive literary career, but it has many similarities to the author's life. In fact, the name of the main protagonist, Khalil al-Imam, resembles the author's name. Khalil is the nickname for Ibrahim, and Imam is a synonym for Faqih in Arabic. Furthermore, Khalil al-Imam, the hero of the trilogy, like the novelist, was born in a Libyan village, moved to Tripoli, and studied theater and literature in Great Britain.

Understanding that most readers are not aware of his work, brief biographical notes of al-Faqih are appropriate before analyzing the themes presented in his trilogy. Al-Faqih was born on December 28, 1932, in a small village in western Tripolitania, called Mizda, which is located one hundred miles south of the city of Tripoli. He studied in his village until the age of 15 when he moved to Tripoli, the capital and largest city in the country. In 1962, he left Libya for Egypt to study journalism in a UNESCO program and then returned to Tripoli to work as a journalist. Between 1962 and 1971, he was offered a scholarship to study theater in London. When he came back to Libya in 1972, he was appointed head of the National Institute of Music and Drama. In 1972, al-Faqih became the editor of the influential *Cultural Weekly.* After that, he returned to England as a Libyan diplomat and began to study for his doctorate in literature. In 1990, he finished his degree and returned to North Africa, where he now divides his time between residences in Cairo and Rabat.[7]

This trilogy, al-Faqih's most ambitious and mature work, presents Khalil al-Imam, a Libyan student who goes to the University of Edinburgh in Scotland to study for his doctorate in literature. His dissertation topic is based on the impact of Arabic myths on English literature, specifically sex and violence in the folk tales of the *Arabian Nights.* The first book of the trilogy takes place in Scotland, where Khalil is thrown into a world of foreigners, especially women, and tries to find a way to deal with the new culture. In the second volume, Khalil goes back to his country, Libya, to teach at Tripoli University. There, as in England, he runs into emotional trouble and becomes severely depressed. With the help of a Muslim healer, he experiences an exciting Sufi spiritual journey to a utopian city of the past. But because of his unpredictable hubris, he destroys his happiness by opening a forbidden door and hence finds himself back in the city of concrete reality, Tripoli, where he faces the actuality of Libyan society while vainly attempting to find his own identity. This trilogy dramatizes through fantasy the depth of the social and political alienation of some Western-educated Libyan intellectuals in the postcolonial period.[8] The problem of alienation from the West and Libyan society is shared by many Arab and Third World intellectuals.

Al-Faqih begins the three books of his trilogy with the statement, "A time has passed and another time is not coming," and ends the third book with the pessimistic statement, "A time has passed and another time has not come and will never come." The novelist is dubious about the possibility of a positive change, because as long as the existing social and political conditions are reproduced, society, like Khalil, is stalled. The trilogy deals effectively with the social and political causes of such pessimism and the troubles experienced by Khalil al-Imam, who is torn between the values of a traditional, patriarchal life in the village and a contemporary, individualistic life in the city. At the very beginning, Khalil enters a new city, Edinburgh. As he is looking for a room to rent, he comes across a couple, Linda and Donald. He rents a room in their house. One night Linda comes to his room, and they begin a love affair. Donald, who is interested in Eastern philosophies, does not mind sharing Linda with Khalil. To further complicate his personal life, Khalil meets another woman at the university, Sandra, who plays Desdemona to Khalil's Othello in the student theater production. One night after rehearsal he and Sandra get drunk, and the next morning, he finds her next to him in bed. When Linda discovers the affair, she decides to end her relationship with Khalil. But Linda becomes pregnant and Khalil realizes that because Donald is impotent, he is the true father of the child. Khalil tries to go back to Linda, but she refuses. He becomes torn between the two women. Linda decides to leave the house and go back to her parents with Khalil's child, Adam. In the meantime, Sandra is kidnapped by a gang of youths who brutally rape her and leave her near death. Fortunately, she is saved and taken to the hospital. Only then does Khalil discover that Sandra's father, who takes her to his own home, is a millionaire. Khalil finishes his doctorate on sex and violence in *The Arabian Nights,* which echoes the same disturbed emotions of his real-life encounters with Linda and Sandra and the tragic rape of the latter. He remembers his family and country and decides to go back to Libya, leaving behind his child, Adam, with Linda. The symbolic meaning of this section of the novel is the creation of a bond between Libyan and British cultures. The name of the child Adam signifies the common origins of mankind, the prophet Adam. Khalil's attempts to pursue love and adopt the values of Western society, however, fail due to his unpredictable cravings and his inability to decide between Linda and Sandra. In the end, he loses both women.

The second book of the trilogy begins, again, with the statement, "A time has passed and another time is not coming." By repeating the same statement, the novelist wants to remind the reader that Khalil is still trapped in a continuous state of hopelessness. Khalil returns to Tripoli where he becomes a professor at Tripoli University. Because of family pressure, he agrees to marry Fatima, a school teacher, to prove his membership in a society that expects young men and women to be married at an early age. However, after three years in this loveless marriage, he becomes very depressed.[9] He tries modern therapy, yet doctors are not able to figure out the cause of his severe psychological illness. Out of desperation, he accepts his brother's advice to see a Muslim healer, a Sufi *faqih,* for treatment.

Desperate for a cure, Khalil goes to his childhood neighborhood in the old city of Tripoli to meet Faqih Sadiq Abu al-Khayrat, whose name, literally translated in English, means "Truthful the father of good life." Notice the significance of this for Khalil. Modern medicine cannot cure Khalil's depression because his illness is not physiological but emotional and spiritual.[10] Only a Muslim healer, whose name and specialty are "Truth and the meaning of good life," can help him. Faqih Abu al-Khayrat burns some frankincense and recites verses from the Quran. Suddenly, Khalil finds himself in a utopian city called Necklace of Jewels, reminiscent of a city in *The Arabian Nights* of the eleventh century B.C. This fantastic city has no prisons, no taxes, no police, no wages. Life is communal, and production is shared. This is a subtle critique of the Arab state, which relies on secret police, as well as the repression of intellectuals and freedom of expression.[11] According to tradition, he marries the princess, Narjiss of the Hearts, and becomes the prince of the city. Yet the princess warns him not to enter a secret room in the palace, as the ancestors have warned people about the curse of the room.

Khalil finds happiness and love in the city of dreams. Then, disturbingly, he meets Budur, a beautiful singer. He falls in love with her and as in the case of the first book, is torn between two women, Narjiss and Budur. Also, as in the case of Linda, Khalil discovers that Narjiss is pregnant with his child. One has to remember that Linda in the first book and Narjiss in the second book both conceived children with Khalil, while his Libyan wife, Fatima, cannot bear children. Love seems to be associated with fertility in the novel. And since Khalil does not love his wife, she cannot bear children with him, while in the first two books of the trilogy Linda and Narjiss both become pregnant after loving relationships with Khalil. Worse for him, his reckless desire leads him to open the door of the secret room. A nasty yellow wind blasts from the room and he suddenly finds himself back again in the present in the city of Tripoli. He realizes he has been in a dream, a beautiful one that he has destroyed. Khalil is unable to commit himself to a normal loving relationship even when he lives in a dreamlike utopian city. Therefore, he returns to brute reality and his life in Tripoli.

The third volume of the trilogy takes place in the city of reality, Tripoli. His wife, Fatima, wants a child, but he is not interested. Once again, he becomes depressed and alienated from his wife's family and from his boring job at the university. Before slipping into a deeper depression, however, he meets Sana Amir, a beautiful and intelligent pharmacy graduate student at the University of Tripoli. She becomes the woman who lights up his life as the title of the third book of the trilogy indicates. When Fatima discovers her husband's new love, Khalil insists on a divorce, but Fatima demands ownership of the flat, which he does not mind relinquishing.

Khalil becomes a free and happy man in love with Sana. One day he meets his childhood friend, Juma Abu Khatwa, who goes to al-Azhar University but returns to Tripoli to become a singer by the name of Anwar Jalal. Anwar invites Khalil to his parties where he discovers the life of music, dance, sex, and drinking. Despite the fact that alcohol, drugs, and premarital sex are restricted by state laws, Anwar's parties are frequented and protected by state officials who seem to be alienated from the official claims of Islamic purity.[12] Khalil sarcastically chastises the hypocrisy of a society in which "People . . . burn trees and replace them with pillars of cement, and . . . camels are slaughtered and replaced by big iron insects called cars."[13] Through Khalil's character, the novelist expresses his distaste not only for some of the tribal and Islamic laws but also for the new consumerism of the modern oil economy, because it marginalizes individuals like Khalil who do not fit in. Khalil is now completely alienated from what he views as the rigid social values of honor and family. He finds the university restrictive and plagued by corruption. One day he drives his car around the city of Tripoli thinking, "My city is no longer a village but not yet a city not Eastern or Western; it does not belong to the past nor to the present, between the desert and the sea, between past time and a time that is not coming."[14] This is a significant statement as it expresses the middle class, cosmopolitan, and modernist views of al-Faqih toward his city, and the fact that Libyan society is dominated by hinterland rural forces. He struggles with his society's historical specificity, the hegemony of the rural and tribal forces of the hinterland over the weak urban centers. This historical specificity in Libya is different from other Eastern Arab societies such as Egypt, Syria, Palestine, and Lebanon where notables and large landowners in big urban cities such as Cairo, Damascus, and Beirut dominate the countryside. Libya has had two leaders after independence, King Idriss al-Sanusi and Muammar al-Qadhdhafi, both of whom came from and were supported by social forces from the hinterland.[15] This historical context is essential in understanding the causes of alienation of a Western educated intellectual such as Khalil al-Imam, who finds his escape in alcohol, sex, and music. The problem of intellectual displacement from both the West and one's own society is not unique to al-Faqih and is shared by many individuals from Third World countries. The causes of this displacement are cultural encounter and social class. Third World societies experienced capitalist colonization by European states and found themselves struggling to figure out their identity. But many Third World intellectuals have come from a middle- or upper-class background and therefore look down at their own peasant/tribal cultures using the language of modernity and progress.

Plagued by conflicting desires in his real city, Khalil cannot wait to be happy with Sana, the woman who now lights his passage through life, but in a wild destructive moment tries to rape her in his apartment. She leaves him, and he must now face himself and his troubles. Torn between dreams and reality, he can no longer teach, and the university fires him. He becomes a full member of Anwar's group, and the trilogy ends with the statement, "A time has passed, another is not coming and will never come." Although the ending is sad and pessimistic, it is nonetheless realistic. Khalil's life and his society are still full of contradictions, and there can be no change in Khalil's life as long as these contradictions exist.

Many other Arab writers have dealt with these questions before from the Egyptian Tawfiq al-Haqim to the Sudanese al-Tayib Salih.[16] Like the Sudan, Libya was a colony of Italy from 1911 to 1943, and from 1943 to 1951 it was occupied by the British and French armies who defeated the German and Italian forces in the destructive battles of World War II. Libyan independence was the product of rivalry between the Allies. At the beginning of the Cold War, the strategic location of Libya was crucial for British and American interests, especially after the 1948 war in Palestine, Nasser's revolution in Egypt in 1952, and the nationalization of the Suez Canal in 1956. Also, two other factors were important: the demands of the exiled Libyan leaders in Egypt for independence and the support of the Arab league of such demands. These interests were not the same.

The British policy then was hostile to the Tripolitanian nationalist demands for a unified country and close ties with the Arab League. Only when a diplomatic alliance between the gradualist and pragmatist Amir Idriss al-Sanusi, the exiled leader of the defeated Sanusiyya order, and the British colonial in Egypt was established did Libyan independence become a real possibility. In 1951, England and the United States engineered the creation of an independent Libyan state in exchange for a political alliance with military bases. Political parties were banned, and the leader of the Tripolitanian Congress party Bashir al-Sadawi was stripped of his citizenship and sent into exile in 1953.

Libyan independence was a major threshold for the Libyan people. However, such independence brought many contradictions. The monarchy faced the heavy task of building nationhood and interacting with the international system after a brutal colonization under the Italian colonial state, which led to the death of half of the population including the educated elite. A Libyan state was created, but one without a strong Libyan nationhood. The monarchy was dominated by tribal shaykhs and urban notables. Also, the state was one of the poorest in the world with an average income of $35 per capita and a 90 percent illiteracy rate, one of the highest illiteracy rates in the world in 1951. The state was dependent on economic aid and rent for military bases for England and the United States. The political structure of Libya was designed by the United Nations as a federal constitutional monarchy with three regional states. The aloof King Idriss lived in Tubruq next to a British military base in Eastern Libya and favored his eastern region Barqa, even though the population of this region made up only 27 percent of the total population of the country, while Tripolitania's population was 68 percent and Fezzan's, the southern region, 5 percent.

The discovery and the exportation of oil in 1961 had a major economic and social impact on the country. Suddenly the Libyan state, which was one of the poorest, became one of the richest in Africa and the Middle East. The monarchy initiated various programs in education, health, transportation, and housing. A new Libyan university was opened in 1955 with two campuses in Benghazi and Tripoli. By the late 1960s, the educational policies led to the rise of a new salaried middle class, a militant student movement, a small working class, trade unions, and modern intellectuals such as al-Faqih. The Sanusi monarchy lasted from 1951 until 1969, when a military coup replaced it and declared a republic, and in 1977, the name of Libya was changed to Jamahiriyya, the "state of the masses" in Arabic.

During the old regime, Libya shared close educational, economic, and military ties with the West, especially England and the United States. Libyan students were sent to these countries and Egypt rather than to Russia or China. Therefore, Khalil al-Imam's trip to Scotland is the result of the colonial and cultural hegemony of Great Britain over Libya after 1943. Al-Faqih's trilogy is similar to al-Tayib Salih's novel, *Season of the Migration to the North.* Both examine the dislocation and alienation of Arab men and their confrontation with Westernization and modernity in different overtones: Sudanese and Libyan. Nevertheless, there are certainly differences between both works. Salih's novel deals with the impact of colonial dislocation, while al-Faqih's trilogy, two decades later, is concerned with postcolonial nationalist culture.

The roots of a torn personality such as Khalil's are not found in the traveling genre of the Arabic novel focusing mainly on East/West encounters, but in the protagonist's fundamental alienation from his own society. Khalil is moody, unpredictable, and violent, as the topic of his doctoral dissertation suggests. That is why this novel is as complex and multifaceted as al-Tayib Salih's *Season of the Migration to the North.* Like Mustafa Said,

Khalil al-Imam faces violence and uncertainties in Great Britain and at home in northern Sudan and western Libya. Moreover, the Libyan novelist brilliantly adopts the style and narration of *The Arabian Nights,* especially in the first and second books. It must be remembered that, unlike poetry, the novel is a new literary form in Libya, but like other Arab novelists, al-Faqih is giving the novel Arab and Libyan voices during a time of capitalist transformation.

But what are the roots of Khalil's troubles and unpredictability, especially his feelings toward women? The novelist suggests that the problem of Khalil is of culture and class. Al-Faqih gives the reader a clue from Khalil's childhood in the village. Khalil almost dies because the man who circumcises him uses an unclean knife, which causes an inflammation of the penis. Due to the lack of medical care and rampant poverty in the village, Khalil cannot be treated before migrating with his family to the city of Tripoli. The physical problem of his penis carries with it the patriarchal wounded male identity to which Khalil refers in the trilogy: "This penis which I almost lost due to my circumcision is the only thing that Sana does not have."[17] Khalil uses violence and sex with women to assert his personality and male ego. He elaborates further, stating, "I know that sex is natural, but I pursue it with a psychology that carries with it old wounds of tribal societies that migrated to the cities. I love and hate every woman. I hold them responsible for the feeling of shame I felt after each time I masturbated. These feelings are the ones that destroyed my relationship with Linda and Sana."[18] This is the root of his sexual and social troubles. He becomes aware of it when he travels to Britain and becomes distanced from Libyan culture when he is able to look back at his society. Khalil's disillusionment is also political since he is alienated from his society, his tribe, his family, the university, and the state. He blames all of them for his emotional, sexual, and political alienation.

The trilogy explodes with all these contradictions and gives no direct clue as to how they can be resolved. According to the author, there can be no happy ending to this complex novel, not until Libyan society itself resolves these conflicts. The author does not apologize for these contradictions, nor does he create a happy ending for his novel. These are not unique contradictions, since other societies experiencing colonialism, economic transformation, and social and cultural dislocation suffer the same challenges. What seems unique to Libyan society is its persisting autonomous kinship and Islamic social organizations, its weak urban centers, and its reluctance to adopt the modern nation-state. Ibrahim al-Faqih dramatizes these cultural and social conflicts from a middle-class modernist perspective and consequently brings Libyan society into contemporary history.

Notes

1. See Catherine Zuckert, "Why Political Scientists want to study Literature," *PC: Political Science and Politics* XXVIII:2 (June 1995): 189–190, and Bradford Burns, "The Novel as History: A Reading Guide," in his book *Latin America,* 6th ed. (Englewood Cliffs, NJ: Prentice-Hall, 1994), pp. 355–362.
2. I relied on oral traditions in my study of Libyan social history. See my book *The Making of Modern Libya, State Formation, Colonization and Resistance, 1830–1932* (Albany: State University of New York Press, 1994).
3. For an introduction to the modern Arabic novel, see Roger Allen, *The Arabic Novel, An Historical and Critical Introduction* (Syracuse, NY: University of Syracuse Press, 1982). On modern Libyan literature, see Muhammad Ahmad Atiyya, *Fi al-Adab al-Libi al-Hadith* (Of Modern Libyan Literature) (Tripoli: Dar al-Kitab al-Arabi, 1973), and for a survey of the Libyan novel, see Sammar Ruhi al-Faysal, *Dirasat Fi al-Riwaiya al Libiyya* (Studies in the Libyan Novel) (Tripoli: Al-Munsha al-Ama Lil Nashir Wa al-Tawzi Wa Illan, 1983).
4. Ibrahim al-Kuni's focus is the opposite of al-Faqih's. He writes about Libyan society from within. Al-Kuni's novels and short stories are about the Libyan Sahara, and its people, animals, and legends, not about urban life like al-Faqih's. For a good introduction to Ibrahim al-Kuni's work, see Ferial J. Ghazoul, "Al-Riwaiya al-Sufiyya Fi al-Adab al- Magharibi" (The Sufi Novel In the Maghrib) *ALIF* 17 (1997): 28–53.
5. For an analysis of the impact of oil on Libyan society, see A. J. Allan, *Libya: The Experience of Oil* (Boulder, CO: Westview Press, 1981), and A. J. Allan, ed., *Libya Since Independence* (New York: St. Martin's Press, 1982). On migration to the city of Tripoli see James Harrison, "Migrants in the City of Tripoli," *Geographical Journal* 57 (July 1967): 415, and Yasin al-Kabir, *Al-Muhajurun Fi Trabulus al-Gharb* (Immigrants to the City of Tripoli) (Beirut: Mahad al-Inma al-Arabi, 1982).
6. For an overview of al-Faqih's publications, see Lee Rong Jian, "Mazij Min al-Hulm Wa al-Dhakira" (A Mixture of Memory and Imagination) *Adab Wa Naqd* (1992): 110–113.
7. Despite al-Faqih's subtle criticism of Libyan politics and his disillusionment with pan-Arab politics, he has served as a Libyan diplomat and wrote an epilogue to Qadhdhafi's collection of short stories, *Al-Qariyya al-Qariyya, al-Ard al-Ard Wa Intihar Raid al-Fada* (The Village the Village, the Land the Land, and the Suicide of an Astronaut) (Zawiyya: Mataba al-Wahda al-Arabiyya, 1993).
8. See al-Faqih's interview in *Al-Wasat* 815 (1995): 60–65.
9. The character of Fatima in the trilogy is represented in a static way. For an alternative female perspective, see the work of the Libyan writer Sharifa al-Qayadi, *Min Awraqi al-Khasa* (From My Private Papers) (Tripoli: Al Munsha al-Ama Lil Nashir wa-Tawzi Wa Illan,1986).
10. On the influence of Sufi Islam on Maghribi literature, see Ferial J. Ghazoul, pp. 28–53.

11. See the interview with al-Faqih in *Al-Wasat,* p. 61, and his essay in *Al-Sharq al-Awsat* 5391, September 1, 1993.
12. On the politics of Islamic laws in Libya, see Ann Elizabeth Mayer, "Legislation in Defense of Arabo-Islamic Sexual Mores," *American Journal of Comparative Law* 27 (1979): 541–559, and her chapter "In Search of Sacred Law: The Meandering Course of Qadhafi's legal policy," in Dirk Vandewalle, ed., *Qadhafi's Libya, 1969–1994* (New York: St. Martin's Press, 1995).
13. Al-Faqih, Trilogy III, p. 256.
14. Ibid., p. 235.
15. King Idriss's social base was in the Eastern region Barqa, while Qadhdhafi was born in the central region and went to school in the southern region, Fezzan.
16. For a comparative analysis of this genre, see Mary N. Layoun, *Travels of A Genre, The Modern Novel and Ideology* (Princeton, NJ: Princeton University Press, 1990). On Arab intellectuals' views of modernity and identity, see the classic critique by Abdallah Laroui, *The Crisis of the Arab Intellectual: Traditionalism or Historicism?,* trans. Diarmid Cammel (Berkeley: University of California Press, 1976); Issa J. Boulata, "Encounter between East and West: A Theme in Contemporary Arabic Novels," *Middle East* Journal (1976): 49–62, and on Taib Saleh's novel, see Saree S. Makdisi, "The Empire Renarrated: *Season of Migration to the North* and the Reinvention of the Present," *Critical Inquiry* 18:4 (Summer 1992): 804–820. For a female Arab perspective on Western cultural encounter, see the Egyptian critic and novelist Radwa Ashour, *Al-Rihla, Yawmiyyat Taliba Masriyya Fi America* (The Trip, Days of an Egyptian Student in America) (Beirut: Dar al-Adab, 1983).
17. Al-Faqih, Trilogy III, p. 195.
18. Al-Faqih, Trilogy I, p. 150.

Chapter 5

Cartographies of Identity

Writing Maghribi Women as Postcolonial Subjects

Mona Fayad

In "Towards the Development of Post-Islamist and Post-Nationalist Feminist Discourses in the Middle East," Mervat Hatem outlines the "old and tired concepts and roles that cannot be expected to deliver new solutions"—traditional approaches to nationalism.[1] Hatem categorizes primarily three traditional approaches: the modernist-nationalist discourse, the national liberation discourse, and the dependency discourse. Hatem argues for going beyond such discourses. Yet, as the search continues for a feminist identity that is local and specific to the conditions that Arab women face, the terms of the debate remain centered on issues of cultural identity. In many senses, this is inescapable, given the so-called postcolonial status of any national subject in the Arabic context seeking to define his or her identity. For, as Saree Makdisi points out in "The Empire Renarrated," the very category of "postcolonial" in Arabic literature implies a crisis, a lack of closure that prevents identity from being fully inscribed within the terms of tradition and modernity that are so much a part of constructing the concept of national identity.[2] This very lack of closure, while apparently traumatic, bodes well from a feminist perspective. The advantage of working in terms of a "postcolonial" identity as opposed to a "national" identity is that the terms of the debate can be seen from a different perspective, allowing women a position that differs radically from the limited and restricted role Arab women have been given within national narratives.[3] For while it would be counterproductive at this point historically to premise identity on a rejection of nationalism, it is clear that from a feminist perspective there is a need for a fundamental rethinking of the terms through which nationalism has come to be defined.[4]

The construction of Arab women's identities consequently partakes in an attempt to construct the postcolonial. In order for such a construction to escape the limitations outlined by Hatem, the subject must relocate or dislocate herself from a particular historical context that has always already overdetermined the subject's identity within the categories of First/Third World, Western/non-Western, margin/periphery. In the case of the writers I am dealing with, Moroccan Fatima Mernissi and Algerian Assia Djebar, such relocation involves rethinking the very terms that the debate has taken for granted. Mernissi and Djebar are currently engaged in revisionary historical projects that draw on the Islamic tradition and articulate a resistance to colonialism that is not simply a response to a particular moment in history (the colonial occupation itself), but is based on a reaction to the cultural erosion that is taking place in many countries in the Arab world as nationalism, itself, either in terms of pan-Arab nationalism or in terms of local nationalisms, becomes engulfed in the demands of a global economy and the slow encroachment of the multinationals.[5]

Christopher Miller, in "Nationalism as Resistance and Resistance to Nationalism in the Literature of Francophone Africa," points out that an integral part of the process of constructing a national "identity effect" in a postcolonial context lies in confronting the colonial constructions through which the colonizer identified the colonized.[6] For, as Miller indicates, "Within the colonial context, in which the means of producing discourse had to be appropriated by colonized subjects in a step-by-step process, new positions had to be invented, and the first of these new positions had to deal with the colonizer in his own terms. . . . Nationalism *is* that battle for the status of truth, for the power to determine dominant lies and truths. In Anderson's terms, it is a battle to decide who will imagine the community" (60). For Arab women, creating a subjectivity for themselves, particularly one that will identify them as national subjects, has required this struggle for the status of truth. Part of this struggle involves confronting the meaning of feminism and its relation to Arab women's desire for liberation. Because feminism has been and continues to be identified as an imported Western notion, what is at stake is the relation of Arab women to Western notions of "modernity," as opposed to their "entrenchment" in tradition and, by implication, their oppression. Modernity, in this construction, is equal to liberation. The argument in *New Left Review* between Ghoussoub and Hammami and Rieker is an indication of the terms through which this issue has continued to be discussed.[7] The terms of the debate itself lock women who are seeking a national identity for themselves into a no-win situation.

Either they abandon their traditions and take up a Western stance, thereby, as the argument goes, freeing themselves but losing in the process their national identity, or they remain "enslaved" within an Islamic tradition that supposedly, in its very essence, denies freedom to women.

However, as Marnia Lazreg has pointed out in "Feminism and Difference: The Perils of Writing as a Woman on Women in Algeria," one of the basic problems of this dichotomy is the persistence in feminist discourses of the "religious paradigm" that is used to define Arab women's status and hence to deny them identity other than that defined by their religion, or by the all-encompassing term "tradition." "Once researchers have decided on a functionalist/culturalist method," Lazreg argues, "they are unable to address anything but religion and tradition. The overall result is a reductive, ahistorical conception of women."[8] Chandra Mohanty, discussing the hierarchical categorization of "Third World women" within feminist studies, uncovers a fundamental difficulty in (Western) feminist perceptions of non-Western women, assumptions that take for granted, for example, that "the more the number of women who wear the veil, the more universal is the sexual segregation and control of women" (209).[9] Such an approach fails to distinguish between the meanings of various social practices, argues Mohanty, falling far short of acknowledging cultural, economic, class, and status differences in such practices: "While there may be a physical similarity in the veils worn by women in Saudi Arabia and Iran, the specific meaning attached to this practice varies according to the cultural and ideological context" (209).

What do studies on "Third World women" or " Islamic women" have to do with the construction of postcolonial identity for women writers in the Maghribi context? To return to Miller, it has everything to do with it. Postcolonial identity cannot exist, in a postcolonial or neocolonial context, without reference to the discourses of knowledge that are propagated *about* Arab women. In constructing the imaginative community that is the nation, the struggle to identify *who* defines the community is the first step toward achieving subjectivity. Since feminism appears to be the means through which this definition can be achieved, feminism becomes a focal point in determining "the status of truth." The harem and the veil, signifiers within the discourse of Western feminism of Muslim women's oppression, lie at the intersection of "liberation" and "oppression," of "modernity" and "tradition." This discourse, while less obviously immediate to Arab women writers of the Mashriq, is of vital and crucial concern to Maghribi women, whose own bilingual heritage itself places woman as subject in the postcolonial crisis Makdisi describes. For Maghribi women, therefore, any self-conscious construction of national identity within the parameters of the *postcolonial* needs to confront these issues, particularly given the connections between the call for women's liberation and the colonial occupation.[10]

Representing Boundaries

It is no coincidence, therefore, that the two North African women writers most obviously concerned with defining women's postcolonial status in the Maghrib focus on the harem or the veil. In Fatima Mernissi's *Dreams of Trespass: Tales of a Harem Girlhood,*[11] the harem forms the basic representation of the boundaries that confront women. However, Mernissi strategically questions the very concept of the harem while at the same time exploring what the notion of boundaries—personal and political—conceals and reinforces. Assia Djebar, in *Fantasia: An Algerian Cavalcade,*[12] uses the veil as a means of representing the barrier between Algerian and Western, tradition and modernity. She, however, deconstructs the concept of veiling, providing it with multiple meanings that outline, like Mernissi's harem, what is concealed behind this conflictive symbol. In the case of both writers, national identity extends beyond the apparent boundaries set up by the two modes of representation to an exploration of conflictive and often contradictory postcolonial identities.

Fatima Mernissi: Dreams of Trespass: Tales of a Harem Girlhood

Fatima Mernissi's autobiographical *Dreams of Trespass* (1994) celebrates the childhood of young Fatima. Set a few years before and after the French withdrawal from Morocco in 1956, it chronicles the search for identity of two communities of women living in two different types of "harems": one belonging to her father's family in the old section of Fez, the other in the countryside, which belongs to her maternal relatives. As the process of defining national identity in the Moroccan struggle for independence takes place, the women manage to find a space for themselves, using the nationalist movement that is sweeping Morocco as a springboard, and constructing subjectivities that the young Fatima draws upon as a means of empowerment. The autobiography shows a marked departure from Mernissi's earlier sociological works, particularly *Beyond the Veil: Male-Female Dynamics in Modern Muslim Society,* which falls into the trap of dichotomizing the opposition between modernity and tradition.[13] Refreshingly free of cliché, the account uses the harem to examine basic questions regarding Moroccan women's postcolonial identities.

To start with, Mernissi associates the harem with both visible and invisible boundaries, representing them as constructs that are specifically located historically. Her positioning on the "threshold," caught between "contesting and fighting" identities, establishes the problematic nature of boundaries from the initial chapter. The title of the chapter, "My Harem Frontiers," is consequently brought into question, since the frontiers are far from being clearly established and are in fact interpreted differently by different adults. Moreover, the concept of *hudud,* in the sense of actual national borders, seems to be constantly shifting, since the boundaries the "Christians" draw up keep changing. Morocco is divided between the Spanish and the French, and as a result, Moroccan identity is forced to accommodate the division:

> "[T]o go north, you needed a pass because you were crossing into Spanish Morocco. To go south, you needed another pass, because you were crossing into French Morocco. If you did not go along with what they said, you got stuck at 'Arbaoua, an arbitrary spot where they had built a huge gate and said that it was a frontier." (2)

The frontier, then, is arbitrarily determined, "an invisible line in the mind of the warriors" (2). The very fact that identity can depend on such an "invisible line" points to the arbitrary rules that establish both individual and national identities. Having established through a complex series of relationships the changing nature of *hudud,* Fatima extends her quest to the notion of the sacred *hudud,* and by extension, to the harem itself. She compares the boundaries of the harems with the borders that contending colonizers draw at various points of time as the map of Morocco is reshaped depending on whether the Spanish or the French have more power. For, as Fatima's cousin Samir phrases it, "the frontier is in the mind of the powerful" (3). It is up to those *inside* the frontier, however, to determine whether or not to recognize the frontier, whether it is established by colonialism or by patriarchal control.

Moreover, to problematize the term *harem* itself, Mernissi introduces in a footnote a distinction between two types of harems: "imperial harems," which disappeared with the fall of the Ottoman Empire (in other words twenty to thirty years before the events of the novel), and "domestic harems" (34). "Domestic harems" cannot be clearly defined. Polygamy is not the common factor, since many harems do not involve polygamy. The closest Mernissi is able to come to a definition of "domestic harems" is that they have in common "the men's desire to seclude their wives" (35). The form the "domestic harem" takes depends on class, geographical location, and the beliefs of both the male head of the household and the convictions of the matriarch. The rural harem in which Fatima's mother grew up, for example, is polygamous, while the one in Fez, which is where Fatima is raised, is not, since neither Fatima's father nor her uncle has married more than one wife. The various women living in the Fez household are relatives and not wives. Beyond the principle of seclusion, any attempt to generalize about "the harem" in the course of the novel proves to be impossible.

The Harem as Nation

As a social structure, Mernissi depicts the Fez harem as an imaginary community that reproduces the nation, a microcosm of the large sociopolitical macrocosm beyond. The disagreement between the women about the value of history and their differing interpretations of what tradition constitutes echo the political schisms in the public sphere. Moreover, their perceptions of the harem itself differ. For whereas Fatima's mother dreams of living, after the liberation of Morocco, in a house made entirely of glass, surrounded only by her nuclear family, Lalla Radia, for example, strongly upholds the harems, which she perceives as "wonderful things" where women can feel privileged and protected. In Lalla Radia's eyes, the colonial invasion poses a threat not only to the glory of Arab history but to an institution of privilege for women. She agrees wholeheartedly with the father's statement that "if Arab women started imitating European ones by dressing provocatively, smoking cigarettes, and running around with their hair uncovered, there would be only one culture left" (180–181). The harem, in Lalla Radia's mind, is a marker of difference, a marker of cultural identity.

From this perspective, the Fez harem is a sanctuary in which the integrity of "tradition," "culture," and "woman" can be protected. The closed walls keep away Western ideological invasion. Under the disciplinarian rule of Lalla Mani, who controls the strictly regulated community, order is maintained and the rhythms of communal living upheld. The Fez harem becomes a government in itself, with the women themselves responsible for being "good citizens," maintaining "public" order, and following clearly dictated codes of behavior.

Mernissi does not restrict herself to a reading of the harem as a contested site of cultural identity, however. As she opens up the meaning of the word further, the harem becomes a representation of any system that is locked ideologically, binding its "inhabitants" and restricting their movement. In a chapter entitled "The French Harem," Mernissi toys with an ambiguity that emphasizes the political ramifications of the term. The title is deliberately left unclear. Will the chapter illustrate a Western appropriation of the harem, fulfilling a Western "dream of trespass," a colonial desire for conquest and possession? Will the Western reader finally be allowed into the territory of the repressed erotic that has been absent so far? The chapter, in effect, reproduces the frustrated "dream of trespass" of the colonizers, providing an inverted harem. It is the colonizers, the ones on the outside, who live in a harem, not the colonized.

The site of the inverted harem is the Ville Nouvelle, the city the French have built for themselves because "they were afraid to live in ours" (23).

Shielded by weapons, afraid to step out, the French have created boundaries that restrict them in a way similar to the boundaries of the harem:

> Their fear was quite an amazing thing for us children, because we saw that grownups could be as afraid as we could. And these grownups who were afraid were on the outside, supposedly free. The powerful ones who had created the frontier were also the fearful ones. The Ville Nouvelle was their harem; just like women, they could not walk freely in the Medina. So you could be powerful, and still be the prisoner of a frontier. (23)

To the child Fatima, the fact that the French, who are powerful, choose to inhabit a world of fear and to set up boundaries to mark their fear seems incomprehensible. In a reversal, it is the colonizers who are "feminized," their weapons the "veils" behind which they hide in order to protect themselves against the "masculine" threat of the men in the Medina. Thus the French occupation, instead of fulfilling a "dream of trespass," ends up constructing a harem of its own.

By expanding the meaning of the word, Mernissi discards any monolithic representation of the harem. She presents it instead as a heterogeneous institution that is subject to interpretation, and consequently no more easily defined than the notion of boundaries, which, the narrator remarks, continues to be elusive (3). For example, the harem of Yasmina, Fatima's maternal grandmother, bears little if any resemblance to the urban harem in Fez. Yasmina's is rural, without walls or enclosures, and the women there are involved in a great deal of outdoor physical activity, including horseback riding and wading in the river. The women there include the Berber warrior Tamou, whom the grandfather marries to save her from French soldiers who are pursuing her as she escapes on horseback. Tamou, as a war heroine engaged in the anticolonial struggle, hardly fits the role of the passive, victimized woman enclosed in the harem, with her dagger, her Berber bracelets "with points sticking out, the kind of bracelets you could use to defend yourself if necessary," and her Spanish rifle (51). Nor do the other women, who are left to their own devices under the supervision of the driver Krisha, who believes that "most of Allah's creatures had enough brains to behave and act responsibly" (71), and is not concerned with asserting control. Young Fatima's complete confusion about the meaning of the word *harem* stems from the incompatibility of the use of the word to apply to two such radically different households.

But as the harem also reflects the nation, the different households come to reflect the contradictory aspects of Moroccan nationalism. As "imaginary communities," the harems bring out the ideological conflicts inherent in the creation of the national subject.

Inscribing Community

It is thus as "imaginary communities" that the harems can construct their own visions of women's identity. In *Dreams of Trespass* Mernissi does not suggest Western individualism and separation from the community as a basis for self-inscription. Rather, she represents Fatima as deeply rooted in a woman's community that creates her identity, providing it with the "dreams of trespass" that enable her to articulate herself. Rather than growing *away* from the harem, the narrator emerges *from* it, drawing from the sense of "women's solidarity" that the women often discuss in the novel. As such, even though the narrator is the young Fatima, and even though the novel does share some of the characteristics of the individualistic *bildungsroman,* it provides the many women who pass through its pages with their own voices as well. Nor does the narrator perceive herself as different from and above the other women. For, as she is told on more than one occasion, she has a clear heritage of strong women who have rejected and resisted oppression in various ways.

The novel, overall, draws on two types of resistance—one individual, and one collective. But ultimately, it is the notion of collective change that permeates the text. In keeping with the political events outside, the household at Fez is undergoing a transformation, much of which is due to the reforms advocated by the nationalists. As such, it is Moroccan nationalism that opens up the space for the women to "dream of trespass." Consequently, the novel represents nationalism as a "dream," a potentially liberating force that introduces the winds of change, enabling the women to demand and realize many of their dreams:

> The nationalists, who were fighting the French, had promised to create a new Morocco, with equality for all. Every woman was to have the same right to education as a man, as well as the right to enjoy monogamy. (35)

It is in this context of "fighting the French" that nationalism becomes a dream of trespass, a means of overcoming boundaries of all kinds. Nationalism in the text, rather than being exclusive, opens up boundaries, offering possibility as an alternative to closure. It becomes the locus of desire, for it is through the nation that a new identity for everyone can be created. As an alternative imagined community, it embodies equality and independence in all its forms, a world where, as in the mother's vision of the glass house with terraces, houses can be constructed from whatever one values most. Because it is amorphous, it is neither gender nor class specific. Thus, in Miller's terms, the women participate in the "battle for the status of truth," constructing a national "identity effect" (60) of their own.

Situated within the euphoria of the nationalist context, the two harems that Fatima describes are not rigidified, stagnant structures but communities that are evolving, engaged in a process of redefinition that is in constant flux. This is particularly true of the Fez harem, where the women actively redefine history and establish a past that both reinforces tradition and breaks away from it. Through storytelling, drama performances, and political arguments, the women of the community produce a history in which women are the center, opening up traditional historical narratives to interpretation. Far from being silent victims, the women are organized, articulate, and determined.

Retelling History

The women's farcical retelling of the origins of the harem itself exemplifies one of the ways in which the women provide a rereading of history. This rereading provides an example of Mernissi's revisioning of history, a project she is engaged in outside her autobiography. Using a parodic approach to history that is both humorous and insightful, Mernissi follows women's actual reinscribing of their identities from the inside. Chama's story, which provides a history of the harem's origin, attributes the founding of the institution to masculine competitiveness and the need to embody power in a figure of authority *(sulta)*. Uncertain how to appoint such a person, men from various parts of the world organize a race in which the man who catches the largest number of women would be given *sulta*. Once they establish the criteria for authority, they are faced with a new problem: where to put the women they catch in order to be able to count them. Their solution: the harem.

Having established why the first harem was built, Chama then presents us with a history of the harem as a symbol of power. According to her account, it was the Byzantine Christians who won the race initially, setting up the harem to symbolize their power. By emphasizing the role of the Byzantines, Chama questions the idea of the harem as a signifier of cultural purity since it was not even a specifically Islamic or Arab institution. As the Arabs came to power, they decided to emulate the Byzantines, learning, like their Christian predecessors, the art of capturing women. Eventually Caliph Haroun al-Rashid (786 to 809 A.D.) was able to defeat the Byzantines and crown his victory by setting up the largest known harem, one that contained a thousand captive slave women *(jawari)*.

With the passage of time, the Byzantines and other Christians changed the rules. Power was no longer manifested in the size of the ruler's harem, and "[c]ollecting women, they declared, was not relevant any more" (44). Instead, power was in the hands of those "who could build the most powerful weapons and machines" (44). According to Chama, the Arabs were not informed of the new rules and they were consequently caught unprepared. She draws on the example of colonialism and the standards of modern day France. The president of the French republic, for example, despite his extensive power, now has only one wife.

> And that single wife spends her time running in the streets, in a short skirt, and a low neckline. Everyone can stare at her ass and bosom, but no one doubts for a moment that the president of the French Republic is the most powerful man in the country. Men's power is no longer measured by the number of women they can imprison. (45)

Chama's interpretation of history is a conglomeration of facts derived from her readings and is all the more significant if we remember that Mernissi's novel is autobiographical. Through her interpretation, Chama indicates how the outmoded harem reinforces not the Arab male's power but his powerlessness to withstand military invasion, which has displaced the ownership of women as signifier of power. In addition, she contrasts the tighter restrictions imposed on recent harems with the looser and more tolerant attitude of earlier times. She sites as an example the highly educated *jawari* of the Abbasid period, when the women competed in the acquisition of knowledge and the arts. Chama's reading emphasizes the changes that the harem has undergone in the course of the centuries, historicizing it rather than accepting it as a never changing sign of fixed cultural identity. Lalla Radia, who, like her daughter Chama, is well versed in history, insists on telling everyone "the correct version of history." She sees Caliph Haroun as a great leader: "He was the prince of all Caliphs . . . the one who conquered Byzance and made the Muslim flag fly high in the Christian capitols" (46). But despite the disagreement among the women as to how to react to Chama's historical narratives, her version is the one that is most widely accepted in the household, as the popularity of her performances testifies.

In *Dreams of Trespass,* Mernissi does a double take. She "remembers" the harem and women of her childhood who in turn "remember" the past. It is because the women can reconceive their past that they are capable of creating collective "dreams of trespass," rewriting themselves as postcolonial subjects. The beliefs of the different women in the novel constitute different forms of resistance that shape young Fatima's vision of the future. Such beliefs include Aunt Habiba's conviction that women have wings and can therefore escape any restrictions imposed upon them, echoed in her embroidery in which she creates birds with gigantic wings; Chama's histrionic retreat into *ham*[14] when her creativity is inhibited or interfered with; the storytelling and theater, which both reinforce positive women's roles and represent women who are in control of their fate; and the firm faith of Mani, the ex-slave woman, in inward strength and her self-reliance against all odds. None of these "trespasses" are gratuitous. They are highly self-conscious acts directed at a particular audience, specifically at the young girls who are expected to internalize these reinterpretations of women's roles and to act upon them in the new space created by the nationalists, who themselves are creating new visions of the future. Thus when Fatima remembers the harem she remembers a narrative of nationalist resistance that mocks both the French occupation and the boundaries established by patriarchy. It is through the harem that she has learned to reconsider history, to recognize the difference between women's perceptions and official discourses, and to take advantage of any openings given to her to construct her own subjectivity. Unlike her earlier, more essentialist feminist critiques of Islamic tradition, Mernissi here places the struggle for identity within a postcolonial context. Through her autobiography, Mernissi resists simplistic attempts at defining national identity and engages instead in an informed reading both of "tradition" and a retrospective view of Moroccan nationalism's encounter with colonialism and its aftermath.

Assia Djebar: *Fantasia, an Algerian Cavalcade*

Djebar also "remembers" the harem but, unlike Mernissi, she perceives it through the eyes and language of her French education. Moreover, her primary symbol is not the harem but the veil. Like Mernissi, Djebar's use of a highly charged Orientalist symbol involves rethinking the ways such a symbol conveys the relation between gender and national identity. The novel is specifically an enterprise of remembering—of recalling the colonial occupation and the suffering it inflicted on the Algerian people, specifically on the women. By "remembering," or what she calls "unveiling" what nineteenth-century French narratives sought to conceal, and by writing a testimonio of Algerian women who took part in the anticolonial resistance movement, she retrieves segments of Algerian history unrecorded in official national narrative on either the Algerian or the colonial side. Moreover, by revealing the eroticized Orientalist depiction of the process of colonial occupation, she reveals the colonial occupation as "an obscene copulation" (19).[15] Thus it is through writing and rewriting history that she hopes to establish a national identity for herself as well as for Algerian women. Specifically, she represents that identity as intimately tied to French colonialism, and therefore possible only as a *postcolonial* identity.

Fantasia establishes a dichotomized image of "tradition" versus "modernity" in the opening episodes of the novel. Tradition is represented by the illiterate, inarticulate women of the harem she knew in her childhood,[16] while "modernity," the means of her salvation, is represented through her schoolmaster father who breaks tradition by naming her mother in writing and by giving the narrator herself access to French education. Through her access to her education, the narrator reflects, the "cries" of her body *(cris)* can be written *(ecrits),* and hence her desire as a female subject can be articulated. Otherwise, the narrator implies, she, like all those others whom she has left behind, would have been silent and voiceless, waiting for someone else, someone like the narrator, to come and tell her story. Because the women of her family cannot write, the narrator suggests, they have no means of articulating who they are.

By positioning herself very clearly within this colonizing discourse, Djebar collapses two projects. One project, a nationalist project that becomes a personal quest, reclaims Algerian women's resistance to colonialism by reading in between the lines of official colonial history, "unveiling" the brutal violence inflicted on Algerian women's bodies during the course of colonial occupation in the 1830s. The other project is enabling Algerian women who were part of the resistance movement of the 1950s to "speak" by interviewing them and recording their stories. Much of the latter project consists of interpreting their silences—providing the words for what was "unspeakable" to women who were forced to undergo the humiliation of rape, torture, and loss.

H. Adlai Murdoch, in "Rewriting Writing: Identity, Exile and Renewal in Assia Djebar's *L'Amour, la fantasia,*" points out the function of writing in the text as an attempt to "reclaim the colonized female body itself, to provide a subjective identity despite the legacies of a colonialist discourse." Such writing, moreover, becomes ambiguous, Murdoch argues, as "the narrative voice becomes plural, fragmented, as the narrator proceeds to write, to speak, in the names of all those women subjected to oppression and exiled from their heritage; writing and identity become practically interchangeable as past and present meet across the abyss of absence."[17] The novel reveals the impossible breach of the "I" the narrator is struggling to establish, an "I" that is impossible to write given the language being used. Djebar is aware of this impossibility. The text writes the postcolonial subject as one that cannot be produced without recourse to history, and the French language, the means of liberation, as a cloak of Nessus that leads to the painful and slow demise of subjectivity through the very desire it seeks to incorporate.

Yet while Djebar does not mince words about the brutality of the colonial occupation, she clearly does not see a belief in traditional nationalism as redeeming in any way. The primary image used to represent nationalism in the novel is the fantasia of the title, the reeling of horses in a ritualized military display of heroic chivalry. The *Fantasia* symbolizes in this sense the Algerian male subject's clinging to forms of identity that are completely ineffective in resisting the onslaught of the West. The *Fantasia* is not only a highly formalized representation of chivalry that seems to have no room in the fumigations and brutal subjugations of the novel. It in fact turns against itself. The final image of the novel, a horse crushing an Algerian woman suspected of having a relationship with a Frenchman, is an image that ultimately reflects the traditional nationalist position. The man crushes a hybrid Algeria that has "betrayed" him in the name of cultural purity. The image represents the violence inherent in any attempt to put back the clock to find an image of a pure, unsullied national past.

Throughout the course of the novel, Djebar reveals that while a simplistic nationalist position cannot successfully capture "Algeria," individual identity cannot be constructed without an appeal to communal identity. In "Resisting Autobiography," Caren Kaplan points out that "autobiographical expression, along with other cultural signposts of individualism, became part of the economy of colonialism, that is part of the division of labor that produced subject positions and the artifacts of subjectivity" (132).[18] An alternative available for postcolonial writers to enable them to resist being positioned within such an economy is to produce what Kaplan calls an "out-law" genre. One such genre is the "cultural autobiography." Assia Djebar produces an "out-law" genre through using a combination of personal and collective narratives and through problematizing the nature of autobiography as a genre with a traditional focus on the individual to the exclusion of communal identity.

Unlike traditional allegorical representations of the nation in which the individual is *subsumed* to a collective national struggle that makes of the individual a symbol of the nation, Kaplan's "cultural autobiography" emphasizes the interdependence of the two in contexts in which their very survival is threatened: "The link between individual and community forged in the reading and writing of coalition politics deconstructs the individualism of autobiography's Western legacy and casts the writing and reading of out-law genres as a mode of cultural survival" (132). Such a link, however, is represented as a conflict rather than as a careful balance of two coexisting elements. The struggle *within* the texts between an attempt to construct a subjectivity that establishes itself *against* the community, specifically the national community, and an attempt to inscribe the community itself, results in completely destabilizing the political subject. As the opposition between autobiography and fiction, or autobiography and testimonial are broken down, the shifting boundaries that reject fixed notions of cultural identity are highlighted to emphasize what Francoise Lionnet has called "*logiques metisses,*" which she defines as "hybrid identities, and interrelated, if not overlapping spaces" (100).[19]

With this definition in mind, I would like to argue that Assia Djebar's *Fantasia: An Algerian Cavalcade* is a cultural autobiography that represents

Algerian women's bodies as irretrievably entangled in the dynamics of colonial rule. Because of this entanglement, the narrator's own body becomes a contested site that both reinforces national identity and at the same time betrays it. The narrator's struggle to write her body into the novel illustrates the limited ability of representational systems to depict the postcolonial condition. The novel is primarily about displacement. The narrator, who is unnamed, has been taken out of her conservative family environment in Algeria, educated in French schools, and is now moving back and forth between France and Algeria, enjoying the sexual freedom her unveiling has provided her, yet trying to retrieve that essential part of herself that was lost along the way.

Redefining the Veil

In the novel, the unveiling of the narrator becomes a strategy that illustrates the elusiveness of cultural definitions. The act of unveiling itself, seemingly a simple physical act, becomes, as it is transcribed into French writing, a hopelessly difficult task. Unveiling, when written in French, represents not only varying levels of violation but also ambivalent feelings of betrayal and humiliation side by side with liberation and self-articulation. Neither is possible without the other, Djebar suggests, nor is there, in fact, any precise way of translating such a culturally defined act into the language of another culture without losing something essential along the way.

Using unveiling as a metaphor, the whole novel aims at making the invisible visible on several levels. It unveils what the French conquerors did not reveal about the process of subjugating the Algerians through presenting historical archival research (the narrator is a historian, as is Djebar herself). It also unveils the historical invisibility of Algerian women, whose resistance to French occupation has gone largely undocumented, by providing us with a series of testimonials told by the women themselves, and inscribed by the narrator.

The narrator's purpose in "unveiling," therefore, becomes what she calls a process of intervention, one that is accomplished "with nomad memory and intermittent voice." By intervening between official French chronicles and the oral histories and marginal documentation that provides another narrative, Djebar provides a "chain" of memories that constitutes a collective vision of the suffering of the Algerian people as a whole throughout the French occupation. As such, she produces a "national consciousness" in the sense that Timothy Brennan uses the word, by striving "to assemble the fragments of a national life and give them final shape. They become documents designed to prove national consciousness, with multiple, myriad components that display an active communal life" (60).

It is the Western colonizing narrative that provides for Djebar the starting point for establishing the historical basis for national identity. By deconstructing this narrative, Djebar foregrounds the internal conflict of postcolonial identity: the opposition between Western paradigms and the essentialist self-portraits that are the result of ideological interpellation. The postcolonial subject thus plays out an acceptance-rejection of what the colonizer has defined, from an Orientalist viewpoint, as essential to the colonized culture, or internalizes, as Memmi has pointed out at length, the master's interpellation of him or her as a subject. Or, as Chatterjee explains, "in Orientalism the Oriental is a passive subject, in nationalism the object has become an active 'subject,' but one that remains captive to categories such as 'progress,' 'reason,' and 'modernity,' categories that are alien to him/her." It is precisely such interpellation that is at work in what Franz Fanon calls "the cult of the veil":

> What was an undifferentiated element in a homogenous whole acquires a taboo character, and the attitude of a given Algerian woman with respect to the veil will be constantly related to her overall attitude with respect to the foreign occupation. (47)

It is when the veil deliberately becomes the target of French attempts at assimilation, as Fanon explains, that the veil comes to be seen as a symbol of identity, a signifier of Algerian resistance to occupation, and the body of the Algerian woman becomes a site of conflict between colonizer and colonized.

Djebar's use of the veil in the novel, however, is a strategic one, bringing into play the complex meaning assigned to it by both the colonial and the Algerian national context. Like words, the veil therefore often assumes a double and contradictory function: it protects while it suppresses; it establishes identity while it erases it. The shifting meanings Djebar assigns to the veil, which in the text often comes to represent language itself, foregrounds the question of whether, as H. Adlai Murdoch phrases it, "language will merely mark desire, or whether it will mask it as well" (78).

I would like at this juncture to examine more closely the ways in which the narrator maps her desire both through and against the representation of woman as nation. The novel brings out the displacement of the narrator through emphasizing images of dismemberment, but attempts to reconnect all the conflicting strands through the idea of remembering, both in the sense of retrieving memory (as oral narrative *and* history) and putting the fragments of the novel together through the actual musical form of the fantasia. The image of the hand at the end of the novel specifically illustrates this process. The narrator "takes" a woman's hand cut off by the colonizers and described by the Orientalist Fromentin and places in it a pen that enables her to rewrite her own (national) desire. The question we are left with is, of course, whose hand does this hand become? The hybrid identity of the woman whose hand is now writing, disembodied as she is (Duras would say "detached"), is emphasized by the three levels of her inscription, reflecting three overlapping spaces in which she exists: (1) as an actual hand, (2) as a hand described by a French colonial writer, and (3) as a hand that is reappropriated by the Algerian narrator who writes in French. Through this process of "passing on" the hand, Djebar is enacting the "link between individual and community" that is an essential part of the cultural autobiography. Yet even as the narrator takes up the hand which Fromentin discards, she betrays the link between the two women by using French.

Dis-covering History

Establishing the link, moreover, positions her at a threshold that underlines the impossibility of private identity. She expresses this threshold in terms of a pendulum: "I swing like a pendulum from images of war (war of conquest or of liberation, but always in the past) to the expression of a contradictory, ambiguous love" (216). War is presented as both public *and* private, while love, which the narrator initially perceives as private, becomes public, both in the sense of writing it out and in the sense that love is not limited to a private sexual realm but involves also the interconnectedness of a whole community and the love of origin that in its most public form translates into love of nation. Both war and desire, therefore, become cartographies (and here I am playing on the notion of *carte* as letter, a central image in the text and one that emphasizes a process of exchange). They are mapped out both through writing back and forth, specifically the exchange of letters, and through the narrator's body. Through that "cartography," the body is able to inhabit a public space that crosses the boundaries of two nations and maps out a history of Algerian women that renders them visible.

Nowhere is this threshold between public and private more apparent than in the notion of veiling and unveiling. Removing the veil becomes a strategy that not only indicates the transition from private to public space but reveals the position of the body as cultural marker, as deriving meaning through being suspended between one culture and another. The illusion that the body is private corresponds to the illusion of individualism. The body, once unveiled, occupies a public space just as when desire is exposed it becomes public property. Betrayal is tied in with this notion of *making public*—exposing to violation, but it is also a *liberation* in the novel because exposing involves *disinterring* the hidden dead bodies of Algerians *concealed* by the French reports, and allows the bodies finally to be "buried" and thereby to be re-covered. (In French, *decouvrir* suggests both discovering and uncovering).

Throughout the novel, Djebar uses the body as an irrepressible marker of a reality that words seek to distort and erase. Following the brutal extermination of a whole tribe of people hiding in mountain caves, the narrator focuses in detail on the bodies themselves, six hundred corpses brought out of the caves and exposed to the sunlight. Yet it is words, and specifically French words, that have led her to the rediscovery of the tragic event: "Pelissier . . . hands me his report and I accept this palimpsest on which I now inscribe the charred passion of my ancestors" (79). As in the case of the exchange of hands of the unknown woman, here, too, it is language that makes crossing the boundaries from colonizer to colonized possible, for, as the narrator remarks, "The corpses exposed in the hot sun have been transmuted into words. Words can travel" (75).

At the same time, for the narrator, those same words have a physical presence that inscribes itself onto her, producing her as a text that is never able to attain the illusion of autobiographical self-sufficiency and branding her in a way that marks her as a product of the colonial past: "[T]hose cinnabar-red words still have the power to cut like a plough-share into my flesh" (78). By emphasizing the duality of the process, Djebar indicates that even while she as an Algerian woman seeks to inscribe her individual identity, she is at the same time inscribed by a language that always already interpellates her as a postcolonial writer seeking her past:

> To attempt an autobiography using French words alone is to lend oneself to the vivisector's scalpel, revealing what lies beneath the skin. The flesh flakes off and with it, seemingly, the last shreds of the unwritten language of my childhood. Wounds are reopened, veins weep, one's own blood flows and that of others, which had never dried. (156)

Consequently, and ironically, she has no choice but to produce a cultural autobiography. Her link with the women who are her ancestors defines who she is and guarantees her existence because their survival is her own.

Cartographies of Identity

The primary difficulty, however, of producing a cultural autobiography when writing in the language of the colonizer is recognizing, again, what is *veiled* by the language. Throughout the text, Djebar engages in questioning her own role as writer and specifically her sense of linguistic betrayal. This betrayal she represents both through the image of language and through cartography, a play both on *mapping* as a way of defining national identity *(cartes)* and of postcards and letter writing. In a gesture that negates the notorious *cartes postales,* the postcards sent home by the French soldiers depicting Algerian women as passive and tamed sex objects,[20] the narrator talks about the love letters she receives, both when she is young and in defiance of her father's orders, and later in life when she is in France. It is through this "cartography" that the writer's ambivalent status as a hybrid subject is revealed.

Djebar illustrates this through the fate of one particular letter. Playing once again on the opposition of private and public, she describes a letter that is extremely private because it is from a lover who describes her body in detail. The letter, written in French, illustrates her inability to contain desire and physical passion within a private space. Like the words telling of the exhumed tribe, the words of passion directed only to her end up crossing boundaries and exchanging hands, becoming the property of someone else.

When she first receives the letter, it conveys nothing to her. She is unable to relate to or understand the man's detailed erotic description of her body. However, the letter slowly acquires importance as she begins to think of the many Algerian women who are deprived of the opportunity of receiving similar letters: "Suddenly these pages begin to emit a strange power. They start to act like a mediator: I tell myself that this cluster of strangled cries is addressed—why not—to all the other women whom no word has reached" (59).

Ironically, the letter does reach other women, or at least one other woman. It is taken by a beggar woman in Morocco who steals her purse: "[W]ere not these words perhaps intended for her—words which she will be unable to read? She has become in fact the very object of that desire expressed in syllables that she cannot decipher!" In a moment that is purely symbolic, the narrator's letter crosses the border from France into North Africa, and the Moroccan beggar woman and the narrator become one and the same, both recipients of a letter they cannot decipher. But at the same time, they are separated by a language, French, that serves to emphasize the difference between the two women, both in class and in identity. As part of the *logiques metisses,* the beggar woman is an extension of the narrator's identity, a mark of that other identity that constantly imposes itself on her despite her attempts to escape it. The beggar woman *takes* the love letter from the narrator, claiming a right to it, but she does so silently and then disappears. Because the letter has no fixed addressee, it turns into a love letter from the narrator to the beggar woman, to the (colloquial) mother-tongue that cannot be translated into written language. Love expressed in French loses touch, becoming rootless. For, as the narrator expresses it in the section entitled "Soliloquy," "the tribal legend crisscrosses the empty spaces, and the imagination crouches in the silence when loving words of the unwritten mother-tongue remain unspoken—language conveyed like the inaudible babbling of a nameless, haggard mummer—crouches in this dark night like a woman begging in the streets" (218).

Her language of love, therefore, contains within it a sense of loss, a knowledge of deprivation: "And now I too seek out the rich vocabulary of love of my mother tongue—milk of which I had been previously deprived" (62). While she seeks to reconnect herself with the history of Algeria, she at the same time searches for a means of retrieving her identity as an Algerian. She represents this in terms of a nostalgic longing for the past: "In former times, my ancestors, women like myself, spending their evenings sitting on the terraces open to the sky, amused themselves with riddles or proverbs, or adding a line to complete a love quatrain . . ." (62). However, she is an outsider to this, unable to participate in the women's gatherings in her family.

This loss of origins is portrayed in terms of a forced crossing from one language to another, describing her relationship with the French language and, by extension, with colonialism, as an arranged marriage, one that was imposed upon her and in which she had no say: "I am vaguely aware of having been forced into a "marriage" too young . . . Did not certain fathers abandon their daughters to an unknown suitor, or, as in my case, deliver them into the enemy camp?" (213). Unlike bilingual writers such as Abdelkabir Khatibi, Djebar does not provide us here with a model in which the seduction of the other language is constructed in terms of an impossible desire that is always deferred. She represents it not as a romance but as a mundane, everyday situation that is the realm of the domestic. Although she has no control over the situation, she is forced to work within the realities of the "marriage," to salvage what she can of past and present. Moreover, her body becomes an embodiment of the political games she is expected to participate in, a marker that is relocated for political convenience. She is forced to play the role of intermediary, but only at the expense, again, of losing her own roots: "[M]arriageable royal princesses also cross the border, often against their will, in terms of treaties which end wars" (214). Consequently, she is always already defined by contending discourses that pass her backwards and forwards without allowing her own subjectivity.

Inscribing Betrayal

On this level, it is not clear who can be blamed for the narrator's sense of betrayal. Although her father tries to liberate her, the gift of education he gives her has turned into a means of betrayal that threatens to burn away her flesh: "The language of the Others, in which I was enveloped from childhood, the gift my father lovingly bestowed on me, that language has adhered to me ever since like the tunic of Nessus: that gift from my father" (217). Replacing the traditional veil, the tunic of Nessus reflects the pain of the narrator:

it is a tunic given unaware to Hercules by his lover Deianira, who does not know that once he wears it, he will never be able to take it off. The tunic slowly burns into Hercules' flesh, leading to his slow and painful death.

The story of Nessus' robe condenses several of the novel's themes. Deianira accidentally betrays Hercules, the man she loves, by giving him the robe that is stained by his enemy Nessus' blood. She believes that the blood is a charm that will prevent him from loving another woman more than her. The narrator's father similarly educates his daughter out of love, believing that she will benefit from the education and not foreseeing that she would be separated from her people because of it. The cloak reflects the clothing/unclothing motif, replacing the veil that the narrator removes, but in its adherence to her body, it is certainly not more "liberating." The bloodstains on the cloak echo the past destruction written into the French language by the occupation of Algeria and are an extension of the winding sheets around the bodies of the disinterred victims. Deianira's act illustrates the duplicity of the gift given to the narrator: while seeking to prevent Hercules from having a double love, she in fact ends up betraying him. The narrator, however, ends up having a double love, a love that in itself is a constant betrayal. Overall, through the story, several divergent spaces are superimposed: the tunic of Nessus destroys the narrator's identity, burning her in a way similar to the exhuming of the two tribes by the French, and branding her as the "cinnabar-red" French words do.

As a result, her body becomes the cartography for two different spaces of desire, one representing her Algerian past, the other representing a more open space that crosses national boundaries but at the same time positions her within a colonizing discourse that does not acknowledge her existence as an Algerian woman:

> And when I sit curled up like this to study my native language it is as though my body reproduces the architecture of my native city: the medinas with their tortuous alleyways closed off to the outside world, living their secret life. When I write and read the foreign language, my body travels far in subversive space, in spite of the neighbors and suspicious matrons; it would not need much for it to take wing and fly. (184)

Her body as inscribed in Arabic becomes a text that maps out her specificity, locating her in a space that is safe from intrusion. It is a space that connects her with her city, and, implicitly, with her community. The enclosed realm of the *medinas* defines identity by excluding outside influence and providing an interiority that furnishes her, at least momentarily, with a sense of stability and rootedness. However, that very seclusion proves stifling to her identity and imposes closure on her search for herself. In the foreign language, she finds the freedom and individuality that she perceives as subversive. But while the experience is positive, she loses her specificity as a result, becoming "detached," like the woman's disembodied hand that is passed on from one person to another. As a bird that takes wing and flies, she has become something other than herself, a being forced to migrate constantly. Neither language, Arabic or French, can provide a satisfactory way of defining who she is.

Consequently, while her body can be grounded in Arabic, it is at the same time constrained by the "tortuous alleyways." In French, she is uprooted. She discovers/uncovers her body *through* French and therefore positions it *within* French culture, placing it textually outside her own because she is not writing in Arabic. However, any attempt to inscribe her desire without also mapping out that of other Algerian women involves an act of betrayal that places her on the same side as the colonizers who "hid" the charred Algerian bodies. Her role as go-between, consequently, makes her "like a messenger of old, who bore a sealed missive which might sentence him to death or to the dungeon" (215).

Ultimately, the novel raises more questions than it answers about the nature of hybridity and the responsibility, betrayal, and uncertainty associated with it. Hybridity has been claimed as a form of resistance to the hegemonic colonial model of center and periphery, whether in terms of "nomadism" (Woodhull), "writing back" (Ashcroft, Griffiths, and Tiffin), as "signs taken for wonders," (Bhabha), "bi-lingualism" (Khatibi), and others. However, Djebar's novel, despite its affirming of hybridity, does not provide any easy answers. If anything, it is an agonized reflection on the difficulty of situating oneself between discourses. Yet, through the novel, Djebar is at least able to forge a "national consciousness," in Brennan's sense of the word, informed by a postcolonial consciousness, collecting fragments and bringing them together to form a collective history of Algerian women.

It is Djebar's articulation of her precarious position, in fact, her representation of the complexities of hybrid identity, her insistence on the interconnectedness of past and present, of history and the individual's story, that turns her text into one of resistance. Mingling archival research, testimonial, and autobiography, Djebar produces a cultural autobiography that explores the nature of subjectivity and subverts the individual political subject produced by Western autobiography. By creating a hybrid genre that brings into question the construction of pure forms, she ultimately creates a cartography in which hybrid identity becomes, through its multiple connections, a means of cultural survival.

Conclusion

It is perhaps ultimately ironic in a sense that in writing themselves as postcolonial subjects, both writers end up writing their communities. For while they are seeking to establish themselves as subjects through autobiographical forms, they nevertheless find themselves forging a sense of collective identity, creating their own "imaginary community." Both writers write "cultural" autobiographies that assert the connection between the individual and community and in which community reflects cultural identity. Writing the "imaginary community" in their case, however, does not depend on traditional forms of nationalism that exclude women and oversimplify North African hybrid identities. Instead, Mernissi and Djebar advocate a postcolonial view of identity that introduces the notion of ambivalence. Ambivalence is able to avoid the problematics of either/or by rejecting the boundaries set up between the dichotomies of modern/traditional and everything they entail. In addition, both writers question history as the foundation of national narratives, rewriting history to include women and pointing out the gaps in traditional historical narratives. In the final analysis, they are engaged in a new process: building a postcolonial female subject that embraces rather than excludes the complexities and contradictions of inescapably hybrid identities.

Notes

1. Mervat Hatem, "Towards the Development of Post-Islamist and Post-Nationalist Feminist Discourses in the Middle East," *Arab Women: Old Boundaries, New Frontiers,* ed. Judith Tucker (Bloomington: Indiana University Press, 1993).
2. Saree S. Makdisi, "The Empire Renarrated: *Season of Migration to the North* and the Reinvention of the Present," in *Colonial Discourse and Post-Colonial Theory,* eds. Patrick Williams and Laura Chrisman (New York: Columbia University Press, 1994).
3. I have discussed the limitations of this role elsewhere. See *College Literature:* Special Issue on Third World Women's Inscriptions 22:1 (February 1995): 147–160. See also "Male Writers Womanize the Nation" in *Aljadid: A Review and Record of Arab Culture and Arts* (Fall 1997), which summarizes the masculinist terms through which Arab narratives define the national subject.
4. Suha Sabbagh, in her introduction to *Arab Women: Between Defiance and Restraint* (New York: Olive Branch Press, 1996), gives specific examples illustrating the "Debate on Arab Women," while summarizing clearly the terms of the dilemma. Of particular interest is her analysis of Western media's "attack on the Arab World under the guise of supporting the rights of women" (xvi).
5. See Winifred Woodhull, "Feminism and Islamic Tradition," in which she reviews Mernissi's and Djebar's revisionist look at Islamic history from a feminist viewpoint. *Studies in Twentieth Century Literature* 17:1 (1993): 27–44.
6. Christopher L. Miller, "Nationalism as Resistance and Resistance to Nationalism in the Literature of Francophone Africa," *Yale French Studies:*

Special Issue on Post/Colonial Conditions 82:1 (1993): 62–85. See also Benedict Anderson, *Imagined Communities: Reflections on the Origin and Spread of Nationalism,* rev. ed. (London: Verso, 1991), for a full definition of "imagined communities."

7. See Mai Ghoussoub, "Feminism—or the Eternal Masculine—in the Arab World," *New Left Review* 161 (January-February 1987): 3–18; Reza Hammami and Martina Rieker, "Feminist Orientalism and Orientalist Marxism," *New Left Review* 170 (July-August 1988): 93–106 and reply to Hammami and Rieker, same issue, 107–109.
8. Marnia Lazreg, "Feminism and Difference: The Perils of Writing as a Woman on Women in Algeria," *Conflicts in Feminism,* ed. Mirianne Hirsch and Evelyne Fox Keller (New York: Routledge, 1990).
9. Chandra Talpade Mohanty, "Under Western Eyes: Feminist Scholarship and Colonial Discourses," *Colonial Discourse and Post-Colonial Theory: A Reader,* ed. Patrick Williams and Laura Chrisman (New York: Columbia University Press, 1994).
10. For reasons of space I will not repeat here the arguments laid out by Leila Ahmed in *Women and Gender in Islam: Historical Roots of a Modern Debate* (New Haven, CT: Yale University Press, 1992), or Marnia Lazreg in *The Eloquence of Silence: Algerian Women in Question* (New York: Routledge, 1994).
11. Fatima Mernissi, *Dreams of Trespass: Tales of a Harem Girlhood* (Reading, MA: Addison-Wesley, 1994).
12. Assia Djabar, *Fantasia: An Algerian Cavalcade,* trans. Dorothy S. Blair (London: Quartet, 1985).
13. Fatima Mernissi, *Beyond the Veil: Male-Female Dynamics in Modern Muslim Society* (Bloomingdale: Indiana University Press, 1987). In her earlier writings, Mernissi takes a stance that is similar to that of many Western feminists: she provides a devastating and totalizing critique of Islam as a patriarchal religion. As such, "modernity" becomes the key operating term, and "tradition" is cast as the culprit for all wrongs against women. *Dreams of Trespass* exhibits a far more self-conscious approach to the problematics of rejecting tradition and embracing modernity.
14. *Ham* is defined by Mernissi as a state few women are prone to but that is an overwhelming and powerful state similar to depression and specific to women living in closed communities.
15. The notion of the eroticized Orient has been dealt with extensively. For more recent discussions of the theme, see Chilla Bulbeck, *Re-Orienting Western Feminisms: Women's Diversity in a Postcolonial World* (Cambridge: Cambridge University Press, 1998), and specifically Meyda Yegenoglu's *Colonial Fantasies: Towards a Feminist Reading of Orientalism* (Cambridge: Cambridge University Press, 1998).
16. Djebar herself at time reveals an Orientalist perception of the "harem" and the women who live in it. This tendency is specifically manifested portraying traditional Algerian women as silent and unable to express themselves. They are thus dependent on the author to find them a voice. Djebar's

"harem" therefore sharply contrasts with Mernissi's, in which women are granted full agency.

17. H. Adlai Murdoch, "Rewriting Writing: Identity, Exile and Renewal in Assia Djebar's *L'Amour, la fantasia*" *Yale French Studies* 83:2 (1993): 71–92.
18. Caren Kaplan, "Resisting Autobiography: Out-Law Genres and Transnational Feminist Subjects," *Decolonizing the Subject: The Politics of Gender in Women's Autobiography,* ed. Sidonie Smith and Julia Watson (Minneapolis: University of Minnesota Press, 1992).
19. Francoise Lionnet, "'Logiques metisses': Cultural Appropriation and Postcolonial Representations," *College Literature* 19:3–20:1 (October/February 1992–1993): 100–121.
20. Malek Alloula, *Colonial Harem* (Minneapolis: University of Minnesota Press, 1986).

Chapter 6

Shadi Abd al-Salam's *al-Mumiya*

Ambivalence and the Egyptian Nation-State

Elliott Colla

When asked to pronounce judgment, Egyptian critics consistently list Shadi Abd al-Salam's *Yawm an tuhsa al-sinin: al-Mumiya (The Day of Reckoning Years: The Mummy)* as one of the most important films, if not the most important film, of Egyptian cinema. Given the film's striking visual style and its impressive production technique, it is not hard to see how this would be so. Yet there is a real dissonance between critical discourse that places the film at the heart of Egyptian cinema and the fact that as a text, its presence in and influence on the Egyptian cinematic canon is relatively negligible. *Al-Mumiya* is a film that, although produced in 1969 within the public sector studio system of the Nasserist state, had no public distribution until roughly six years later. When at last *al-Mumiya* was commercially released in late January 1975—an unlucky week, as the Arab world was awaiting the news of Umm Kulthum's impending death—it failed to draw audiences and was quickly pulled from circulation. In other venues such as television or video, *al-Mumiya* might have enjoyed a life in Egypt that extended beyond its brief theatrical release. But that does not seem to have been the case. Likewise, as much as Egyptian filmmakers reverently invoke the name of Shadi Abd al-Salam in interviews, they have not been so apt to apply elements of his cinematic style that appear in the film. In short, for all the talk about the centrality of *al-Mumiya* within the Egyptian national cinematic canon, the actual film enjoyed only a brief moment of commercial release in Egypt, no lasting public venues there, nor much visible influence on subsequent schools of Egyptian film. My point in raising these issues is not to say that Shadi Abd al-Salam's film does not deserve critical attention. Quite the contrary. However, when the special circumstances of its release and reception are taken into consideration, the film's relationship to the Egyptian nationalist canon appears more ambivalent. The first part of this essay begins with these circumstances in order to speculate about its initial moment of significance. The second part argues that the film needs to be reconsidered and resituated within the state-centered rhetoric of aesthetic Pharaonism. As I hope to show below, *al-Mumiya* both recapitulates and deviates from the dominant themes of an elite nationalist discourse concerned with images and narratives rooted in a very particular aesthetic style of treating ancient Egyptian artifacts.

Al-Mumiya and Audiences

There are different mechanisms by which texts gain a lasting reputation and significance within a cultural formation. Popular audience reception—whether or not the result of aggressive marketing—raises the value of a text most immediately. Or, in a more dialectical fashion, when subsequent artists "recognize" a work by referring to and reproducing its style and themes, the value of that text seems to accrue with each citation. Reception, reference, and reproduction are perhaps the most common ways by which films come to have a place within a cinematic canon. In the absence of such factors, a text can become "significant" by the discourse of critics—backed by the institutions that give their discourse legitimacy—who struggle to assert its value against the ravages of time, ideological opposition, popular disinterest, or cultural invisibility. *Al-Mumiya* is one such text, for its lasting cultural significance has been the product of critical rather than popular reception. Moreover, I would argue that the peculiarity of its status as a "critics' favorite" raises the first questions about its meaning.

In a sense, the fact that the cultural value of *al-Mumiya* has been the product of critical assertion means that its significance was constructed in a more deliberate way than other more popular films within the Egyptian canon. Admittedly, within any given cultural formation the value of a text is always constructed. However, when the significance of a text is tied to popular reception, the process by which value has accrued is relatively obscure since it is determined by factors (audience composition, reader response) that are often quite difficult to distinguish and weigh. Similarly, when a text becomes significant because of its influence on subsequent texts, the process by which value has accumulated is highly mediated, fluctuating, and relational in nature, the result of an ongoing series of citational performances each of which retroactively transforms the significance of the text in question. But the value of texts also accrues by critical assertion. That the contemporary significance of *al-Mumiya* has been constructed by critical insistence rather than commercial or popular reception is not a remarkable fact in itself. What is striking however is the heterogeneous composition of the body of critics who have most loudly asserted its significance. If we can say there is a community that has been established by discourse about the film's significance, it is a community that is both cosmopolitan and local, both limited and split, composed of a thin elite of Western film critics of world cinema, Orientalist academics and Egyptian partisans of national culture, each with its own distinct way of talking about the film.

There are good reasons why I cannot separate the history of the film from the discourses of Orientalist academism and European cinema. In my own experience, which was probably not significantly different from other American students of Arabic, I first came to know the film in the context of language instruction: for years *al-Mumiya* has been a standard teaching text in Arabic language programs since its dialogue, unlike that of other Arabic films, takes place in a classical register. Thus, the text has come to have a value in North American area studies programs, albeit with certain radical qualifications: its significance in this context has not been tied to plot, cinematic style, or relevance to wider cultural issues; rather it has been the peculiar accident of its language that has served to make it such an important text. But that has not been the only extra-Egyptian forum in which the film has circulated: not only did Shadi Abd al-Salam work with a number of foreign *auteur* directors on productions both in Egypt and Europe, but according to him, it was the Italian director Rossellini who played the decisive role in winning approval for the project with Tharwat Akkasha, then-Minister of Culture.[1] Rossellini also helped secure the aid of Italian studios for postproduction and, later, for screenings at European film festivals where it went on to win a number of awards. Since the early 1970s, *al-Mumiya* has figured prominently as one of the most sophisticated examples of Third Cinema from the Arab world.[2]

Meanwhile back in Egypt, the film initially languished between bureaucratic hostility and public disinterest. *Al-Mumiya* was not released to theaters because the very governmental institution—the Cinema Organization within the Ministry of Culture, which had funded and overseen its production and owned all the movie houses by that time—deemed that it was not suitable for general distribution.[3] The film was screened a number of times within the exclusive confines of the Cinema Club where it attracted the attention of small audiences there. It was only after *al-Mumiya* had won a number of awards at European film festivals that the ministry was humbled into reconsidering its quick dismissal of the film. At the time *al-Mumiya,* a different *infitah,* was commercially released in 1975 (2), Egypt was distracted by other events and the film seems to have quickly disappeared from the public eye. Even though during the eighties the film reappeared in the video stores of al-Shawarbi Street in Cairo, it seems to have attracted a small market composed not so much of Egyptians as foreign scholars on library purchasing forays. Finally, if the decisions of television formatters to include the film were only rarely any indication of its significance in that medium, then we would have to concede the enormous gap between the critical discourse celebrating the film and the resounding silence it has met with at the usual sites of Egyptian cinematic culture. The unpopularity of the film has not been lost on critics, although it has entered their imagination only in a negative way: when critics acknowledge the fact that Egyptian audiences have avoided the film, they explain it as a failing on the part of a vulgar public that craves melodrama and action.

However, while the film may have made a brief and low appearance in the forums of mainstream Egyptian film culture—theaters, television, and video—it has enjoyed a persistent and high profile there in elite print discourse on film. Since the 1970s, there has been something of a consensus in Egypt about the significance of *al-Mumiya,* a consensus that makes the film out to be a straightforward story about the eternal spirit of Egypt, an ancient spirit that was reawakened and nurtured by the modern nation-state. Within this discourse of cultural criticism, the film text functions as a transparent example of the anticolonial struggle, a variation upon the tried and true theme of the struggle of the modern, urban national liberation movement caught between the forces of foreign oppression and the tradition-bound peasantry. This interpretation of the plot is more or less the gist of the European cineaste discourse on the film as well. But the point at which these two discourses depart from one another is perhaps the most telling: whereas European critics have chosen to talk about the film's most striking cinematic techniques (the real-time shot, slow pacing, lingering close-ups, and silences) in terms of *estrangement,* Egyptian critics—and Abd al-Salam himself—have discussed them largely in terms of *authentic history.* European critics have watched the film and commented glowingly on its unusually slow, lingering sense of cinematic time and alienating camera effects. These critics, not wholly attuned to the nature of nationalist culture in Egypt, have focused on the film's formalist questions while almost completely ignoring its specific sociohistorical claims. For their part, Egyptian critics have instead foregrounded discussions of plot and character while backgrounding the complications brought on by its exaggerated stylistics. For these Egyptian critics, the film—despite its estranging formalism—portrays its subject, the peasant culture of Upper Egypt, the "true" national culture of Egypt, realistically and authentically; if it seems estranged, it is because under colonial pressure the local culture has become alienated from itself.

Obviously, the main points of each critical version have their merit, but as I will argue, the rich significance of the film needs to take both plot and style into account. Moreover, it needs to be placed within the long history of invoking ancient Egyptian symbols and themes on which *al-Mumiya* explicitly draws. In light of these issues, the film appears as a key text within the Egyptian cinematic canon, not for the reason that Egyptian critics contend (i.e., that it is an unambiguous allegory of national liberation), but rather because it reveals the violence and ambivalence of the national culture it depicts in addition to the relations of domination that undergird the official *effendi* culture of Egypt, both in the colonial period and in the specific moment following the defeat of 1967. In arguing for an ambivalent reading of the film, I am hoping to transform the central use the film has had for Cairene critics. I am not suggesting that the film is not about national liberation, cultural authenticity, and resistance to colonialism, but rather that it also shows the limits of the Cairocentric, elitist categories embedded within that nationalist narrative.

Al-Mumiya and the Rhetoric of National Authenticity

At first glance, *al-Mumiya* appears to be a straightforward narrative about the importance of conserving Pharaonic antiquities within nationalist culture. The film, set in 1881, on the eve of colonial rule in Egypt, is based on the true story of the Abd al-Rusul clan of Qurna.[4] Throughout the 1870s, the Abd al-Rasuls robbed a cache of royal mummies, enriching themselves by selling ancient relics to traders who in turn sold them on the black market to European collectors and museums. The Antiquities Service, led at the time by Gustave Maspéro, learned that the artifacts had come on the market and became interested in finding out their source, especially because the pieces, from a relatively unknown dynasty, had come from a location unknown to them. During their investigation, the service began to suspect a middleman, Mustafa Agha Ayyat—the local consul of England, France, and Belgium—who, because of diplomatic immunity, could not be fully pursued. Instead, the police went after two brothers, Muhammad and Ahmad Abd al-Rasul, arresting the younger Ahmad and holding him in jail. When no evidence could be found to prosecute, Ahmad was released. Upon his return, Ahmad demanded as recompense for his jailtime the lion's share of the artifacts then still in his clan's possession. Whereas Ahmad wanted to continue in the trade, Muhammad had decided to quit. After quarrels with Ahmad (and with the consul Ayyat, who demanded money for his silence) Muhammad went to the police and confessed everything. Muhammad eventually found part-time employment with the Antiquities Service and later helped to discover a number of other important royal tombs.

The film creatively recasts the events of this story by situating the moral center of gravity squarely within the Antiquities Service. The film tells the more or less heroic tale of how the Antiquities Service breaks up the illicit activities of the clan of backward, traditionalist tomb robbers who sell Egypt's artifacts, via greedy middlemen, to European collectors. The film ends with the officers and soldiers of the service moving in to save the sarcophagi and mummies of the tomb from destruction at the greedy hands of the "Harbat" clan. However, the nationalist timber of the film is complicated in a number of ways. The struggle between the two chief protagonists—Ahmad Kamal, who is an inspector in the Antiquities Service, and Wanis, of the Harbat tribe—is a highly ambiguous one and ends with Wanis betraying the secret of his people to the Service. The murder of Wanis's brother by members of his clan and Wanis's own estrangement from them complicate matters even further. Finally, while the film ends with the victory of the Antiquities Service, it also gives a sense of the tragedy that this event poses for the world of the vanquished Harbat.

The film retells the Abd al-Rasul story in terms of a struggle between two opposing camps, the first represented by the *effendi* officers of the Antiquities Service, while the other camp is led by the patriarchs of the Harbat and the traders and smugglers with whom they traffic. And since the film is about the control of the trade in antiquities, the two sides, the state and the tribe, serve as figures for more deeply embedded opposing styles of culture, community, and political organization. On the one hand, there is the *effendiyya,* representatives of the enlightened state bureaucracy—modern, rational, transparent, orderly, benevolent, scientific, and historical—that seeks to preserve antiquities for public good and scientific benefit. On the other hand, there is the tribe—traditional, ignorant, secretive, tyrannical, violent, and superstitious—that seeks to maintain its ways at all costs. It needs to be added that this sharp set of oppositions is in fact completely congruent with the director's own accounts of the film. In interviews, Abd al-Salam describes an Egypt that is completely bifurcated, one that is split by a struggle between the enlightened capital and the rural South. This struggle is admittedly complicated by the fact that the South, for all its backwardness, is also the site of the great cultural legacy represented by Pharaonic artifacts:

> [Le film] c'est l'histoire de deux Égyptes qui se recontrent, l'une qui finit, l'autre qui commence à s'imposer. La première, une Égypte anachronique, encore vivante, se heurte au progrès scientifique venue de la ville dévoreuse, Le Caire. Si les gens des deux Égyptes se ressemblent physiquement et parlent la même langue dans le film (l'arabe littéraire), les uns, archéologues, ont tarbouches et bateaux à vapeur venant d'un monde totalement différent; les autres ont des bâtons et le pillage de tombes incompréhensibles pour toute subsistance.[5]

> (It's the story of the two Egypts that meet, one who ends and the other who starts to assert itself. The first one, an anachronistic Egypt, still alive, collides with scientific progress that has come from the devouring city, Cairo. If people of the two Egypts resemble one another physically and speak the same language [literary Arabic], some, the archeologists, wearing the tarboosh and using steamboats come from a world altogether different, while the others have sticks and the pillage of tombs are their sole means of subsistence.)

The temporality of these two Egypts reveals a particularly Cairene conception of enlightened modernity and its vanguardist, pedagogical mode of nationalism: the scientific, developed present/future Egypt of Cairo able to teach the rest of Egypt, which, despite efforts to educate it, remains in the past. In fact, "ignorance"—that necessary feature of the discourse of modernity that invites pedagogical intervention—plays a central role in Abd al-Salam's comments on the film. In the nationalist struggle to regain control over antiquities, imperialist Europeans can succeed only by the unwitting collaboration of "ignorant" peasants. Thus, the mission of the *effendi* protagonist in the film is twofold: to repossess antiquities and to teach their value. And in teaching the true value of the artifacts, the *effendi* restores to the rural peasant his original culture:

> With me the protagonist is the protagonist. Not that I tell the story of just any character . . . but so that I can tell the story of Egypt: the role of Egypt in the Middle East, in Africa, or in the Mediterranean. Or the story of someone in relation to Cairo, or the countryside in relation to Cairo, or Upper Egypt and Cairo—so that two different civilizations can encounter each other. An old civilization which stopped advancing at a certain stage and withdrew from the world because of those imperialist currents which focused on the capital and ignored [the development of] Upper Egypt. And so, for its part, Upper Egypt withdrew itself until the Europeans arrived. If those Europeans happened to know something about antiquities, they bought them . . .
>
> The Europeans would go to the inhabitants [of Dayr al-Bahri] and ask to buy artifacts at prices which were inconceivable to this impoverished, closed society. So they began to sell [antiquities] without meaning to, or without knowing what they were doing. A European would come to him and say, "Give me this piece of stone for this much money," and the Upper Egyptian would give it to him without realizing that he was selling a piece of his own flesh. This continues until the present day.
>
> In the film *al-Mumiya,* the educated Cairene comes to Upper Egypt and meets this other Egyptian on the other's ground. But the two—even if they are joined by a single Nile . . . and shared language—are separated by a huge difference between their respective cultures. The meeting of these two cultures is the axis of the film . . . It is an encounter in which the two sides don't come

together in a single history or even in terms of economy—for one of them searches for antiquities and the other trades in them.[6]

This binary split between peasant-traditional and urban-modern stands upon a notion of false consciousness. It is a representation of Egypt that is seconded by many of Abd al-Salam's critics who describe the film in terms of a "search for identity" and "authenticity."[7] To explore the dynamics of this conceptual formation, I would like to touch briefly upon a number of terms that reappear both in Abd al-Salam's comments on the film and in the critical discourse of others. These ideas—resurrection, identity, redemption, authenticity, and unity—are revealing in that together they express the rubric of the nationalist discourse in which Pharaonic artifacts come to have an identificatory value.

Interestingly, the film directly addresses the topic of identity only in a cursory way. The credits and the opening scene, which serve as a framing sequence, refer to identity and resurrection. The film's credits open with lines taken from the Egyptian *Book of the Dead:* "O ye departed, you shall return! / O ye asleep, you shall awake! / O ye perished, you shall be reborn! / Glory be to you!" After the credits, we fade into a scene in which the character of Ahmad Kamal reads another passage to his Antiquities Service colleagues in Cairo. We then hear Maspéro's voice stating that to forget one's name on the Day of Judgment is tantamount to losing one's identity *(al-shakhsiyya)* forever: each body must know its name if the soul is to return and each mummy must have its identity if it is to be resurrected. These words, which do not recur in the film, nevertheless cast a long shadow over the events that follow: to remember one's name, to repossess one's own spirit and body—are these tasks not the sacred mission of the service? In discussions of the film, Abd al-Salam and his critics use this frame scene to argue an interpretation of the film as allegory, as Egypt's search to remember its true name, redeem its identity, and to be resurrected anew.[8] Their consensus on this allegorical interpretation about the redemption of identity begins to explain the importance that Abd al-Salam (and his critics) place on authenticity. This occurs not only on the surface of the film's theme, namely Abd al-Salam's assertion that the recovery of Pharaonic culture was a return to Egypt's original culture, but on many other levels as well: his (and others') claims about the film's absolute "historical accuracy" in using "real" historical events and characters such as Kamal or Maspéro (despite the fact that Maspéro was absent during the Abd al-Rasul affair and that the actual career of the Egyptologist Ahmad Kamal did not begin until some time after the events of the film); Abd al-Salam's exceptional attention to using only "authentic" costumes, actors, and sets,[9] as well as his desire for precise lighting and color, in "the search for the true Egyptian dramatic element, [one that is] removed from the themes of borrowed or false cinema."[10]

Thus, while the claim to an authenticity awarded by an aesthetic-historical "appreciation" of ancient Egypt and the claim to an authentic indigenous cinema appear to be separate from one another—or at least, of different orders—they actually work together to create a conceptual continuum whereby past and present, aesthetic appreciation, historical accuracy, scientific method, and production technique find a coherent unity. Indeed, as Abd al-Salam and his critics claim, the film lays the foundations for a culture of redeemed origins. The paradox of this claim is that the categories of the rural and the traditional serve to lend authenticity to those of the urban and the modern but only when the traditional has been reminded—by the more developed *effendiyya*—of its own true, ancient origins. The result would be a culture in which all differences would be sublimated into unities and continuities.[11] Abd al-Salam remarks,

> The events of the film are of secondary importance to me. In *al-Mumiya* I have essentially dealt with the problematics of national culture. That is what was important to me. Accordingly, I purposely structured my film on a number of levels. We can find in the text the description of the awakening of a character and the dramatic situation created by this awakening. Wanis—who has been entrusted with the secret that generations of his tribe have passed down—is torn between his loyalty to his civilization [*al-hadara*] which has survived for thousands of years, the culture [*al-thaqafa*] of his grandfathers, and between the demands of the modern world and its sciences. He realizes that there is some mistake in the predicament and lifestyle of those around him.
>
> But, even though I support progress, I cannot condemn the tribe of [tomb] robbers. This tribe represents people who have maintained national culture and all that means. Furthermore, they respect that culture and help it develop. I wanted to make it clear through the film that, even though Wanis and the young Egyptologist [Ahmad Kamal] had never spoken to each other before their meeting, they are two brothers who represent two poles of Egyptian society. There will come a day in which all the Egyptian masses will share one culture, that is, the culture [*al-thaqafa*] of customs that are particularly Egyptian, but developed [modernized]. This is the deeper meaning of *al-Mumiya.*[12]

In Abd al-Salam's account, as in the accounts of his critics, the relation between civilization and culture—*al-hadara* and *al-thaqafa*—is one of balance and complementarity: *al-hadara*—associated with the distant past—functions as the deeper, inertial force that unifies the more superficial differences of *al-thaqafa,* local knowledge, culture, and custom; *al-thaqafa* may serve to unite smaller social groups of shorter geographical and temporal dimensions but, as these critics would have it, a "nation"—like Egypt—needs to be founded on *al-hadara.* It is on this point that we can see why ancient artifacts appear so crucially in Abd al-Salam's vision: as material objects, they function as markers that testify unequivocally to the obscured past of *al-hadara;* and as signs, they connote the possibility—through the aesthetic-scientific discourse of appreciation—of a recuperated *al-hadara* transcending existing regional, class, and historical-developmental differences.[13] However flexible Abd al-Salam's account of Egyptian civilization may seem at first glance, when set in the context of nationalist discourses on antiquities, its rigidity begins to show. Indeed, for all his claim to sympathize with the tribe and Upper Egypt in general, Abd al-Salam's account of civilizational unity recapitulates some of the more elite aspects of *effendi* nationalism. Because it is the modern and the urban that have the monopoly on the interpretation and representation of antiquity, this idea of the local *al-thaqafa* melting into the more universal *al-hadara*—like the Antiquities Service that enforces it—begins and ends in Cairo: in the film, this comes across most visibly in the transport of Pharaonic artifacts to their rightful place in the capital museum. Thus the call to dissolve local "culture"—the "tradition" of the tribe within the film—within the transcendent "civilization" of the nation-state seems to reiterate the essential terms of elite nationalism: to subordinate the South to the needs of the North, to remake the rural according to the imagination of the urban.

The temporality of this model needs further elaboration: *al-hadara,* insofar as it suggests ideas of accomplishment and development, places it within a time that links the *distant* past directly to the (future) time of modernity. In the film, *al-thaqafa* is related to the more *recent* past, to retarded development, to an incomplete present dominated by an unchanging tradition of repeated imitations *(al-taqalid).* Or more directly, from the earlier quote, "C'est l'histoire de deux Égyptes qui se recontrent, l'une qui finit, l'autre qui commence à s'imposer." As I noted in passing above, this temporality implies a certain pedagogy, one aesthetic consequence of which is the tendency of nationalist texts to develop an aesthetic that is split in terms of its representational goals. On the one hand, these texts are committed to asserting the claim to represent social relations as they *are*—in the terms of Lukacsian realism, "the typical,"[14] the "manners and customs" of a community as they exist.[15] On the other, they are equally committed to a pedagogy that represents the exemplary or the desired (as opposed to what is) in order to express what *should* be. As Homi Bhabha has pointed out, the difference between the rhetoric of "what is" and "what should be" is a difference of temporality between a present state (of lack) and a future state (of fulfillment).[16] Moreover, this antagonism between "is" and "should be" proves irresolvable within the terms of realism: it creates a split image of the nation. We will return to this ambivalence after briefly touching upon the wider context of scientific-aesthetic institutions by which the trade and consumption of Pharaonic material objects—and mummy objects in particular—were regulated in nineteenth- and twentieth-century Egypt.

The Mummy and the Nation-State

It may seem peculiar to use mummies—both as material objects and as discursive figures—to explore the colonial struggle between Egypt and Europe or to get at the processes by which the Egyptian nation-state asserted itself over Egyptians. But just as shifts in the value of other commodities (such as cotton or labor) give some indication of wider transformations in market relations, so too do ancient Egyptian objects—for which there had long been a developed economy—mark the site of fierce competition between European and local traders and a simultaneous struggle between the emerging Egyptian nation-state and those groups *within* Egypt who contested the state's efforts to bring territory, inhabitants, and things under a single, centralized authority. Part of this peculiarity may be due to the fact that while the European fascination with mummies is persistent and more or less familiar, the mummy figures only very marginally in Egyptian elite and popular cultures. There was a brief heyday, predating and following the discovery of King Tutankhamun's tomb in 1921, during which mummies, along with other Pharaonic figures and themes, appear in middlebrow print culture.[17] But for the most part, they are not a literary (or cinematic) concern, which partly accounts for the striking originality of Abd al-Salam's film. Yet when we glance at antiquities laws in Egypt, a certain narrative about mummies begins to emerge, a narrative that suggests that state control over the exchange of objects implied certain relationships not only between people and things, but between people and the state as well.

For centuries, mummies were extracted and sold in Egypt by the ton, nearly all for export to markets in Europe. However, during the nineteenth century, the trade of mummies changed drastically: the mummy object moved from being a common commodity to being a singular artifact, and its economy shifted from mass circulation and unregulated consumption to one of increased restriction and sacralized display within specialized institutions governed by discourses of aesthetic and historical appreciation. In short, the mummy moved from the margins of the local souq to the center of the Egyptian Museum. Throughout this process, the state was involved on a number of levels.

In the opening years of the nineteenth century, new laws were enacted on the trade in antiquities that gave the agents of European powers a near monopoly in excavation and extraction rights.[18] Although local officials did not enforce these concessions evenly, from the 1810s onwards, it is European agents who dominate the legal excavation of major antiquities centers—and this included, significantly, the extraction of mummies for export.[19] This did not happen without resistance: the village of Qurna near Luxor regularly took up arms to resist these concessions, which they saw, more or less correctly, as an infringement on the local monopoly they had established since the mid-eighteenth century.[20] Nevertheless, by the 1820s, European archaeologists, collectors and adventurers had begun to dominate the excavation and trading markets to the point at which local entrepreneurs were increasingly driven underground. It is important to note also that hereafter these laws set the tone for legislation on the antiquities trade between Egypt and Europe: such trade remained permissible as long as it was for public (or national) interest; trade for personal profit became illicit.[21]

Most histories of the laws and institutions governing antiquities in Egypt look to the Vice-Regal Ordinance of 1835 as a point of origin.[22] The decree cut in two directions. On the one hand, it was prohibitory, forbidding the export of all antiquities from Egypt. And on the other hand, it was constructive, establishing a "special place" *(mahall khass)* in Rifa al-Tahtawi's School of Translation, located in Ezbekiyya, for the collection and display of antiquities for Egyptians, but "particularly for European visitors." These two principles—prohibition and construction—came together most explicitly in the Third Article, which stipulated that the State expressly sees fit "not only to prevent hereafter the destruction of ancient monuments in Upper Egypt, but also to take measures to insure their conservation throughout."[23] Accompanying the decree were a number of orders directed to the local governors *(mudirs)* of the Said, orders that partly clarified the guiding principles of the decree: that they hand over all found antiquities to al-Tahtawi; that they not allow any defacing of monuments; that they suspend all current excavation projects, using armed soldiers if necessary; that they henceforth rigorously prevent the unregulated export of antiquities from Egypt. The other orders detailed the organizational hierarchy of the state museum and the protocol by which local *mudirs* would interact with museum officials and museum inspectors on their annual visits. This decree was accompanied by at least one other, aimed not at the trade with Europe but at the practices of Egyptian peasants who "destroyed monuments" in order to build habitations.[24]

As Antoine Khater has pointed out, the terms of the 1835 Ordinance were not effectively realized, and the excavation and export of antiquities continued apace: first, antiquities "discovered" before 1835 were exempted by the law's nonretroactivity; second, there remained a number of questions within the law itself, questions as to the definition of antiquities or to the implementation of conservation and prohibition. Interestingly, mummies figured as an important test case for the legal definition of antiquities. In response to an 1835 inquiry from the governor of Qusayr (on the Red Sea) about the legal status of a mummy and wooden sarcophagus that had been loaded onto an English ship bound for India, the Council of the Pasha replied: "Since the decree on antiquities is mute about the subject of *infidel* mummies . . . the Council does not oppose their export, insofar as there is no formal prohibition."[25] Khater notes that the absence of a precise definition allowed for "human products," but not human bodies (however embalmed), to be defined as antique objects. Mummies continued to be exported without even formal resistance until the state reclassified them as antiquities in 1851. There is another point to be made about the wording of the council's ruling: it implies that the export of mummies was permissible on the grounds of their religious status as *kufar* bodies. It is perhaps the only moment in the state's administration of Pharaonic antiquities that moves out of an explicitly secular register.

As if these interpretative and legislative problems did not weaken enforcement of the law enough, official exemptions on the part of the pasha and governors—the granting of special *firmans,* the predilection for gifting antiquities to curry favor with European powers—quickly made the prohibition a purely formal matter. And whereas the establishment of the museum perhaps did help centralize the conservationist aspect of the antiquities ordinance, it also facilitated the old habit of royal benevolence: its collection depleted over the years by gifting, the Ezbekiyya "museum" ceased to exist in 1855 when Abbas Pasha bestowed the remaining pieces to the Archduke Maximilian.[26]

Without a permanent administration, the principles laid out by the 1835 Ordinance had decreasing effect. As Khater and others have argued, this begins to change in 1857 when, at the behest of Ferdinand de Lesseps, Said Pasha employed Auguste Mariette as director *(mamur)* of antiquities in Egypt. Given the necessary funds to rejuvenate the antiquities administration, and the vice-regal authority and steamboat with which to make inspections in Upper Egypt, Mariette began to implement changes. In 1858, the Khedive established the Bulaq Museum under Mariette's management. By 1862, local governors were given explicit orders to submit to the authority of Mariette during his inspections. However, the widened scope of Mariette's authority is best evidenced in an event that took place in the wake of the 1867 World's Fair in Paris where the Egyptian pavilion, designed by Mariette, had been celebrated as a wild success. After the fair, the empress of France wrote to Ismail Pasha asking him for the jewels that had been on display. Ismail, who agreed on the condition that Mariette approved, is said to have written, "There is someone in Bulaq more powerful than I [in this matter], and it is to him you must address yourself."[27] When Mariette refused, the jewels returned to Bulaq. From this point on, the principles of conservation were sharpened and expanded by an increase of legislation—both on the level of Egyptian law and on the level of Ottoman law—that helped to augment innovative institutional changes within the service.[28]

Whereas the highest official of the emerging Antiquities Service was French—this was to remain the case through the first half of the twentieth century as well—the largest number of employees and officers in the service were Egyptian: they served as guards, excavation foremen, guides, and porters. While there were hundreds of Egyptians involved in the conservation and policing of antiquities, by and large they answered to a management that was European. That is to say, that while Egyptians worked to unearth, guard, and display the artifacts of ancient Egypt, it was almost exclusively Europeans who interpreted those artifacts. After the closing of al-Tahtawi's school of translation, the state attempted to expand the ranks of Egyptians in the field of archaeology by opening the first Egyptian school of Egyptology in 1869. But the school, headed by the German scholar Heinrich Brugsch, was soon closed when French archaeologists led by Auguste Mariette, angered by the Franco-Prussian war—and hostile to the encroachment of Egyptian intellectuals in "their" field—pressed for the expulsion of German scholars from Egypt and effectively closed the school for good. Although the school's existence was brief, it did produce a number of Egyptian scholars, such as Ahmad Kamal, who were systematically discriminated against in the major institutions of archaeology, even those financed by the Egyptian state. Kamal and his colleagues were eventually hired by Mariette's successor Gustave Maspéro, who allowed Kamal to teach Egyptology through the museum to a handful of Egyptian students. This and another experiment in 1910 were short-lived and without lasting results. It was not until 1925, with the formation of an ongoing Egyptology program within the new Egyptian University, that the study of ancient Egypt was available to Egyptians on their soil.

However involved the state may have been in administrating the trade and display of antiquities and mummies, this should not imply that there was a consensus on the issue among late nineteenth-century intellectuals. In fact, something of the opposite was probably true: by and large, figures of ancient Egypt were negative in the older literary tradition, which equated the Pharaoh with tyranny, vanity, and sacrilege. In the early 1900s there was a public debate about the usefulness of antiquities: some intellectuals suggested that all Pharaonic antiquities—including the Pyramids—should be sold to European museums, because Egyptians did not need them, and only Europeans would be crazy enough to pay for them. Thus, Egypt would be able to settle its foreign debt, placating and expelling its foreign rulers at one and the same time. Such a debate occurs in a hilarious exchange taken from Muhammad al-Muwaylihi's episodic work, *Hadith Isa ibn Hisham,* published in 1900. In this passage, a character argues about the value of Pharaonic antiquities:

> The reason why people in [Europe] are so proud to cherish antiquities in their museums is that they consider them symbols of victory and conquest . . . But what sign of glory and honor is there in these decaying corpses of ignorant and tyrannical people who numbered among the ancient kings of the past? . . . These relics don't come to us by conquest and victory, but merely by digging up graves. . . . Almost every year some new cache of these relics is discovered somewhere in Egypt . . . It wouldn't do any harm for Egyptians to get rid of some of this excess . . . They could put the money to good use on public welfare projects, and there would still be enough relics left in the Egyptian museum to satisfy the requirements of ostentation and national rivalry.[29]

While the nineteenth century ended with a real ambivalence about the status of antiquities in Egyptian culture, by the 1920s, and especially after the discovery of Tutankhamun's tomb, secular intellectuals earnestly embraced symbols from ancient Egypt. The period of the 1920s and 1930s marked the zenith of the political and literary movements that drew inspiration from this ancient past: in the theater of Tawfiq al-Hakim, Ahmad Shawqi, and others; in the poetry of Ahmad Shawqi and others; in the novels of al-Hakim, Naguib Mahfouz, and others; in the sculptures of Mahmud Mukhtar; and finally, in essays, memoirs and speeches of Lutfi al-Sayyid, Muhammad Husayn Haykal, Saad Zaghlul, Salamah Musa, and Ahmad Husayn. It is during this period that an identificatory culture of "Pharaonism" emerges, a culture in which the state of modern Egypt finds its origins in the symbols of ancient Egypt.[30] In the struggle with imperial occupation, Pharaonist culture created new spaces for Egyptians to legitimate their claim to sovereignty. Artifacts, such as mummies, served to concretize the problem of colonial dispossesion and mobilize a symbolic system that was as specific and actual as it was inspiring.

Because the discourses about antiquities and artifacts were initiated, underwritten, extended, and policed by the Egyptian State, it becomes necessary to address the question of the state more or less explicitly. But this will not be easy for a number of reasons. Foremost among them is the fact that for the rather long historical period I have invoked, there is nothing like a single "Egyptian state." Rather there are periods in which at least three different forms of state authority emerge, thrive, and transform: relative autonomy within the Ottoman Empire, joint British-Khedival rule, and joint

British-Khedival-Parliamentary rule. Each of these implies a different rhetoric of legitimacy and corresponding concept of the state. And as all these examples suggest, these instantiations of the state were neither wholly unified nor self-contained: at each moment the Egyptian state was compelled to mediate between antagonistic forces that were both internal and external in nature.

Insofar as the state is a reification of a more complex set of social relations and political antagonisms, my invocation of it as a concept needs serious qualification. Recent critics have pointed out that on the one hand, the state exists merely as a formal concept, and on the other, as an administrative system by which legitimate rule—authority and sovereignty—is produced and extended.[31] Paradoxically, these theorists acknowledge that there is both far *less* to the state than we would suppose since it is merely an abstraction; and there is far *more,* insofar as the aura of the state seems to exceed the mere sum of its numerous administrative functions.[32] Thus, for analytical purposes, the state can be said both to exist and not exist.[33] What all this suggests is that the study of the state is hindered both by the nature of the object of study and by the methods that focus too much study upon that object.[34] That is, both the disperse nature of the state and the habits by which the state is studied obfuscate rather than illuminate.

Foucault has argued that the conceptual problem posed by the state is embedded in the overvaluation of its repressive capacities or, equally, in the overestimation of its administrative functions.[35] Either way, at best "the state" can be only a misleading metaphor for discourse on social and political relations, and for the ongoing process of subject formation. While Foucault's argument is based in a specifically European history—namely the replacement of medieval concepts of legitimate political authority by eighteenth-century ideas of political economy—the trajectory of his argument suggests that the theory of governmentality at which he arrives is meant to get around the analytical problems inherent to the study of the state. In Foucault's account, instead of seeing the state as an extension of sovereignty over a territory and its inhabitants, "government" works upon things—resources, wealth, health, customs, and social relations—by subordinating their administration to ever increasingly specialized forms of knowledge and techniques of security.[36]

Making use of these ideas, I would like to return my attention to the Egyptian Antiquities Service, whose continuous institutional existence from the 1850s becomes all the more remarkable when juxtaposed with the real discontinuities within the history of the Egyptian State during the nineteenth and twentieth centuries. Following Foucault's lead, certain aspects of the Antiquities Service come into sharp relief: the superspecialization of archaeological knowledge; the increasing intricacy of institutions of conservation and display; the ever-growing body of legal discourse governing the uses of antiquities in formal ways; and expanding enforcement of antiquities laws in material ways. Most importantly, the management of antiquities becomes more than just the management of things: it encourages certain dispositions, especially the disinterested scientific-aesthetic mode of relating to Pharaonic artifacts or the interested nationalist mode of identification with the objects as the signs of one's own history.

The cultivation of normative social relations between modern Egyptians and the objects of ancient Egypt is inseparable from the nationalist project of forming ethical, aesthetic citizen-subjects.[37] This idea of a cultivated subject position with regard to the objects of antiquity was manifested on the institutional level by the formation of different organizations devoted to Egyptology: some were governmental (the Antiquities Service, the Egyptian Museum, the short-lived School of Egyptology), some private (the program in Egyptology at the Egyptian University), all of which helped to administer the culture of Pharaonic artifacts. The field of Egyptology was dispersed by other complementary organizations—at the elite level, by the Khedival Geographical Society or L'Institut d'Égypte, or, at a more popular level, by the establishment of formal and informal institutions in which cadres of museum guards, antiquities caretakers, and skilled excavating laborers—and later archaeologists—were trained, supported, and promoted. Furthermore, in no less a real way, the positive notion of a relation to ancient artifacts was put into practice in the emerging institutions of domestic tourism.[38] It is in the sum of these institutions and practices that one can make sense of the emerging representational formations—in literature and in politics—that encouraged, through this relation to artifacts, a relatively abstract identification with ancient history or national culture.

The cultivation of this identificatory relation to artifacts was never disarticulated from prohibitions: just as the discourses of law and literature normalized certain relations, so too did they greatly delegitimize other sorts of relations Egyptians could (and did) have with regard to the objects. In the laws concerning the excavation, transport, sale, and export of antiquities, the actual practices of Egyptians were put under increasingly strict governmental supervision, under an implicitly prohibitory rhetoric that defined what was permitted and under what conditions. When the terms of permission were breached, there were punitive consequences. Thus the excavation or transport of artifacts without a permit was subject to criminal punishment.[39] So too was the sale or export of objects without the necessary government permits tantamount to theft of public property.[40] Some of these restrictions, such as those on sales exports and graffiti, mostly affected Europeans.[41]

However, there is ample evidence that the ban on unauthorized excavations was directed chiefly at two practices that were associated primarily with non-Europeans: on the one hand, the fairly systematic excavations performed by local Egyptians—such as the residents of Qurna—who had long been engaged in the harvest of artifact-commodities for European markets; and on the other, "treasure seeking" ventures, associated with Maghribi searching for gold and jewels on their passage through Egypt. This second type of practice was so widespread that the Antiquities Service commissioned the Egyptologist Ahmad Kamal to edit and translate a collection of Moroccan manuscripts that pilgrims on the Hajj had been using as guides for digging around Pharaonic monuments. At the end of his preface to the collection Kamal writes:

> Allow me to state the reasons behind why the Antiquities Service decided to undertake this publication. One can say, without exaggeration, that this practice [of treasure seeking] has ruined more monuments than war or the centuries: even today, hardly a season—or month—passes without some Maghrebian, or professed sorcerer, coming to recite magic incantations, or burning incense in front of a bas relief on the wall of a lonely temple or tomb, attacking it with a pick, or even dynamite, in order to extract the treasure that he believes to be hidden inside. In spite of not finding anything, they persevere and, since they don't have the money to do the work at their own expense, they always find gullible people to underwrite the operations.[42]

While it is not clear how the publication of this work would actually prevent the practice, it does give some indication of the extent to which the service saw treasure seeking as a problem.[43] In addition to Maghribi treasure seeking and unauthorized local excavations, the Egyptian state expressly prohibited a number of other practices by which antiquities were put to nonscientific or nonaesthetic ends. In particular, the use of stones and debris to build homes was prohibited, and the use of temples as inhabitations was put to an end.[44] Finally, the old practice of using debris mounds (containing disintegrated mummy corpses, pottery, stone, etc.) as fertilizer, known in Egypt as *sibakh,* was greatly restricted and, by the early twentieth century, prohibited completely.[45] The scope of these prohibitions was not confined to formal legal discourse: in the contemporary writings of travelers, tourists, archaeologists, and Antiquities Service employees, one finds many moralizing echoes.[46]

It is important to note that each state decree established an administrative branch of bureaucrats, archaeologists, and inspectors who oversaw enforcement. And, as a quick glance shows, a singularly loaded word recurring in these texts is *surveillance.*[47] When one begins to recast the legal and moral prohibition of certain practices in terms of a regime that surveils relationships and dispositions, encouraging some and prohibiting others, one begins to see within the mission of the Antiquities Service the outlines of both a state-led pedagogy and a disciplinary order: a pedagogy inculcating a specific set of legitimate concepts and practices—practices and concepts that implied a certain subjectivity, and a disciplinary regime actively policing the fields of its jurisdiction and punishing those who crossed it.

What is most telling about the legal discourse on antiquities is that although the language of prohibition was always *universal,* it prohibited practices and economies that were quite *particular* in scope. That is to say that although the law addressed *all* Egyptians as it attempted to regulate and restrict the excavation, trade, and transport of antiques, in practical terms the law could specifically prohibit only those Egyptians who had been engaged in or were in a position to engage in the antiquities trade. It is no exaggeration to say that the majority of these prohibitions were explicitly directed at the peasantry of Upper Egypt, in particular at those who lived near the rich antiquities sites around Beni Hassan, Luxor, Kom Ombo, Edfu, and Aswan. Indeed, the bans on excavation could be put into effect in very few places other than Upper Egypt. The moralist equivalent of legal discourse also specifically targeted the rural peasantry of Upper Egypt, as we find in Ahmad Najib's 1895 guide for Egyptian tourists to Upper Egypt. Najib prefaces his text with a long argument about the benefits of antiquities and the importance they should have for "cultured, modern Egyptians." It is a didactic text that attempts to translate the European model of antiquities appreciation to the lettered classes of Cairo and Alexandria, to encourage those who rarely travel to Upper Egypt to see the wonder of its monuments. But with regard to the peasants of Upper Egypt, Najib writes:

> Among the reasons which pressed me to write this book is that when I was appointed to the Antiquities Service to protect historical monuments throughout Egypt, I went to Upper Egypt to perform my duty [and there] I found ignorant people—uncultured mobs—attacking monuments to destroy them. Nothing can prevent them from doing this, and nothing can protect the antiquities from those people who listen not to sound advice and who have no shame. . . . They meddle with the dead and scatter their bones. They rip up towering monuments and bring them down, they pull apart the joints [of mummy bodies] and sell them. They deface papyri. They lay their hands on the tombs of kings, now unknown, as if these were not the remains of their forefathers. I searched for reasons [for why they do this] . . . and realized that they are a people who do not know the difference between ugly wretchedness and beautiful value. They know neither science nor the general good.[48]

Save for Najib's nationalist identification with aspects of the Pharaonic past ("the remains of their forefathers"), it is hard to distinguish between his contempt for the peasantry and the usual contempt shown to them by European travelers and archaeologists.[49] Nor can we say that there is a pedagogical telos to his comments. On the contrary, the peasants of Upper Egypt appear to be beyond teaching, which would suggest that rather than figuring as the subjects of the pedagogical discourse on antiquities, they are the objects of its corresponding disciplinary rhetoric. Not surprisingly, the village of Qurna holds a particularly low place in Najib's account:

> You people of Upper Egypt, and especially the Shantara Arabs and inhabitants of Qurna: don't you realize that once you have completely robbed Upper Egypt of its antiquities, visitors will stop coming? Don't you fear the wicked result, you who are more aware of this than anyone else?! In a few years, with so few visitors, you will grow rebellious, you will rant and rave, send delegations and claim "economic depression" and the spread of "corruption" and "poverty." And the national papers [in Cairo] will sympathize and your cries will go out. Whenever there are hordes of foreigners in your neighborhood, you destroy monuments and sell them away. You're like the one who cuts down the tree to pluck its fruit![50]

The tone of Najib's account—which is unexceptional in the nationalist discourse on antiquities—gives some indication as to the specific social class nature of the legal-moralistic discourse on antiquities. That is to say, the positive—appreciative and/or identificatory—subjectivity with respect to artifacts begins to show its underlying Northern, urban, lettered, and elite character, while the prohibitive and repressive rhetorics of the discourse begin to show the outlines of its irreformable target, the Southern rural peasantry. Thus, we can begin to see within the discourse on antiquities an opposition that dominates elite nationalist writing, a bias that can be conceived of in terms of Gramsci's arguments about the Southern question: that is, the subordination of economic development in the rural South to the needs of the industrializing, urbanizing North and the political domination of the South by the North.[51]

Al-Mumiya: The Ambivalence of 1967

In light of this history, the ways in which the text of *al-Mumiya* is implicated within the nationalist discourse on Pharaonic objects should appear more obvious. From its identification with symbols of the ancient past, to its assumption of a normative urbane sensibility toward antiquities, and to its acceptance of the "natural" legitimacy of the nation-state as conservator over the objects and economies of the South, the film is very much a part of a much longer and more complicated history than most critics acknowledge. Nevertheless, as much as the film participates in this statist discourse on antiquities—and the Cairocentric elitism in which it is rooted—it also deviates most significantly from that discourse. To conclude, I would like to return more closely to the film in order to spell out the ways in which the film departs from the major themes of Pharaonism.

I have already suggested that the realist-pedagogical mode of nationalist discourse is an ambiguity traversing the text of the film and that it splits the image of the nation into two temporalities and two voices—one, the nation as it is, the other as it should be—that are rejoined only with great difficulty. I would like to consider four other sites of ambivalence within the film that seem to me to both undermine the coherence of the text's nationalist surface and announce paths for breaking away from the deeper structures of realism that support that surface. These ambivalences occur at various levels in the text—in language and sound, image and pacing, character and plot. These points are never far removed from the basic elements of the film's story, however: as Abd al-Salam's commentary on the film concedes, each of these ambivalences marks a point of contention with realism.[52] I will begin my discussion of each ambiguity with Abd al-Salam's own commentary—where he discusses his nationalist vision—in order to show that the actual articulation of the text diverges and begins to rub against his apparent intentions. Along the way I will suggest that the point of each departure is tied to the moment of 1967.

The Estranged Univocity of the Nation

Unlike the vast majority of Egyptian films, *al-Mumiya* takes place in a classical rather than colloquial idiom. This was no accident, nor was the director's decision driven by the desire to create a film for export to non-Egyptian Arab markets. On the contrary, Abd al-Salam affirms that the language of the film serves to unify the characters into a single family, nation, and culture:

> [An aesthetic of strict] realism would have dictated that Wanis speak in a different style from the urban intellectuals, but I preferred that they all spoke in the same style so as not to reconfirm unnecessarily the social difference between them. For Egypt contains both of these cultures. . . .
>
> I relied on removing the differences between the cultures, even in the use of make-up: their skin color is the same, even though the skin of peasants is dark from the rays of the burning sun. I wanted to say that Wanis and the archaeologist belong to a single family . . . When we see the film we sense that Wanis and the archaeologist are not really enemies, but they are searching for the same thing. . . . My hope is that in the future Egypt will have a unified culture throughout. We have suffered so long from the cultural division of the Egyptian people. These divisions have diminished and I believe that one day they will disappear.[53]

In Egyptian cinema of the period, which, unlike print media, was dominated by an aesthetic of relative linguistic realism, characters are usually differentiated in terms of heteroglossic classes and regions. What makes Abd al-Salam's choice of the classical register so interesting is that the unification of his characters within an homoglossic community is accomplished through a distancing of the text from the thing—Egypt—it claims to represent.[54] The language the characters speak does not mimic language actually spoken in Egypt; rather, it is an exaggerated, stylized idiom. This distance from the everyday and the colloquial is the condition for Abd al-Salam's image of the univocal nation but it also marks something of a limit: within this model, the social-cultural differences between speakers are transcended by the language of each utterance, but the utterances themselves remain somewhat estranged from the speakers and the situation they claim to represent.

It is only by acknowledging the sense of distance embedded within the spoken dialogue that we can begin to account for the long silences—broken by the cries of mourning women, the distant horn of a steamboat, or the howl of the wind over empty spaces—that only increase the distance of the words by setting them against a background of hollow sounds. Thus, it is not simply that the image of the unified linguistic nation comes at the expense of simple realism, but its silences—oddly in tune with the distanced effect of the register—begin to show the hollowness of the spoken language in the text. The play of estranged language and distanced sound also serve to intensify the richness of the text's visual images and to isolate them from the rest of the film, an issue to which we will now turn.

Real Time and the Disconcerting Image

Abd al-Salam has remarked on the glacial pace of his film a number of times: "The style of *al-Mumiya* approaches poetry more than a simple narrative. To a certain extent, it is inspired by eastern *muwashshahat.* The slow pace of the events is an effect I wanted in order to arrive at a hypnotic rhythm."[55] If we are to trust Abd al-Salam's comments, this is just as much an aesthetic principle as an aspect of the thing he wants to represent:

> The slow rhythm expresses hypnosis in the film . . . It tells the story of a young man who thinks, and imagines and suffers from the reality which surrounds him . . . I was inspired to use such a slow pace because life in Upper Egypt is so slow, since the severity of the heat leads to relative inactivity and a tendency towards depression.[56]

These last remarks—which should recall our comments on Northern chauvinism toward southern Egypt—betray the supposedly realist motivation behind the film's sense of time: the camera moves slowly in order to capture the essence of Upper Egypt.

The pace of the film works to intensify the image-quality of the text in disconcerting ways. In fact, the film's pace clearly has more to do with a specific cinematic style than it does with the supposed "inactivity" and "depressed" speed of the underdeveloped South. What sets this film off from the dominant aesthetics of the period's melodrama and social realist cinema is precisely Abd al-Salam's avoidance, when possible, of the more common time-condensing and editing-intensive techniques of montage and shot-reverse-shot. In contrast, Abd al-Salam's reliance on long tracking shots, deep-focus, and dense visual composition is unique in Egyptian cinema—creating a text in which the time of action, rather than being compressed through editing, figures centrally within what the lens of the camera registers. The editing of the film never takes away from temporal duration even in the more elaborate sequences of the film—the opening funeral, the sarcophagus opening, the arrival of the government steamship, the procession of the sarcophagi—that are composed of multiple points of view and countershots. On the contrary, each of these sequences is composed of images that seem to record first a sense of time passing and then, only secondarily, narrate a plot of events.

Abd al-Salam's attention to time recalls the remarks of the film critic André Bazin in his reaction to the artifice of early cinema—in particular, to the techniques of montage and shifting camera point of view—that produced images and narratives at the expense of time. Bazin poses a different aesthetic of shots in which time, uncondensed by editing, could begin to show itself as a pressure within the medium. This is because, for Bazin, what sets film apart from other art media is its special capacity for recording objects and events as they offer themselves to the camera: hence, techniques that sacrifice this recording capacity for visual effect transgress upon the special quality of the medium. Instead, Bazin repeatedly pleads for "a film form that would permit everything to be said without chopping the world up into little fragments, that would reveal the hidden meanings in people and things without disturbing the unity natural to them."[57] In Bazin, this aesthetic is a realism "capable once more of bringing together real time, in which things exist, along with the duration of the action, for which classical editing had insidiously substituted mental and abstract time."[58] But the insistence on "real time" is not as easy an aesthetic principle as it might sound. On the contrary, Bazin acknowledges that this aesthetic is disconcerting: "Take a look at the world, keep on doing so, and in the end it will lay bare for you all its cruelty and its ugliness."[59] In particular, it is the lingering close-up shot—a technique that recurs often in *al-Mumiya*—that, as time passes, begins to appear disturbing. Bazin explains this by noting that the effect of real-time cinema is that it begins to draw attention to its own recording capacity. That is, within the real-time shot there emerges a sense of the image's supplemental relationship to the thing it represents—a sense that the cinematic image is always the ghost-image of the text that it is recording.

Bazin has described his realism—a sort of negative theology, an aesthetic in which the representation wears on the surface its distance from the object of representation—in terms of mummification, rooted in the particular temporal nature of the photographic still image that, he argues, records an object by embalming it:

> If the plastic arts were put under psychoanalysis, the practice of embalming the dead might turn out to be a fundamental factor in their creation. The process might reveal that at the origin of painting and sculpture there lies a mummy complex. . . . The first Egyptian statue, then, was a mummy, tanned and petrified in sodium. But pyramids and labyrinthine corridors offered no certain guarantee against ultimate pillage.[60]

In Bazin's account, there are two representative "ambitions" in art: "the primarily aesthetic, namely the expression of spiritual reality wherein the symbol transcended its model" and the "purely psychological, namely the duplication of the world outside."[61] What is unique about the photographic image is that it marked the first moment in which the duplicative ambition could be definitively separated from the symbolic. But what concerns us here is something connected to the problematic status of the photographic image: namely that as a duplicate of the world, the photograph represents something at a particular moment. In a sense, it embalms objects of representation in a more exact and enduring cast than other media—indeed, it does not represent them so much as supplement them by putting alongside them copies that are (more or less) faithful. What seems especially rich in Bazin's account of the photographic image is this uncomfortable juxtaposition between the copy and the original, a juxtaposition that begins to rub against the conceptualization of "realist" representation as the mere duplication of things as they are. For Bazin, even the most precise photographic image creates, by the act of duplication, an uneasiness between original and copy, an uneasiness that he aptly describes through the metaphor of the mummy: it preserves the body only through embalming it.

In order to illustrate the applicability of Bazin's ideas on time and image with regard to Abd al-Salam's film, I would like to concentrate on the second scene, the funeral of the father. This scene, which is approximately two minutes in length, is almost exclusively visual in nature: there is no dialogue and the only sounds are that of the wind and a pitch that resembles mourning women. What occurs in the scene—the funeral procession to the graveyard and the burial of the father—is narrated through the lens of a camera that constantly moves. While there are nine cuts in the scene, insofar as the shorter cuts (six shot-reverse-shots) are interspersed with long tracking shots, the overall effect is fairly continuous and smooth. The first shots of the procession are long, followed by middle-range shots that focus on the women and finally a lingering close-up of the two brothers in front of their father's grave. Although it is clear that the elapsed time of the procession and burial has been greatly condensed by editing, nevertheless the pace of the scene remains slow—we see characters walking, standing silently, watching the bier as it passes. In fact, the temporality of the scene suggests a sense of waiting more than movement. The effect is indeed hypnotic, as Abd al-Salam might say, not because it reproduces the slow essence of the South, but because the camera's attention to the passing of time problematizes the status of the image on screen. Nowhere is this more manifest than in the close-up shot that ends the scene: the lingering pace—what Bazin would call "real time"—makes visible the artifice underlying the cinematic shot; the image—which seems to remain too long on the screen—begins to show the constructedness of its composition. These effects are based in an aesthetic of distance and estrangement, an aesthetic that, when looked at closely, runs against the grain of Abd al-Salam's own rhetoric. The very technique of pacing that Abd al-Salam claims as necessary to represent his object "realistically" becomes the very mechanism by which the representation peels away from its object.

The Mummification of Wanis

There is a strange undecidedness to Abd al-Salam's own comments on the struggle within the film. In interviews, Abd al-Salam has stated that the film depicts Egypt's enlightenment during "a moment of consciousness or conscience."[62] The underlying terms of this enlightenment need to be mapped out as a series of binary oppositions—rationality versus superstition, progress versus stagnation, etc.—in which the discourse on ancient Egypt played a significant role. But on this subject, Abd al-Salam is also conflicted: at times he admits to a real ambivalence about the desirability of the "progress" associated with statist enlightenment and discusses the project in terms of tragedy and loss. This shows itself quite explicitly in the character of Wanis, the character who effectively abandons the traditions of the tribe but whose "enlightenment" remains somewhat opaque:

> Le fils du chef décédé de la tribu, voyant que ces hommes venus de la capitale peuvent déchifrer les secrets, incompréhensibles pour lui, des tombes dont sa famille vit, se sent étranger à son village, à son propre monde. Il comprend que ces objets leur appartiennent et que leur existence sera eternelle, comme

> l'existence de toute œuvre d'art, et que ces hommes en tarbouches, sur leur vapeur, sont les messagers d'une machine qui vient inexorablement transformer le pays, le progrès scientifique que l'on ne peut arrêter, bien qu'il écrase beaucoup de gens, sur son passage.[63]
>
> (The son of the deceased tribal chief, seeing that these men who come from the capital can decipher the secrets of the tombs, for him incomprehensible, tombs that his family live off, feels like a stranger in his own village, his own world. He understands that these objects belong to them and that their existence will be eternal, like the existence of all works of art, and that these men wearing tarbooshes standing on their steamboats are messengers of a machine that comes to transform inexorably the country and brings the scientific progress that cannot be stopped even though it crushes many on its path.)

Wanis's estrangement from his village and world begins with the death of his father, the tribal patriarch. After this death, Wanis and his brother are brought into the secret of the clan's livelihood. In an early scene, which depicts a ritual of initiation, Wanis and his brother are led into the secret tomb to take part in the family economy, are invited—as their father was—to become men of the tribe. But rather than embracing the tribe's system of values, the two men break from it. They turn in horror as they watch their uncles dismember the body of a mummy. It is not just that Wanis turns away as they roughly hack at the body of the mummy. Instead, there is a remarkable shift that transpires during the scene when Wanis is ordered to take a piece of jewelry to the antiquities trader Ayyub. The piece of jewelry—a necklace adorned with a large eye—seems to return Wanis's gaze: by the end of the scene, he is the one who appears possessed, transfixed by the eye of the object. It is as if the eye of the past stares back in judgment at the present.

The scene is a watershed for Wanis's character: it precipitates his exit from the tribal culture, a culture in which mummies have value largely as inanimate objects to be traded for profit. In confronting the tribe, both Wanis and his brother assert that mummies, as human remains, demand the respect of ancestors. However, when Wanis's brother confronts the elders and tells them it is shameful to traffick in the dead, they murder him and thus reinstate their notion of ancestral loyalty to the tribe. In contrast to his brother, Wanis leaves the tribe passively, more through madness than will. He wanders the Theban landscape, pursued by uncles who want to silence him and by antiquities officers who want to question him. If the tribe and the Antiquities Service represent two opposing systems and two opposing modes of subjectivity, then we can say that although Wanis has left the first position, he never arrives at the second. Instead, he wanders among colossal ruins throughout the course of the film. His character marks a liminal space between the despotic traditionalism of the tribe and the enlightened modernity of the nation-state. It is this very in-betweenness that makes Wanis seem unhinged or undead. In short, the film tells the story of Wanis's transformation into a mummy.

Wanis's narrative is about this figurative mummification and is underscored by the many uncomfortable close-ups that intensify the embalmed quality of his visual image. The mummy figure that emerges signals loss more than preservation and death more than resurrection. Visually, this loss of self is represented most powerfully in the scenes in which Wanis wanders through ruins, scenes in which his character falls under the shadow of the objects that surround him, the rocks and statues that come to possess him. The monumental ruins do not serve as a backdrop to the development of Wanis; rather, as the film progresses, it is as though these monuments become the true focus and he gradually fades into the background. Thus, the film's obsession with loss inverts the themes of identification with and possession of antiquities: the Antiquities Service project of repossessing ancient artifacts—artifacts that are the stuff upon which identities are founded—becomes linked with the more frightening excesses of identification and possession we find in Wanis's character.

Patrimony, Melancholia, and the Funerals of 1967

To conclude, I would like to consider how the narrative of the film is framed by two funerals: in the first scene the patriarch is buried, while in the film's closing scene it is the bodies of mummies that are figuratively laid to rest by the state. This doubled ritual of burial casts a melancholic shadow over what comes between: melancholic rather than mournful, because Wanis's character chooses to honor the loss of the father (and then brother) by specifically refusing to attach himself to the order that would compensate for their loss, and melancholic because the experience of their deaths precipitates an internalization and inversion of his feelings into despair, shame, and self-hatred. This is particularly visible in the final moments of the film after Wanis appears—almost sleepwalking—at the door of the antiquities inspector to whom he reveals the tribe's secret. The antiquities department dispatches soldiers and archaeologists who, under the cloak of darkness, work to save the mummies from the tribe. The film closes with Wanis waking from his stupor and realizing that by helping the Antiquities Service, he has condemned his tribe to poverty. He watches as the soldiers lead a solemn procession of sarcophagi from the tomb to the government steamship for transport to the Cairo museum. On the one hand, this final scene marks the triumph of the benevolent state over the tyranny of the tribe: the rich visual quality and slow pace of the final procession is extended by the detailed composition of the shot in which the members of the defeated tribe stand in front of the powerful steamship. But on the other hand, the film enacts this victory as a funeral ceremony: this procession marks the beginning of the tribe's own death march as it confronts modernity.

We can read the doubled framing ritual of burial in another way, as expressive of competing notions of patriarchy and competing economies of reverence. In a sense, the burials are about one patriarchal system giving way to another: the tribe's literal sense of patriarchy is replaced by the more figurative one of the state; fathers are replaced by forefathers; local customs are supplanted by the more abstract principles of civilization; and finally, family inheritance gives way to national heritage. This transition is a victory of the nation-state, but it is an empty victory: it remains unclear what has been won in the struggle over artifacts. The film begins to seem a meditation on loss and bereavement rather than recuperation and salvation. The note it ends on is so uneasy because by recapitulating and drawing out the ambivalences within the nationalist discourse on antiquities, it begins to lay bare those irreducible social antagonisms which underlie it.

I would like to consider the funeral scenes further in light of the tension between the nationalist, redemptive surface of the film and the sense of ambivalence and melancholia just underneath. I would speculate that this tension exists chiefly between the film's screenplay and its production and that it is partially explained by the peculiar conditions of the film's production. As I noted above, the screenplay for the film was complete and funding guaranteed by the Ministry of Culture by early 1967. Most likely, the casting, sets and locations were also decided by that spring. This was soon followed by the disastrous war which took place in June. As Abd al-Salam notes:

> I wrote [the film] right before the collapse [of 1967]. Then I began shooting six or seven months after it. Of course, [the event] had a great impact on me. Especially since my father had died a couple months after the collapse, which plunged me into deep grief. I could not avoid the effect these two calamities had on me. I remember that when I shaved each morning, I was truly afraid to see my face in the mirror.[64]

The film was then shot in 1968 and completed the next year. With this chronology in mind, one could propose another reading of the film with special reference to the interpretive struggles in which Abd al-Salam, the post–1967 director, exercised his authority to revise the work of Abd al-Salam, the Nasserist screenwriter. This at least might begin to explain the disjuncture between the naive nationalism of the text's screenplay (which passed the first censors) and the complications of its melancholic cinematic style, much of which could be the result of post–1967 choices. Moreover, this would at least partially explain the Ministry of Culture's surprise at the final product and its cool reception: the melancholic, distanced aesthetic of the text does not seem to have been lost on the bureaucrats who decided to shelve the film in 1969.

I would like to conclude by juxtaposing the film's funerals with the historical context in which the film was produced: to think of the film as a meditation on loss taking place in a political and cultural situation of profound loss, as an oblique rumination on the perceived collapse of the Nasserist nation-state. Indeed, early audiences link their experience of viewing the film to general feelings of defeat and loss. One of Abd al-Salam's critics describes what it was like to watch the film in Cairo at the time:

> I first saw the film on December 16, 1969, in one of the private screenings at the Cinema Club . . . I saw the film in the midst of difficult circumstances. The nation was weighed down by anxiety and a heavy sensation of defeat, our breasts were filled with shame. Huge crowds of youth stood in lines outside embassies in the hopes of emigrating.[65]

For this critic, as for others, the film was the sort of powerful text that could redeem a fallen national culture:

> Everyone [in the audience] realized that when an aesthetic piece was presented by an eloquent cineaste like Abd al-Salam who carried within his mind and heart the culture of his ancient forefathers; its message should reach out to his people and kin.[66]

That neither the state nor the public took to this interpretation seems to indicate just how estranged the film was from its context.

Yet, the special circumstances surrounding the general release of *al-Mumiya* on January 28, 1975, reconnect us to the film's funereal themes. The film's appearance on the Egyptian cultural scene is almost too neatly framed by a series of mass funerals—al-Nahhas in 1965, Nasser in 1970, Umm Kulthum in 1975, and finally Abd al-Halim Hafiz in 1977—in which millions of Egyptians mourned something more than the death of public individuals. While it would be incorrect to think that those larger events need be read solely as the public mourning of the passing of Arab nationalism, nevertheless they do seem to figure in the background of Abd al-Salam's text. As such, they suggest a different reason for thinking of the significance of *al-Mumiya* within the nationalist cinematic canon—and allow us to recognize its special place in that tradition while not betraying its internal ambivalences or the richness of the ambivalences posed by its historical moment.

Notes

1. See Shadi Abd al-Salam, "Counting the Years: Shadi Abd al-Salam's Words," *Discourse* 21:1 (1999): 130.
2. For example, see Guy Hennebelle, "Chadi Abdel Salam une brillante exception," *Les Cinémas Africains en 1972* (Paris: Société Africaine d'Édition, 1972).
3. Sami al-Salamuni, "Hiwar lam yunshir fi hiyat Shadi," *Al-Qahira* 159 (February 1996): 351.
4. The story appears in Gaston Maspéro, *Les momies royales de Deir el-Bahari,* pp. 511–787.
5. See the interview "Chadi Abdes-Salam: le duel tradition-modernité" in Yves Thoraval, *Regards sur le cinéma égyptien* (Beirut: Dar al-Machreq Éditeurs, 1975), p. 81.
6. Al-Salamuni, pp. 347–48.
7. See Muridi al-Nahhas, "Shadi Abd al-Salam: shua min Misr," *Al-Qahira* 159 (February 1996): 7–12, and Viola Shafiq, "Al-Bahth an al-Hawiyya," *Al-Qahira* 159 (February 1996): 118–120.
8. "*Al-Mumiya* expresses Abd al-Salam's attempt to cling to his roots. Not in the sense of proudly boasting that he owns the antiquities. But that truly, those thousands of years that extend behind him have not slipped from his grasp, and that they assist him in rising up from his fall no matter how difficult or long that fall may have been." From Saad Abd al-Rahmsn, "Rawat al-mur'iyyat fi-l-Mumiya," *Al-Qahira* 159 (February 1996): 206. See also Majdi Abd al-Rahman, "*Al-Mumiya* abr thalath tawarikh," *Al-Qahira* 159 (February 1996): 229.
9. See for example comments Abd al-Salam (1999, p. 136) makes with regard to the costumes and casting of another Pharaonic film, *Akhinatun,* he was set to make at the time of his death:

   Before starting to shoot, I will teach the cast the gestures and rhythms of those who lived three thousand years ago. They will need to learn to walk very naturally barefoot in burning sands. I've asked the finest artisans in Moski in old Cairo to make for me exactly what was made for Tutankhamen . . . decorated with jewels . . . the very colors . . . the same weights . . . the same material, or something close to it. I am using the finest materials in order to approximate the real thing. I want you to understand me . . . the actors aren't professionals . . . I met the person who will play the role of Akhenaton while walking in the streets of Cairo. . . . I've met more than one young woman who would work for the role of Nefertiti. Now I have to choose one of them. . . . Most who act with me are inexperienced. . . . I can influence them. . . . They're not tied to things that distance them from us. . . . For this reason, when they decorate themselves with jewelry and wear wigs like the ancients . . . wigs made of wool, wearing Pharaonic robes made of Egyptian cotton, or the priest's garment of cheetah skin. . . . At that moment, the blood of our kings and queens and princes and soldiers and storytellers and writers will flow in their veins. It's the blood of memory. They won't be acting roles, they will be inheriting them.

10. See Muhammad Ibrahim Adil, "*Al-Mumiya* bayn al-tashkil wa-l-tajsid," *Al-Qahira* 159 (February 1996): 189.
11. There is a long history of nationalist writing that sees a singularity and univocity within Egyptian culture from the ancient past through the present. With specific reference to the film, see the rich architectural study by Abd al-Salam and Salah Mari, "Al-Bayt wa-l-khayma fi rif Idfuh," *Al-Qahira* 159 (February 1996): 90–118; see also articles by Majd Abd al-Rahman, al-Nahhas, and Shafiq, op. cit.
12. Guy Hennebelle, "Hadıth an *al-Mumiya*," *Al-Qahira* 159 (February 1996): 243.
13. While Abd al-Salam's vision of civilization and culture is unique with regard to his generation of intellectuals, it nevertheless builds upon an established body of earlier discourse that attempted to make sense of the relevance of the ancient or pre-Islamic world within the cultures of modern Egyptians. See for example, Husayn 1996 (1938), #270.
14. "The central category and criterion of realist literature is the type, a peculiar synthesis which organically binds together the general and the particular both in characters and situations." Georg Lukács, *Studies in European Realism* (New York: The Universal Library, 1964), p. 6.
15. "The function of costumbrismo was 'to make the different strata of society comprehensible one to another.'" Susan Kirkpatrick as quoted in Doris Sommer, *Foundational Fictions: Traditional Romances of Latin America* (Berkeley: University of California Press, 1991), p. 14.
16. See Homi Bhabha's distinction between performative and pedagogical subjects in "DissemiNation: Time, Narrative and the Margins of the Modern Nation," in *Nation and Narration* (New York: Routledge, 1990), p. 302.
17. See for example: "*Al-Mumiya,*" *Majallat Ramsis* 10:4 (1921): 314–20; "Yaqzat firawn," *Majallat Ramsis* 12:9–10 (1923): 696–67; and "Al-Yadd al-muhannat," *Majallat Ramsis* (1924): 47–48.
18. See Brian Fagan, *The Rape of the Nile* (New York: Scribners, 1975); Peter France, *The Rape of Egypt: How the Europeans Stripped Egypt of its Heritage* (London: Barrie and Jenkins, 1991), pp. 27–57.
19. For two examples of travel accounts in which the trade appears, see G[iovanni] Belzoni, *Narrative of the Operations and Recent Discoveries within the Pyramids, Temples, Tombs and Excavations in Egypt and Nubia* (London: John Murray, 1820) and Wolfradine Von Minutoli, *Recollections of Egypt* (Philadelphia: Carey, Lea and Carey, 1827).
20. Al-Qurna (also: Gourna, el-Gourney, Curnu, etc.) is exceptional in the accounts of eighteenth- and nineteenth-century travelers: its proximity to the important sites of the Colossi of Memnon, the Memnonium (or Ramesseum), Dayr al-Bahri, Medinat Abu, and the Valley of the Kings meant that travelers and archaeologists had to negotiate for the assistance and labor of locals, in addition to the artifacts they had excavated in secret.

More interestingly, al-Qurna people's organized and militant refusal to concede ground to the central state and foreign explorers set it apart from other regions where antiquities were found. The early history of armed encounters between European visitors and local villagers can be traced through travel accounts. See Richard Pococke, *A Description of the East and Some Other Countries* (London: W. Bowyer, 1743), pp. 78–98; Frederick Lewis Norden, *Travels in Egypt and Nubia* (London: Lockyer Davis and Charles Reymers, 1758), vol. II, pp. 71–74, 194–95; Charles Nicolas Sonnini, *Travels in Upper and Lower Egypt: Undertaken by Order of the Old Government of France* (London: John Stockdale, 1799), vol. III, pp. 239–50; Vivant Denon, *Travels in Upper and Lower Egypt, During the Campaigns of General Bonaparte* (London: J. Cundee, 1803), vol. I, p. 216; and Belzoni.

21. France, pp. 58–80.
22. A complete French translation of the Ordinance of August 15, 1835, appears in Antoine Khater, *Le Régime juridique de fouilles et des antiquités en Égypte* (Cairo: Imprimerie de L'Institut Français d'Archéologie Orientale, 1960), pp. 37–40. The state Arabic translation of the Ottoman text may be found in Dar al-Wathaiq: Abhath Box 127: Folder 9: Diwan Khidiwi, wurida: Daftar 816: Number 148: Page 175: Date: 6 Rabi al-Thani, 1251.
23. Khater, 38, translation mine.
24. See Abhath Box 127: Folder 9. Correspondence from the Sublime Porte to Mukhtar Bey, Nazir of the Royal Court. Date: 21 Rabi al-Thani, 1251.
25. See Khater, p. 45. See also Dar al-Watha'iq: Abhath Box 127: Folder 9: Document "Al-Tasrihat li-naql juthuth al-kufar."
26. Ibid., p. 57.
27. Ibid., p. 61.
28. Donald Reid, "Indigenous Egyptology: The Decolonization of a Profession," *Journal of the American Oriental Society* 105:2 (1985): 233–246; and "Nationalizing the Pharaonic Past: Egyptology, Imperialism, and Egyptian Nationalism, 1922–1952" in *Rethinking Nationalism in the Arab Middle East,* eds. James Jankowski and Israel Gershoni (New York: Columbia University Press, 1997), pp. 127–49.
29. Muhammad al-Muwaylihi, *Hadith Isa ibn Hisham* (Cairo: Dar al-Shab, n.d.), pp. 197–98.
30. See Israel Gershoni and James Jankowski, "The Egyptianist Image of Egypt: III. Pharaonicism," in *Egypt, Islam, and the Arabs: The Search for Egyptian Nationhood, 1900–1930* (New York: Oxford University Press, 1986).
31. See Philip Abrams, "Notes on the Difficulty of Studying the State," *Journal of Historical Sociology* 1:1 (1988): 58–89; Ralph Miliband, "Marx and the State" in *Class Power and State Power* (London: Verso, 1983), pp. 3–25; and Michael Taussig, "Maleficium: State Fetishism" in *Fetishism as Cultural Discourse,* eds. E. Apter and W. Pietz (Ithaca, NY: Cornell University Press, 1993), pp. 217–247.

32. Millband, p. 6.
33. Abrams, pp. 69–70; Taussig, pp. 220–23.
34. Abrams, pp. 61–65.
35. See Michel Foucault, "Governmentality" in *The Foucault Effect: Studies in Governmentality*, eds. G. Burchell, C. Gordon and P. Miller (Chicago: University of Chicago Press, 1991), pp. 87–104.
36. Foucault, pp. 103–104.
37. David Lloyd and Paul Thomas describe more fully this process by which a cultural canon and ethical subject are articulated by the State:

    [Culture] refers in part to the objects that constitute a "culture" [Kultur], in the sense of the ensemble of artifacts and aesthetic practices of a developed civilization rather than to any given 'mode of living,' but designates primarily the disposition of the human subject in relation to those objects and to nature. It thus extends the purview of the prior concept-metaphor, "Taste," and the philosophical elaboration of the "aesthetic" comes to consider culture as a process of cultivation, the gradual formation of an ethical human subject, characterized by disinterested reflection and universally valid judgments (*Culture and the State* [New York: Routledge, 1998], p. 2).

38. See, for example, Ibrahim Mustafa, *Al-Qawl al-mufid fi-athar al-Said* (Bulaq: al-Matbaa al-Kubra al-Amiriya bi-Bulaq, 1893); Ahmad Najib, *Al-Athr al-jalil li-l-qudama wadi al-Nil* (Bulaq: al-Matbaa al-Kubra al-Amiriya bi-Bulaq, 1895).
39. In particular, see Khater, Decrees of 1835 and 1869. Transportation laws seem to have been the medium for regulating ownership and possession. See the Decrees of 1869, 1883, 1891, and the 1901 railroads bylaw also in Khater.
40. The bylaws of 1912 are the most elaborate of the laws on exchange. Besides the 1835 and 1869 Decrees, see the bylaws of 1880, 1912, and 1921. See Khater.
41. As it appears in the above Decree of 1897 and, more specifically, in the Decree of 1909.
42. Ahmad Kamal, *Livre des perles enfouies et du mystère précieux au sujet des indications des cachettes, des trouvailles et des trésors* (Le Caire: Imprimerie de l'Institut Français d'Archéologie Orientale, 1907), p. 8.
43. Treasure seeking—al-matlab—is addressed also in the 1869 Ottoman antiquities bylaws, Articles 7, 11, and 13.
44. See the 1835 Decree in Khater. The vagueness of the 1869 Ottoman bylaws on antiquities allowed the state to lay claim, in the name of conservation, to all sorts of land. One such example is Article 23: "Dans le cas où le Gouvernement voudrait exécuter lui-même des fouilles sur des points qui ne sont pas mulk, ni dépendents de localités habitées et où la découverte d'antiquités serait probable, ces endroits ne seront cédés à personne" (Khater, p. 277).

On the expulsion of the permanent settlement from the ruins of Edfu, see Auguste Mariette-Bey, *The Monuments of Upper Egypt* (Alexandria: A. Mourès, 1877), p. 247.

45. See the Decrees of 1909 in Khater.
46. On *sibakh,* see Khater and Najib. Also, many nineteenth-century writers describe with horror the practice of burning mummies as fuel. See, for example, Frederick Henniker, *Notes During a Visit to Egypt, Nubia, the Oasis Boeris, Mount Sinai and Jerusalem* (London: John Murray, 1824); Minutoli, op. cit (1827); and John Lloyd Stephens, *Incidents of Travel in Egypt, Arabia Petræa and the Holy Land* (Norman: University of Oklahoma Press, 1970 [1835]). Mark Twain claims to have heard that Egyptian locomotives used mummies instead of coal in *The Innocents Abroad* (Oxford: Oxford University Press, 1996). While it is easy to suppose that such a use of mummy would have been prohibited under existing law, the fact that it is never alluded to by Antiquities Service officers makes one at least doubt the extent of the practice. Nevertheless, as an image, it was striking enough to resurface in the "mummy torch" scene in Rider Haggard's novel *She.*
47. Article 3 of the 1835 Decree stipulated the posting of armed soldiers around sites, whereas Article 9 subordinated local officials to the authority of Antiquities Inspectors, and Article 10 authorized inspection tours throughout Upper Egypt. Article 6 of the 1869 Ottoman bylaws authorized government agents to guard monuments while Article 9 placed all authorized excavations under the direct supervision of government agents and Article 21 stipulated: "Si l'emplacement à fouiller se trouve séparé des localités peuplées par une distance qui rendrait difficile toute surveillance continuelle de l'autorité, un employée sera adjoint au possesseur d'autorisation aux frais de ce dernier" (Khater, 277).
48. Najyb, p. 5.
49. See Mariette-Bey, p. 57, or for an earlier account, Moyle Sherer, *Scenes and Impressions in Egypt and in Italy* (London: Longman, Hurst, Rees, Orme, Brown and Green, 1824), pp. 116–17.
50. Najyb, p. 81.
51. Peter Gran, *Islamic Roots of Capitalism: Egypt, 1760–1840* (Syracuse: Syracuse University Press, 1998), p. xxxv.
52. Majdi Abd al-Rahman asserts that the first draft of the screenplay was "realist," the second "melodrama" as opposed to the fourth, the version that was finally produced, which was "visual poetry" (al-shi'r al-mar'i). See Majdi Abd al-Rahman, p. 227.
53. Shadi Abd al-Salam, "Al-Iqa al-Misri al-bati," (interview *in Al-Qahira* 159 [February 1996]: 246.
54. Majdi Abd al-Rahman, op. cit, p. 228.
55. Hennebelle (1996), p. 243.
56. Abd al-Salam (1996), p. 247.
57. André Bazin, *What is Cinema?* (Berkeley: University of California Press, 1967), p. 38.

58. Ibid., p. 39.
59. Ibid., p. 27.
60. Ibid., p. 9.
61. Ibid., p. 11.
62. Shadi Abd al-Salam (1999), p. 131.
63. Thoraval, p. 81.
64. Al-Salamuni, p. 349.
65. Majdi Abd al-Rahman, "Ya man tadhhab sataiud," *Al-Qahira* 159 (February 1996): 306.
66. Ibid.

Part IV

Nationalism, Islamism, and Hegemony

Chapter 7

Islamism and the Recolonization of Algeria

Marnia Lazreg

In November 1988, during a visit to the shrine of Sidi Abderrahmane, a popular sufi and guardian of the old city of Algiers, I noticed two apparently "mad" people (or as they are called in colloquial Arabic, *madroubin,* meaning "stricken"): a young woman dressed in a hijab and a man in his late thirties dressed in Western clothes. They were unrelated, but their presence in the small terrace overlooking the Mediterranean and their delirium brought them close to each other. She spoke to herself about God and his wrath; he spoke to the few visitors about injustices perpetrated by an unspecified "them," of history that will be remade. Addressing me, he also asked a rhetorical question about the meaning of women's "oppression" (or *hogra*) without seeming to see the young woman walking to and fro, absorbed in her soliloquy. In many ways, he was a throwback to the North African tradition of the illuminated man who speaks his mind about the powers that be in a more or less metaphorical fashion. She was brought to the saint's mausoleum to regain her sanity and stop mumbling about the divine. In June 1991, as I was waiting for the bus at a stop on the heights of Algiers in Hydra Square, a middle-aged woman wearing a hijab stood next to me. She appeared to speak to herself, in a low voice, unintelligible words interspersed with a recitation of the *shahada.* I had noticed in the cab that had taken me to Hydra that the driver played a cassette of an imam who broke into loud sobs in the middle of his *khutba,* moved by his own words.

I began to ponder the meaning of these unrelated episodes in the context of the emergence of the Islamist opposition and the rise of a new religiosity. Radio and television were replete with religious news and messages. The loudspeakers in every neighborhood, which, as is customary, announced the time for the regular five prayers, seemed to blast warnings of an impending doom rather than reminders of one's duty towards God. I wrote in my diary, "Algeria has become saturated with religious symbols." I meant to remind myself of the official references to God, as well as the individual ones, such as the sudden concern among friends and acquaintances for the validity of their daily activities measured against this or that tradition.

Algerians have been Muslims since the eighth century—whence comes, then, this ostentatious display of religiosity and the delirium it seems to provoke? Algerians have traditionally considered their attitude towards religion a private matter that could not be legislated by any group or man. Now, it is not only a public matter, but judging by the violence that has erupted since 1992, it is also coercive. The religious discourse has turned into a political discourse, and personal expression can only occur in the delirium mode.

I would like to take the case of the nameless young woman at Sidi Abderrhamane as a metaphor for the Algerian crisis since 1992. At present, Algeria can be apprehended only as a society in a state of political and cultural delirium. The nature of the violence whereby children, women, and men have been hacked by power swords, saws, axes and double-edged knives has a haunting, nightmarish, delirious quality to it. Social delirium is defined in this chapter as the loss of control over the ability to reason by segments of the population, accompanied by discursive excesses. These excesses are marked by an obsession with selective historical experiences such as colonialism and result in actions that are meant to redress mythical rather than real grievances. For example, civilians are massacred today for not conforming to the myth of the ideal Muslim or for being part of a society that is deemed un-Islamic and in a state of *jahiliya* (or ignorance). The Algerian government is regarded as heretical and un-Islamic.

Colonialism looms large in the Islamist discourse of deconstruction of Algeria's culture and politics. It has acquired mythical proportions referring to all that does not conform to a religion-based model of behavior. It is a constructed standard against which to measure happiness, justice, and change. Colonialism has become an ideological concept that helps to remake Algeria's historical map. On the one hand, the Front of Islamic Salvation (or FIS) intended to present itself as endowed with the mission of relinking the society with its anticolonial past, thus forging an historical continuity that somehow bypasses the colonial era. This meant cleansing society of the colonial legacy as exemplified by the continued use of the French language, a constitution defined as "secular," unveiled women, and coeducation. On the other hand, the FIS attempted to *reshape* people's lives by insisting, just as the French did, on the superiority of its vision of culture, society, and politics. The "civilizing mission" advocated by the colonists in the nineteenth century preceded what might be termed the "recivilizing" mission of the FIS. The Islamists' aim is not to "re-Islamize" people as is often said.[1] Rather, it *recolonizes* private and public spaces by infusing them with new meanings and norms derived from ideational and behavioral sources that sound familiar to individuals because they are expressed in the Arabic language and refer to a monolithic "Islam," but that are in effect alien to the historical and daily experiences of individual Algerians. In the end, Islam as understood by Algerians prior to the emergence of the Islamist movement undergoes a transformation that changes its meaning by distorting it. This is a complex and often ambiguous task that plays itself out on several registers: emotional, cultural, social, and political. It capitalizes on Algerians' attachment to their religion, their thirst for dignity, and their desire for equality. I am referring to this process as one of recolonization because of its targeting of Algerians' cultural space in a manner similar to the French who, in the nineteenth century, attempted to displace local norms and values to suit their political purposes. Just as the French hoped to make a *tabula rasa* of Algerians' culture, Islamists intend to impose new models of behavior and attitudinal changes to replace existing ones deemed neocolonial and un-Islamic because they do not conform to Islamists' political conception of religiosity.

This paper examines the process through which Islamism in Algeria has "recolonized" individuals' "life world."[2] The social changes that have taken place in Algeria since its independence—as represented by the spread of education, a slow but real transformation of the structure of the family, an evolution of women's consciousness of their rights, and social pressure for political democratic reform—have been perceived by the Islamist movement as challenges that needed to be controlled. I will argue that the Islamist movement means to redirect the sociopolitical evolution of Algeria through cultural recolonization. In so doing, Islamism has in effect imposed on Algerians a new belief system and created a new counterculture that thrives on nihilism—a blatant disregard for human life that cannot advance any political cause as is expressed in the Armed Islamic Group's attacks on defenseless and innocent civilians, admittedly to emphasize the government's inability to protect its citizens.

The use of colonial methods of social control is not the monopoly of the Islamist movement. The state, too, has adopted colonial strategies, especially in its dealings with the institution of religion, which it attempted to place under political control. However, the Islamist movement has provided a total ideology using colonial strategies of acculturation for political purposes, just as the French did throughout the colonial era. This paper does not delve into the multiple reasons that led to the emergence of the Islamist movement. Nor does it condone any party involved in the ongoing civil war. It is primarily concerned with the ideological uses of the historical reality of colonialism and the transformative impact of Islamism on indigenous culture. It is an analysis of the reproduction of the colonial idea, an obsessive idea that the state failed to deconstruct and the Islamist movement succeeded at appropriating in a mythic form.

Theoretical Considerations

Since 1990, when the Front of Islamic Salvation won municipal elections, Algeria has been studied as a nation that has gone awry, "choosing" the path of tradition over modernity, Islam over secularism. The fact that it is precisely Algeria's experiment with "secular" democratic rules that enabled the Front of Islamic Salvation to spread its message and come close to winning parliamentary elections was often lost on journalists and political scientists ready to capitalize on the apparent "turn" away from "nationalist" rhetoric. It is not the much touted "nationalism" that failed in Algeria. Rather, it is the ideal of what Malley calls "thirdworldism" within the contexts of national crisis and international change that did.[3]

It is fruitful to explore the notion of "crisis" to make sense of the rise of the Islamist movement in Algeria. The crisis of the late capitalist state studied by Habermas bears strong similarities with that of the Algerian state in 1965–1984. Habermas revealed that the late capitalist state undergoes a loss of legitimacy due to its increased intervention in the economic sphere to shore up flagging business or sustain private enterprise. The state seeks to compensate for its lack of legitimacy due to its forsaking the universal good by appealing to residues of tradition.[4]

In the Algerian context, the state directly performed economic functions while at the same time it fulfilled a political role. This double function was necessary in a first stage to permit the emergence of new social classes—a professional, political, and a business class—linked to the state through access to power holders. The sale of the formerly state-owned economic enterprises to private individuals in the past few years, as a result of structural adjustment, has benefited former members of the government and/or their affiliates. In other words, the Algerian state up until 1978 acted as an incubator of social classes while at the same time preventing class conflict from emerging by providing social services such as medical care, free education, and subsidized foodstuffs made possible by petrodollars.[5] By the mid-eighties, the state could no longer satisfy the needs it generated for more and better services. In addition, it could no longer maintain mass loyalty as the ideology and practice of socialism were dealt a severe blow by the collapse of the Soviet Union. This was compounded by a loss of status in the wake of the collapse of the nonaligned movement, in which Algeria played a pivotal role, and greater vulnerability to the dictates of the global economy.

Until 1978, the state monopoly over the economy meant not only a restructuring of social classes but also a brake on cultural development. On the one hand, the state appealed to religion as a reliable institution to secure social consensus already made possible by the provision of social services. On the other hand, it secured mass loyalty through a progressive foreign policy that acted as a substitute for political participation. Social consensus collapsed when the oil crisis of the mid-eighties made it difficult to hide class inequities and even more difficult to stem the tide of protests from those most affected—the urban, disenfranchised youth, and women—by a state that claimed to be universalistic in its aims but was privatistic in its practice. Thus, the crisis of the state became a crisis of identity and motivation.[6] Identity in the sense that the state in the eighties lost its socialist facade, because President Chadli Bedjedid essentially legalized the black market when he took power and slowly moved toward a market economy under the guise of economic adjustment required by a newly discovered foreign debt of $26 billion.[7] Having secured the emergence of postcolonial classes, the state could hope to motivate the public by the introduction of formal democracy, which it did in 1989. Mass loyalty without participation of the seventies gave way to the fetishism of democracy in the late eighties. Lacking the experience necessary to make the democratic game at least enjoyable if not useful, the electorate realized the contrived nature of this new phenomenon that brought it 58 parties all claiming the virtues of the polls. Voters elected those they knew best because they understood their language, although they may not have been convinced by their message. Thus, the Front of Islamic Salvation candidates won the municipal elections of 1990 and the first round of parliamentary elections of 1991.

In sum, the crisis that brought the Islamist movement to the forefront of politics was caused by the preeminence of the political sphere under the cover of which social inequality deepened, new classes emerged, and social conflict could no longer be contained. The state's appeal to religion in its attempt at securing social cohesion backfired for two reasons: (1) new religious leadership resisted its subjugation by the state and created "new mosques" within which it mounted a counterdiscourse of liberation of what it presented as a neocolonial state;[8] and (2) the social inequities laid bare by the oil crisis of the eighties made it easier for the new counterdiscourse to be heard.

Islamism and Colonialism

The Islamist discourse in its manifold expression centers on the colonial past, intends to erase it, and promises to reconstruct a future that reaches back to a mythical primordial era by reconstituting the present on principles deemed anticolonial. That Algeria is no longer a colony does not deter the proponents of this view. The Algerian state is defined as just an extension of the colonial state that must be dismantled. Ironically, the Islamist discourse proceeds along lines similar to those followed by the colonial discourse, by privileging the cultural and the political over the social and the economic. The Bible (used to convert Algerian orphans in the nineteenth century) and the values of the colonial version of the Enlightenment have been replaced by the Sunna and the Hadith, the Quran being given short shrift, notwithstanding its invocation when convenient. Thus, rules governing every aspect of everyday life are explained in mosques and in pamphlets on sale in bookstores. For example, a woman's duties toward her husband, children, relatives, and friends are codified.[9] Similarly, a man's business behavior is also codified down to how much he should charge without losing money or appearing to take advantage of his clients. At the same time, class consciousness is introduced in business transactions in the sense that the customers' social positions figure into the price they are charged.[10]

Just as the colonial project of social engineering was alien to the customs of the Algerian people, the Islamist project of reconstructing social life by giving it a new normative framework expressed in the familiar language of God, his Prophet, and the Traditions is equally alien to Algerians. It is not uncommon to hear Algerians wonder whether the scrutiny of everything they do in everyday life is part of the religion they have practiced since birth. The difference between the colonial and the Islamist projects lies in the Islamists' manipulation of familiar religious symbols and the identification of the new language of religion with a collective "us," the people, and "them," the government. Essentially, the Islamist discourse as expressed by the former Front of Islamic Salvation and the Armed Islamic Group redefines the relationship between the Muslim and God from unobtrusive worship and individual piety to exalted display of public religiosity; from awareness of multiple interpretations to submission to one interpretation of the texts, if not reinterpretation, chosen by the movement; and from tolerance of different modes of being Muslim to a rejection of all deviations from a normative way of being Muslim.

The new discourse on religion is not religion but politics under a religious garb. Thus, crossing the line between religious militancy and direct action to topple the government, Said Mekhloufi, a former chief of the Army of Islamic Salvation, called for civil disobedience. He justified his call by pointing to social injustice caused by "Judeo-Christian laws" and warned that whoever did not heed his call would be guilty of "treason and crime against Islam, against Muslims and against the future of this religion."[11] In this amalgamation of religion and politics, religion is typically invoked as punishment for not engaging in political action. Similarly, Imam Ikhlef

Cherati, founding member of the FIS, issued a fatwa in the summer of 1992 authorizing the jihad against the state on grounds that mix colonialism with state despotism. He pointed out that "while Muslims are hounded everywhere, the old colonists whom our fathers booted out yesterday are welcomed with fanfare; they have come back thanks to their children [meaning the leaders and possibly Western foreigners working in Algeria], to combat our religion and customs, to degrade our culture and personality, to appropriate our wealth, and enslave our people. God orders us to fight, too, and warns us against their assistance."[12]

Injustices, social inequities, and social problems are criticized not as products of an incompetent or misguided government but as the outcomes of a government identified as ruling by proxy—a colonial institution headed by native men. This use of colonialism as a factor of political destabilization transcends the actual nature of the policies undertaken by the state since 1962. It is meant to establish a new historical periodization by occulting the war for independence in order to justify a new war of decolonization. By the same token, an appeal to native colonialism questions the legitimacy of the war for independence; the implication is that it should have been waged against local enemies. In other words, the postindependence state is illegitimate, alien, and must be fought as such. Within this context, acts of violence against members of the government, the military, and the police resemble those committed against their French counterparts by the FLN during the first year of the war for independence. Similarly, the random acts of violence inflicted upon the civilian population by the Armed Islamic Group since 1993 evoke urban guerrilla warfare waged by the FLN against the civilian colonists. However, the use of the colonial imagery by the Islamist movement founders on the issue of democracy. While the wartime FLN invoked the democratic principle of self-determination to legitimize its struggle against the French colonists, the Islamist movement scorns democracy.

The state based on God's commandments does not represent the kingdom of God on Earth. Rather, it is a formal institution established for its own sake, independent of the actions and policies of the existing state. It does not address individuals' spiritual life as such. Rather, it aims at reordering the social and political spheres. Salvation, the soul, compassion, forgiveness, love, and affection are not central to the new life under the Islamic republic. God is invoked within the context of struggle, rebellion, and war. Demonstrations, general strikes and sit-ins have all been used between 1990 and 1992 as so many methods to "destroy the primary obstacle, this offspring of colonialism, born out of our own blood."[13] Having entered the political arena as contenders for power, Islamists appeal to God and religion not to liberate people from mundane cares, but to justify their own search for power. Where they delve in daily matters of morality, Islamists do so through a combination of unrelenting exhortation and coercion, browbeating (especially of women, generally less versed in religious texts than men), and social pressure. The definition of the existing state as a colonial institution dispenses with the formulation of a viable alternative. If being colonial means being "Judeo-Christian," the alternative can only be an Islamic state.

Islamism and Historical Re-Mapping

Islamists have made the claim that they are the heirs of the Ulama movement of the 1930s and see Abdehamid Ben Badis as their spiritual leader. However, there are more differences than similarities between Ben Badis's social project and that of the Front of Islamic Salvation. Ben Badis lived and preached under colonial rule, which he did not repudiate. His goal was a reinvigoration of a culture that had become largely oral due to the dearth of schools that taught Arabic, the popularity in rural areas of sufi leaders whom he despised and accused of spreading superstitions, and the acculturation of young Muslim men who went to French schools and often married French women. His cultural program included teaching Arabic to boys and girls, extending education to girls in order for them to become suitable matches for acculturated men, and returning to a strict application of the Quran and the Sunna as guides for everyday life.[14] Ben Badis did not call for the independence of Algeria, nor did he advocate the overthrow of colonial rule through peaceful or violent means. In fact, he appeared to have favored a renewal of Algerian culture within a colonial framework, an implicit separate-but-equal treatment for the native population. Thus, he argued that to become a French citizen did not mean to commit apostasy. He distinguished between political and cultural citizenship. The former could be French, but the latter is Muslim.[15]

The area of overlap between Ben Badis's so-called reformist project and the Front of Islamic Salvation's plan for the establishment of an Islamic republic lies in the advocacy of purified religious mores, a break with popular sufism, and a stricter application of the foundational religious texts. Yet, even here, the similarity breaks down insofar as Ben Badis and the Ulama movement did not use coercion to achieve their aim, although they did mount scathing verbal attacks against sufi orders. The Ulama movement meant to save a society from cultural neglect, not from development, as seems to be the case with the Islamist movement. Initially, the FIS perceived the reemergence of sufi orders that had been all but repressed under the Boumediene government as a threat to its attempt at monopolizing religious activity. The FIS rejected the developmentalist policies of the state, its secular education, and technologies of communication such as dish antennas. However, it is noteworthy that Ben Badis found little support in many rural areas where being a Muslim also meant being a sufi. If the FIS achieved a measure of success among the urban population, it was due less to its religious message than to the historical conjuncture that pitted a disgruntled people against an increasingly unpopular government. It is instructive to note, however, that the Ulama as well as the FIS were essentially urban movements. The FIS's claim to the Ulama ascendancy constitutes another attempt to remap history, redraw its contours, and present itself as more indigenous to Algeria than the Front of National Liberation party.

A second instance of historical remapping is provided by writers who unwittingly bolster the legitimacy of the FIS's opposition to the state. Increasingly, Algerian scholars who attempt to interpret the present crisis within the history of the nationalist movement argue that from its inception, the Front of National Liberation had included among its members a number of Ulama sympathizers who were excluded from government after independence.[16] This view legitimizes the notion that the Algerian revolution was a religious revolution, somewhat reminiscent of the Iranian revolution, which had been appropriated in 1962 by a group of secularists bent upon "Westernizing" the nation. The caricatural nature of this approach is a measure of its ideological import. The Algerian revolution was a peasant revolution led by lower-middle-class (or petty bourgeois), generally French-educated men who also saw themselves as Muslims. Islam was a dimension of the revolution insofar as the majority of the people involved in it were culturally Muslims. But the revolution was not fought to bring about an Islamic republic even if some religious symbols were used to define the struggle for decolonization as pitting non-Muslim *(kuffar)* oppressors against Muslims.

Colonial Imagery and Cultural Reterritorialization

The symbolic significance of the colonial imagery in the Islamist discourse has played a functional role in *re-territorializing* Algerian culture. I am borrowing the concept of re-territorialization from Gilles Deleuze and Felix Guattari to refer to the phenomenon of displacement of symbols from one terrain into another by mapping familiar events and actions onto a different historical or social reality.[17] For example, democracy is hailed as a "Western" secular invention that is meant to confuse Algerians and perpetuate colonial rule by proxy. At the same time, it is also claimed that democracy already exists in Islamic thought as the old institution of *shura.* In so doing, relations of power that underlie both the Islamists' claim to be the legitimate heirs to postcolonial sovereignty are glossed over, and Algerian political culture is displaced from its present space and projected onto a new plane—the history of Islamic political thought that Algerians as a whole have not experienced at least since the sixteenth century.

Thus, concrete relations of power between government and its Islamist opposition, as well as their social foundations, appear abstract, and their abstraction becomes reified. The colonial imagery helps to naturalize the cultural model that is essentially "sneaked" into the existing culture. Consequently, the model affects a de-territorialization of the existing culture, which it provides with a new symbolic territory.

This process is best studied in gender relations. Bypassing the changes that were made possible by the war of decolonization, the FIS as well as the Armed Islamic Group have insisted that women's roles in society be redefined according to a strict reading of the *sharia.* That the sharia does *not* legislate the modalities of the veil currently imposed on women has not seemed an obstacle to the Islamists' desire to erase women's cultural/historical break with the tradition of the veil. Similarly, the introduction of the *shii* custom of temporary marriage *(muta)* constitutes an attempt at re-territorializing Algerian culture. Women have been forced into *muta* marriage by guerrillas belonging to the Armed Islamic Group eager to satisfy their sexual desires in a "licit" fashion. They could have sex with an unwilling woman under the cover of "temporary marriage." In so doing, they actually distort this old custom (which is based on the consent of both partners) and create a forced continuity between *sunni* Islam, prevalent in Algeria, and *shii* Islam.[18]

The renewed concern for the veil as a tangible mark of faith for women has been accompanied by coercive practices from some men who now insist that their brides must wear it. In 1991, I interviewed two newly married women in Algiers who had never worn the veil prior to their marriage but had to comply with the custom because it was included as a nonnegotiable condition of their marriage contract. Increasingly, young men seeking "virtuous" wives require their future brides to wear the veil. As the leader of the Islamist party Hamas, recently renamed the Party of Peace in Society, put it, "A woman clad in a hijab is to me preferable to a thousand Friday sermons. She is a moving tank."[19] Whatever the meaning of this war metaphor, the fact remains that women's role in society is redefined in terms that overturn the changes that had slowly made it possible for women to worry no longer about veiling and focus on education and jobs instead.[20]

Similarly, the insertion of religiosity in everyday life as a result of the weekly *khutba* in the free mosques has caused religious norms to displace work norms. Thus, workers in state-owned corporations have in 1990–1993 taken unauthorized breaks to pray between noon and six P.M., often leaving their office buildings for a nearby mosque. Once more, Algerian culture was displaced and re-territorialized in an effort to create a new social order under the pretense of re-establishing an old one purportedly displaced by colonialism.

Finally, the Armed Islamic Group's destruction of schools throughout the country on grounds that they teach secularism is meant to be an answer to the colonial policy of imposition of French cultural norms in schools seen as still operating in present-day Algeria. The fact that some religious education has actually been the norm in elementary schools has passed unnoticed, the reason being that religious teaching must be done according to the new (Islamist) interpretation of the texts.

Why Islamism and Not Reformism?

It might be argued that the paramount importance of the colonial imagery that underlies the thinking and strategies of the Islamist movement in Algeria makes sense not only within the Algerian context, but also elsewhere in the Middle East. Indeed, a theorist of Islamism, the Pakistani Abu Al 'Ala Al Mauwdudi, specifically defined one type of *jahiliya* as being caused by the colonial impact on native Muslim culture.[21] Even Muslim reformists of the nineteenth century formulated their thoughts within the context of the encounter of their societies with Western imperialism. This is true. However, it does not explain why contemporary Islamists chose to recolonize the life world of their country men and women (in a manner reminiscent of the cultural policies of the former colonizers) rather than bring about a renaissance of Islamic culture.

A renaissance might build on the achievements of early Muslim societies in the fields of science, medicine, social solidarity, and tolerance. This would mean not simply a return to the foundational texts but a critical reading of the evolution of Islamic thought in philosophy, politics, and the law. It would also mean a critical evaluation of the causes of the Muslim world's vulnerability to colonial conquest and an understanding of the mutual impacts of the colonizers qua Christians and the colonized qua Muslims. Finally, a renaissance would pave the way for a synthesis of some of the Western cultural achievements that cannot be dispensed with, as well as Muslim contributions to social relations, especially race relations. The Western-derived institutions that cannot be dispensed with are science, technology, and citizenship. The FIS has benefited from and used high-tech devices to campaign in the 1991 elections when lasers flashed slogans at political rallies. The use of computers, fax machines, and cellular phones is widespread among Islamists in Algeria and elsewhere. However, the adoption of these devices is seen as purely instrumental and divorced from any cultural content. There is no reflection on the cultural and social changes that had to take place in the West *before* technology could develop. Nor has there been reflection on how to create autonomous scientific development in Algeria. If technology is good enough for Islamists regardless of its cultural origins, so should be other allegedly Western inventions, such as respect for man-made laws and citizenship.

The mythification of colonialism has resulted in an attitude that thrives on a form of cultural revenge, focused on mapping Algeria's history onto a mythical past achievable through an erasure of the present. Erasure takes place in two modes: lapse into formal religiosity centered on an ostentatious display of the implementation of the Five Pillars of Islam, and violence against those deemed imperfect Muslims. The FIS has engaged in both. The Armed Islamic Group refined the art of violence while paying lip service to an eclectic assortment of practices combining neofundamentalist *sunni* and *shii* traditions. The ultimate project of the Armed Islamic Group is nihilistic in the sense that it is linked to no concrete or practical sociopolitical goal. The deaths inflicted upon innocent civilians of all ages and both sexes, especially during Ramadan of 1997, cannot provide their perpetrators with legitimacy. Yet, they can be explained in terms of the achievement of a mythic society peopled by mythic neofundamentalists that never existed in Algeria prior to the colonial incursion.

Man-made laws (or what Islamists refer to as secularism) mean respect for due process, equality before the law, and an end to arbitrariness. These laws cannot be established if oppositional groups respond to government failures with their own arbitrariness. Calls for civil disobedience made by various FIS figures in 1991, which included destroying street lights, thereby plunging Algiers in darkness and making it difficult for people needing emergency hospital care to move about, betrayed a fundamental disregard for the law deemed illegitimate because alien to the *sharia.* To argue, as some American political scientists have, that the FIS's methods were a response to a ruthless and illegitimate government is inaccurate and wrong. The tactics adopted by the FIS were extreme and belligerent *before* the government crackdown, as the history of events throughout 1990 and 1991 demonstrates. Algerians did not question the existence of their state. Rather, they questioned the ability of their leaders to manage the economy. Unlike their Egyptian counterparts, Algerian Islamists provided limited social services in urban centers such as Algiers, and they began to do so only in the 1980s as the oil-based economy suffered from significant shortfalls that affected state subsidies. It cannot be claimed that Islamists were needed by the people and somehow fulfilled functions that the state ought to have taken care of—hence their power is legitimate.[22]

The notion of legitimacy that has been bandied around needs redefining. Does it refer to the existence of democratic institutions? If so, very few countries of the Third World have legitimate governments. Does it mean that the authority of leaders is grounded in a social consensus? In this case, Algerians have agreed in 1962 that they ought to have a government comprised of Algerians. The form and orientation of this government was a matter of dispute that, nevertheless, did not affect Algerians' acceptance of their government.

One can only recall the massive popular effusion during the funerals of the late president Houari Boumediene in December 1978 to realize the extent to which Algerians have, by and large, accepted their government. The tendency to take the present experience of the U.S. government with legitimacy as normative, and subsume the Algerian form of government under it, clouds the specificity of the Algerian experience and prevents an understanding of how Islamism emerged. One can only bemoan the failure of the FIS to formulate oppositional strategies that would have pressed for political reforms in a peaceful fashion. The banning of the FIS after the parliamentary elections of 1991 is often invoked as the cause of the militarization of the FIS and the rise of its radical offshoot, the Armed Islamic Group. Yet, as a party that claimed to represent an alternative to the existing government, it was incumbent upon it to distinguish itself from its opponent by opting for peaceful means in a society that had barely recovered from a bloody war of decolonization. Violence, within the context of postindependence Algeria, victimizes those who supported the FIS in the hope that it would bring about changes in their lives, primarily young people in search of a better life as well as meaning. In this, the FIS differs from the theologians of liberation in Latin America who used religion to defend the oppressed and the disenfranchised. The FIS seems to have represented only itself if one considers that its pronouncements were antisecular, not liberationist, their references to injustice notwithstanding.

Citizenship is perhaps the most important principle that the Islamist movement must come to terms with. Citizenship concretizes the rule of law by stressing that all individuals are bearers of rights and obligations that must be protected by the state. The *nonimplementation* of citizenship in Algeria is most evident in gender relations. Women are nationals (individuals who carry Algerian passports) but not full-fledged citizens. Their citizenship rights are curtailed by family law as spelled out in the 1984 Family Code, which legalizes gender inequality in violation of the constitution.[23] Being subject under Algerian family law, despite protection of full citizenship under the constitution, accounts for women's vulnerable position in society. The FIS would have rationalized women's legal status by removing their formal citizenship and more thoroughly and unambiguously making them subjects of the *sharia.*

As harbingers of a new sociopolitical order, the FIS had a chance to evaluate the gender question in light of the heroic period of Islam when women are said to have played a significant public role. The principle of *ijtihad (*or "striving to do better") could have helped to show that the FIS, a religion-based group, could improve women's status where the state failed by lack of will. Instead, the FIS chose to deny women the rights they had won after the independence of their country by systematically calling for their confinement to the home. This violation of the concept of citizenship cannot be said to be motivated by Islamists' fundamental opposition to gender equality only. It betrays a deeper opposition to all practices that in one way or another are linked to the notion of "secularism." Hence, Islamists' aversion for democracy.

Democracy is rejected not only because it is the rule of the majority, which may exercise tyranny over the minority, but also because it is the *rule of the people*. A critique of the formalism of democracy as practiced in many industrial societies is legitimate. However, the rejection of formal democracy as "heresy" in the words of the FIS co-leader, Ali Benahdj, because it is based on the sovereignty of the people rather than God, is problematical.[24] The rejection of the entire state, regardless of whether it is democratic, is seen as a matter of course. Thus, in attempting to legitimize civil disobedience, an Islamist *imam* pointed out that "admittedly, we could argue about whether we have the right to rebel against an unjust government, but the people did not pay allegiance to this government since it is not based on God's commandments, the Sunna and the Caliphs. . . ."[25] In other words, rebellion is advocated independently of the actions and policies of the government; it is advocated for the purpose of establishing a new institution. It is the expression of a pure will to power. The state founded on God's sovereignty begs the question of who, among members of the FIS, has the right to decode God's will? The *sharia* does not provide a treatise on political philosophy or guidelines for political rule. The inclusion of the divine as the source of sociopolitical institutions that have traditionally been secular leaves open and unresolved the question of the legitimacy of the human medium through which God rules. Countries (as exemplified by Saudi Arabia, the Sudan, Iran, and Afghanistan under the Taliban) where the sovereignty of God has been upheld as a legitimating factor of political rule are fraught with abuses of categories of people deemed imperfect, be they women, "secular" men, or other minorities. The Islamist movement does not promote a theology of liberation from existing needs and wants, but translates these into a political language that aims at making the divine an earthly authority. Indeed, the Islamic republic that is often invoked is a republic of men by men using God as a trope in the struggle of men for legitimizing the political.

No alternative to Western-style democracy has been offered that might be more suitable to Algeria, except for references to the principle of *shura* or consultation, which leaves open the process by which members of the council of *shura* are chosen to represent groups such as women.[26] Citizenship connotes the acceptance of the notion of equality of rights that in this beginning of the twenty-first century is of paramount importance. It is the stumbling block for Islamists who wish to supplant equal rights with difference and complementarity. In gender relations, for example, anatomical difference is seen as a ground for social and political inequality regardless of its impact on the individual as well as society. The Islamists' claim to institute the realm of justice is seriously compromised by their belief in unequal legal standards. The notion that equality is a Western idea that promotes the individual at the expense of the group is a lame defense for the social and political conservatism of a movement that equates change and evolution with colonialism.

It is often claimed that the Islamist movement in Algeria as elsewhere expresses a desperate search for *identity* in a world that is increasingly dominated by cultural symbols and practices originating from former imperial powers. Algerians born before independence know only too well the meaning and effects of French policies of cultural assimilation. However, these policies did not change their belief in their religion despite attempts at conversion to Christianity made by the Franciscan order of the "White Fathers." It is nevertheless true that Algerians' identity was problematized by being politicized by the colonists. Colonial authorities created the category of "Muslim natives," who were deprived of equal rights because of their religion. In the colonial encounter, Islam became the most salient feature of Algerian identity. However, after Algeria recovered her independence, Algerians took their affiliation with Islam for granted and began to emphasize other dimensions of their identity such as social class, profession, gender, etc. This process was thwarted by a re-problematization of identity by the Islamist movement, which, just as colonists did before it, politicized religion and made it the only form of identity an Algerian could have. Islamism does not provide a solution to the issue of identity; it is less about identity and more about power politics, just as colonialism was less about a "civilizing mission" and more about power. The "native Muslim" was succeeded by the "Islamist," who is not a citizen but a new subject of a theological discourse of power. Identity is a very complex phenomenon that cannot be reduced to one dimension only. Throughout the colonial era, Algerians managed their identity by keeping their religious beliefs while negotiating their way through the colonial system by taking advantage of its educational opportunities, as limited as they were. There is no reason why they should be told today that their identity was a lie. All identities are unstable. Fixing them, whether in a restricted view of Islam, race, or ethnicity, is one of the major problems in contemporary societies. The debate over identity politics is one expression of the abuses that identity can suffer. There is no reason to claim, as Islamists do, that identity is founded on the *sharia,* which in its essentials means the subjection of the female population—no more, no less. If a Muslim ethic is to suffuse a new, industrial society, Islam must cease to supplant the political. Rather, it must attempt to act as its conscience.

In sum, the Islamist movement in Algeria has not brought about a renaissance in Muslim thought and institutions. It is neither a reformist movement, nor a social movement bent upon sociopolitical and economic transformation. It is an oppositional movement overthrowing the existing order by using religious symbols familiar to Algerians, but infusing them with different meanings in order to reestablish a mythic society untainted by colonialism. The unrealistic character of this project qualifies it as political delirium.

Why Recolonization?

The major role played by the colonial imagery in the Islamist movement and the consequent strategy of recolonization of the life world need to be explained. Why is it that a movement that could have successfully challenged the government by focusing on its failures and formulating concrete, viable alternatives consumed itself in the mythification of colonial history? Tactical and structural reasons may have been operative. The FIS was eager to motivate people to undertake action against the government. Considering Algeria's recent history, Islam and colonialism were the most powerful symbols of mobilization. The appeal to Islam stirred up a latent anger with the condition of being a Muslim in a global context. News of racist practices against Algerian immigrants in France, the Gulf War, and American attacks against Libya were so many reminders that Islam is under siege. The appeal to colonialism was more risky but equally powerful. It was risky because the rank and file of the Islamist movement is comprised of young people who were born at the end of or after the war of decolonization and who, therefore, have no experience or memory of the colonial period. Symbolically, the linking of Islam with colonialism fulfills the function of uniting the constituency of the FIS, thereby occulting serious class differences. The typology of the membership of the Islamist movement in Algeria formulated by Gilles Kepel reveals a wide spectrum of classes, ranging from the commercial bourgeoisie to the chronically unemployed.[27] In a historical replay of the configuration of the wartime Front of National Liberation, the FIS also perceived itself as a front. As such, it needed to gloss over and contain class differences and interests by choosing the symbols of Islam, the common denominator of Algerians, and colonialism, a phenomenon that historically elicited resistance. The nihilism of the Armed Islamic Group is a function of the lack of understanding and experience of the postwar generation of people who were mobilized by a slogan that mythified what was once a lived historical reality. Colonialism for them means absolute evil as embodied by the state and those who do not rebel against it. In this sense, the Armed Islamic Group simply pushed to its logical conclusion the FIS's use of the colonial imagery. Indeed, the unbridled violence that has been claimed by the Armed Islamic Group may be understood in Fanonian terms as providing a cathartic function. Blood and sex seem to cleanse the imputed colonial traces in Algerians' culture and behavior, just as the state's repression is meant to cleanse the country of political Islam.[28] Violence has acquired the characteristic of delirium by its lack of focus, its randomness, and its arbitrariness.

The saturation of Algerian life with symbols laden with religion and mythified history can only give more poignancy to the plight of the anonymous young woman pacing Sidi Abderrahmane's terrace while mumbling the name of God. This symbolic saturation has further confused Algerian history and confounded Algerians' sense of the future. The recolonization of Algerians' life world and the reterritorialization of their culture serve as a reminder that Islamism may not be a movement for a renaissance of Muslim culture or an alternative to existing forms of government. To attain these goals, it must rise above its thirst for power politics and come to terms with a world it has not made but in which it must live. It must analyze Algeria's colonial past as it actually happened and attempt to overcome it rather than mythify it.

As social scientists from the Middle East, it is incumbent upon us to take a hard look at the power that lurks behind movements that at first glance may excite our latent expectation of meaningful change in our societies, our unsatisfied hunger for a sense of belonging, and our frustration with having made time, not history. The Islamist movement has given us a jolt. Here are people who tell governments things many intellectuals refrained from saying. But speech can be oppressive. It can also kill, as the Islamist discursive remapping of Algerian culture can demonstrate. If God is after all clement and merciful, is any word, concept, or discourse worth dying for anymore? To think that it is can only make us repeat history. The point is to learn from it.

Notes

1. This concept is frequently used by analysts of Islamist movements such as Gilles Kepel and Olivier Roy.
2. For a discussion of this notion, see Jurgen Habermas, *Legitimation Crisis* (Boston: Beacon Press, 1973), chap. 1.
3. Robert Malley, *The Call from Algeria: Third Worldism, Revolution and the Turn to Islam* (Berkeley and Los Angeles: University of California Press, 1996), chap.1.
4. Jurgen Habermas, *Legitimation Crisis,* part 2.
5. See Marnia Lazreg, *The Emergence of Classes in Algeria: A Study of Colonialism and Sociopolitical Change* (Boulder, CO: Westview Press, 1976). See also Hassan, *Algerie: Histoire d'un Naufrage* (Paris: Le Seuil, 1996), chap. 7 and 8.

6. Habermas, chap. 7.
7. See Smail Goumeziane, *Le Mal Algerien,* Economie Politique d'une Transition Inachevee (Paris: Fayard, 1994), especially chap. 4.
8. Amine Touati, *Les Islamistes a L'Assaut du Pouvoir* (Paris: L'Harmattan, 1995), p. 256.
9. See Noureddine Touaba, *Wajibat Al Mar'a Fi'l Kitab Wal Sunna,* 3rd edition (Qasantina: Daar Al Baath, 1989).
10. Information obtained from two Algiers cab drivers in 1991.
11. Amine Touati, *Les Islamistes a L'Assaut du Pouvoir,* p. 250.
12. Ibid., p. 254.
13. Ibid., p. 257.
14. For an analysis of Ben Badis's thought, see Marnia Lazreg, *The Eloquence of Silence: Algerian Women in Question* (New York, London: Routledge, 1994), pp. 81–88.
15. Lhouari Addi, "Religion et Politique dans le Nationalisme Algerien: le Role des Oulemas," *Revue Mafgrebine d'Etudes Politiques et Religieuses,* Universite d'Oran, #1, October 1988.
16. An example of this view is provided by Mohammed Harbi's revisionist conception of the history of the Algerian war.
17. Gilles Deleuze and Felix Guattari, *Anti-Oedipus: Capitalism and Schizophrenia, vol. 1* (New York: The Viking Press, 1985).
18. For a discussion of forced *muta* marriages in Algeria, see Karima Bennoune, "S.O.S. Algeria," in Afnaz Afkhami, ed., *Faith and Freedom* (New York: Syracuse University Press, 1995).
19. See Marnia Lazreg, *The Eloquence of Silence,* p. 217.
20. The fact that some women have joined the FIS hardly makes it an advocate of women's rights.
21. John L. Esposito, ed., *Voices of Resurgent Islam* (New York: Oxford University Press, 1983), chap. 5.
22. This line of thought is represented by John Entelis, who perceives the Islamist movement as a legitimate movement responding to people's aspirations. Talk given at Drew University, Madison, New Jersey, April 14, 1997.
23. For an analysis of the Family Code, see Marnia Lazreg, *The Eloquence of Silence,* pp. 150–57.
24. See Kamel Hamdi, *Ali Benhadj, Abassi Madani, Mahfoud Nahnah, Abdellah Djaballh: Differents ou Differends?* (Alger: Chihab, 1991), p. 75.
25. Amine Touati, *Les Islamistes a L'Assaut du Pouvoir,* op. cit., p. 257.
26. For a discussion of Islam and democracy, see Azizah Al Hibri, "Islamic Constitutionalism and the Concept of Democracy," *Case Western Reserve Journal of International Law,* 24, I, 1992.
27. Gilles Kepel, "Islamism and the State in Algeria and Egypt," *Daedelus* 124 (Summer 1995): 109–127.
28. For a discussion of the cathartic value of political violence, see Frantz Fanon, *The Wretched of the Earth* (New York: Grove Press, 1963).

Chapter 8

Economic Reform and Tunisia's Hegemonic Party

The End of the Administrative Elite

Stephen J. King

I argue that during a period of accelerated economic liberalization, from 1986 until today, Tunisia's hegemonic party abandoned its representation of a broad segment of society and became a vehicle representing the interests of the rural bourgeoisie and urban manufacturers, many of whom had been rural notables. In addition, an increasingly globalized economy and stagnant, state-led growth strategies within Tunisia led to constraints on state autonomy as international forces pressed for increased market reforms. An Islamist movement serves as the strongest organized resistance to the hegemonic party.

In the four decades since Tunisian independence in 1956, a single political party, under different names and leaders, has monopolized the political system. I interpret Tunisia's state party historically as a political movement led by an administrative elite[1] that was capable of resisting social forces both domestically and internationally in the sense that state policy reflected the needs and preferences of the elite. These state authorities had a strong influence on socioeconomic change in postindependence Tunisia. The administrative elite is defined here as the provincial elites, especially those from the Sahel, who in the 1930s took over national leadership in Tunisia from the traditional elites in urban areas. The new administrative elite, mostly embodied in the Neo-Destour party, were characterized by their modern, usually French, education and a commitment to creating a modern economy with greater social equity. Their mission was to transform Tunisia economically, socially, and technologically. Among the administrative elite, there have been differences in strategies to attain an industrialized economy. They have tried both a state-led growth strategy and liberal economic policies to reach their goal.

The administrative elite's autonomy, however, has always been vulnerable to one powerful social group: the rural bourgeoisie. The postindependence policy process has frequently reflected the elite's vulnerability to the vested interests of the rural bourgeoisie. Until relatively recently, however, the administrative elite attempted to use its control, first of the nationalist movement and then of state patronage and state policy, to create an umbrella political organization that attempted to respond to all constituencies in Tunisia, while still formulating an overall development strategy according to their own ideologies and goals. Their actions led to a populist nationalist movement and a populist political party, the Neo-Destour. At independence, the administrative elite led by president Habib Bourguiba took control of the political apparatus of the state. Party leaders and the bureaucratic establishment form the membership of the administrative elite.

The inability of a single party to represent all social groups in Tunisia even modestly well was apparent by the 1970s, but the current identity of the state party was solidified during the economic reform process of the past decade. The party's increasing link with the rural bourgeoisie and its urban offshoot as well as its ties to transnational capital ends the era of an administrative elite in Tunisia that was willing and able to challenge the interests of the most powerful social forces within and outside of the country. Any pretense of a populist party that represented all Tunisians has ended. In terms of the literature on Tunisian and North African politics, international political economy variables and class analysis probably deserve more attention than the earlier emphasis on political elites, regime types, and ideology.[2]

During economic reform, the state has remained authoritarian, leaving few options in the formal political system for the abandoned constituencies of the once-populist party. This dire political picture is partially alleviated by relatively strong overall economic growth rates during the structural adjustment era[3] and by the civil war in neighboring Algeria, which the current regime uses to justify a frozen political system. The regime has banned the participation of the only opposition political party with significant public support, the Islamist al-Nahda party, and smothers the development of any other significant political threat, while society continues to change rapidly both politically and economically.[4]

To maintain political coherence and stability, the regime appears to be relying on market reforms to produce rapid economic growth (with little regard to equity in the distribution of benefits), and has assumed an adversarial position against an Islamist movement through use of repression. While Tunisian state authorities fundamentally reorganize the distribution of economic and political assets in favor of more dominant social groups, no political parties representing the interests of the peasantry or labor have been allowed to develop.

The Neo-Destour and Modernization Theory

A generation of scholars, largely working within the modernization school, provided a base for an understanding of Tunisia's single (now hegemonic) party system. Modernization theory provided a liberal, pluralist interpretation of change. There was an optimism in this approach which in most versions predicted a nonviolent trajectory culminating in liberal democracy.[5] Developed partly as an alternative to Marxist approaches, political change was not tied to economic forces. Also, very little was done to integrate the realms of domestic and international politics.

In the Tunisian version of modernization theory, the Neo-Destour "became Tunisia's key instrument of modernization."[6] In this line of thinking, a single party with a quasi-monopoly on political power could lead the march toward modernity and liberal democracy by "maintaining national cohesion and mobilizing the people along national and modernist lines while exercising a minimum of constraint and allowing a reasonable amount of discussion."[7] Political change entails an elite committed to modernization. This elite maintains national cohesion, mobilizes and educates the masses, and transforms values and structures. Eventually, the elite moves aside for the full operation of liberal democracy.[8] I differ with this linear, relatively nonconflictual view of change by asserting that in the course of the evolution of Tunisia's hegemonic party system, a transformed rural bourgeoisie has overtaken the administrative elite, and for various reasons the international arena has become central to economic policy making.

If they underestimated the vulnerability of the administrative elite to powerful social forces and missed in the predictions of the trajectory of the political system, modernization theorists were absolutely correct to be impressed by the dynamic group of new elites from the provinces that arose in the early part of the century to take over the nationalist movement from the stagnant, traditional urban elite. The Neo-Destour founded in the 1930s by Habib Bourguiba and his colleagues began as a break from the Destour party, which was the first to challenge French colonial rule. The Destour was essentially a party of Tunisia's traditional leadership based in the capital, Tunis: the administrators, religious leaders, and notables of the Ottoman Beys. Carl Brown described the Destours, a distinctive social class, which emerged to lead Tunisia's first national political party just after the end of World War I:

> Like medieval Islamic society in general, this class was urban centered, but it was not the instrument of a commercial, industrial, or any other kind of revolution. It included the following: the religious leadership or ulema; the religio-judicial leadership, or muftis, caids and aduls (notaries); prominent merchants; leaders of the most respected crafts; and the informal leaders of various quarters of the cities. This traditional group was the most self-contained and thus the least open to western influence.[9]

Ultimately the Old Destour failed to mobilize popular support from rural areas in its struggle against the colonial regime. Popular nationalism could not be accommodated within the framework of the first nationalist organization. Instead the Destour was supplanted in the 1930s by the Neo-Destour. This party, largely, had its power base in the provinces.

The nationalist movement in Tunisia was captured by a new generation of elites who had little in common with the leadership of the Old Destour. The Neo-Destour leadership was comprised of a new intelligentsia of modest social origins, educated in Franco-Arab schools, especially Sadiki College. Founded by the Islamic reformer, Khaireddine, prime minister of Tunisia from 1873 to 1877, Sadiki College was to bring Western education to Tunisia in order to meet the challenge of European powers.

Sadiki College served as an important channel to elite status for bright young people from rural areas. These new elites mastered French, learned to negotiate the colonial administration, and frequently went to France for advanced education in one of the liberal professions. The new party leaders were distinct due to the premium they placed on intellectuality in social leaders,[10] organization and activism in all sectors and areas of the country, and social control in a centralized hierarchical structure.

The most important Sadiki College graduate was Habib Bourguiba, the son of a low-ranking government functionary in the Sahel town of Monastir. Trained in political science and law in France, Bourguiba became the founding father of modern Tunisia and the charismatic leader of the nationalist movement. He was deposed in 1987. Other French-educated founders of the party included Mahmoud Materi, Taher Safer, and Bahri Guiga, who all returned from France in the late 1920s. The group originally participated in the Destour party, but early on it became apparent to this young cadre that a nationalist movement would require more than the Old Destour had to offer. The new party they formed included some members of the traditional elite but, significantly, reached beyond the old social order to the new proletariat in urban and rural areas.

The original Neo-Destour party animators were men of ordinary Sahelian origin who had taken full advantage of opportunities in modern education. The Sahel, an area of settled agriculture on the eastern coast of Tunisia, had experienced less of the negative effects of colonization than had other areas. Its strong village life, coupled with a high concentration of private ownership, prevented foreigners from buying land.[11] The region developed a tradition of sending its brightest sons to Sadiki College. "The widely distributed yeoman class of olive tree cultivators living in Sahel villages made thrifty sacrifices to send their sons, ambitious and hardworking students on the whole, to modern secondary schools and French Universities."[12]

The party also had strong ties to commercial agriculture in the Sahel, which provided much of the early party funding. Gallicized and intellectual, party elites aimed to overhaul the old social order. Their aim was to guide a mass nationalist movement toward socioeconomic change that would nevertheless remain under the guidance and control of the intellectuals at the top of the party. Various social groups—indeed, all social groups from all areas of the country—were considered legitimate constituents of this one party and social movement.

The emphasis of the Neo-Destour party was on modernization under the tutelage of intellectuals, the corporateness of society, and the ability of the party to represent all interest groups. In spite of the mass appeal of the party, major political decisions in the beginning reflected the ideologies and interests of state authorities. The notion of the relative independence of the Neo-Destour from vested interests is contestable, and certainly has not been the case throughout the history of the party's dominance of the Tunisian political system. Still there is some truth to characterizing the Neo-Destour as a party of modernizers who adopted a historical mission to transform their own society and were willing at times to challenge any group to achieve those ends. The transformation was to be guided by rationality and by use of the most modern technologies available. The administrative elite, through the bureaucracy and the new party, sought to guide the transformation in a hands-on controlling manner.

Elite Versus Class Analysis: The Administrative Elite and the Countryside

At some points in postindependence Tunisian politics, the administrative elite has been powerful enough to pursue policies independent of various social classes. The state, however, has always been linked in varying degrees with large landowners, making class analysis a tempting alternative to a focus on party and state elites. Teasing out the relationship between the state and the countryside, especially large landowners over time, will help clarify the relationship between the state and the rural bourgeoisie.

In a general sense, the Tunisian development process itself conditioned a tie between the state and the countryside since it was provincial elites who overthrew their urban forebears. The triumph of the Neo-Destour over the original Destour required funding from large landowners and the mobilization of the rural masses. Samuel Huntington has noted the pivotal role of rural mobilization for political stability in the developing world.[13] Governments in late developing countries, or what Huntington termed changing societies, that have rural support are better able to withstand the widespread instability engendered by economic development and the socioeconomic changes of modernization. In an analysis that emphasized social control in order for political institutions to develop, Huntington viewed the countryside as the source for political stability. The combination of rural majority and urban growth in the Third World gives rise to "a distinctive pattern of politics in modernizing countries." The growing urban areas have different attitudes from the countryside and are more likely to be the source of opposition to the government.

Huntington mentions several countries as following the pattern of opposition support in cities, including Tunisia, India, Venezuela, Korea, Turkey, and Pakistan.[14] Winning rural support is the way governments withstand this opposition until they are able to build urban support and until urban areas grow to constitute the majority of the population. This task is more difficult because most political elites are from urban areas and hold attitudes similar to those of their urban counterparts. The ideal and unusual situation is a melting-pot party able to build support in both rural and urban areas simultaneously.

Tunisia fits Huntington's scheme for stability during the tumultuous times of modernization, as the author has noted.[15] A rural-urban struggle characterized the party at the outset. Unlike political parties in most of the late developing world, the core of Neo-Destour leadership came from the countryside. Lisa Anderson notes that the new elite was largely provincial, "the sons of or younger brothers of minor or government functionaries, like Habib Bourguiba of the Sahil, or of provincial landowners and merchant families, like Yusuf Rouissi of the Jarid and Salah Ben Youssef of Djerba."[16]

In the beginning of the party, the support of large landowners was probably more important than the backing of the rural masses. Important large landowners and rural merchants chose pragmatic collaboration with the French as the one sure way to get rich since the protectorate controlled the country's purse strings. Those who cooperated with the French were anathema to both the Destour and future Neo-Destour leadership,[17] but in a strategy that helped the nascent Neo-Destour take over the nationalist movement from the Destour, the administrative elite sought the backing of the rural bourgeoisie.

In 1933, the year prior to the formation of the Neo-Destour, Muhammad Chenik, one of Tunisia's wealthiest businessmen, president of the Tunisian Chamber of Commerce, and president of the only exclusive Tunisian banking facility, the Coopérative Tunisienne de Crédit, found himself in a major conflict with the protectorate government, which ironically had advanced the funds to start the bank. The conflict arose when Chenik appealed directly to Paris for changes in protectorate policy as Tunisian agriculture faced the grave problems of the 1930s depression. Most of the bank's business came from the olive growers and textile manufacturers of the Sahel. Angry at the appeal to Paris, protectorate authorities accused Chenik of diverting funds from the Credit Cooperative. Opposed to the stance of most of the Destour leadership, Bourguiba defended Chenik and accused the Protectorate administration of sabotaging the self-help efforts of Tunisians at the instigation of the *colons.*[18]

Within a year Bourguiba and his supporters broke with the Destour leadership. The success of the dissident Destourians was facilitated by Chenik's support. He was to provide the nationalist leaders with financing. Chenik and most of his bank's clients, the rural bourgeoisie and large landowners particularly of the Sahel, gave their financial and political support to the newly formed Neo-Destour. This backing was critical to the party's ability to take over from the Old Destour and launch a nationwide movement against the Protectorate.[19] Thus, strong ties with large landowners, the landed commercial farmers centered in the Sahel, were central to the Neo-Destour at its inception and during national liberation. Historically, this has been the party's main source of support.[20]

However, not all of the administrative elite was happy with the incorporation of the rural bourgeoisie into the fold. In reaction to Bourguiba's defense of Chenik and the Credit Coopérative, party leader Hedi Nouria wrote in a personal letter to Bourguiba, "It is a delusion and great folly to pretend that our policy would attract the discontented bourgeois elements, and to found hope on those elements, which have been the allies if not the basis of colonization; it is to display an absence of political sense and a total incomprehensibility of our movement."[21] The incorporation of the rural bourgeoisie into the nationalist movement, as I will illustrate, meant that the state party would be gradualist and accomodationist in its policies that affected this group and would eventually capitulate to most of the group's political demands in the 1980s and 1990s.

The Administrative Elite and the Rural Masses

As a national liberation movement, the Neo-Destour attempted to bring all Tunisian social forces into its sphere for the fight against the French. In rural areas, in addition to large landowners, they sought support from small- and medium-scale peasants. The administrative elite had several advantages in regard to eliciting the support of the rural masses. First, it was aided by the rural roots of many members of the party and its familiarity with the small villages of the country. The party also aided in the establishment of an agricultural union in 1949, the Union Générale des Agriculteurs Tunisiens, and deliberately organized a liberation army composed of peasants.[22] Rather than focusing on economic concerns, the union established a political goal of national liberation. The general effectiveness of the party's organization aided the union in its efforts. Party branches were installed throughout the countryside to recruit, discipline, and politically educate the new members.

The efforts of the Neo-Destour at rural mobilization were largely successful; both large landowners and the rural masses joined the party's liberation movement. If large landowners supplied the finance, "its most reliable shock troops were country peasants and Tunis plebs."[23] Rural mobilization permitted the formation of a mass organization and also provided the future state party with a strong source of support.

The Neo-Destour would follow either of two basic strategies to maintain rural support in the years following independence in 1956: either it could try to dominate the countryside by directly dealing with the peasantry and providing it with state patronage; or it would deal with the small and medium peasantry through the intermediation of rural notables.

The Neo-Destour achieved what Huntington considered ideal for a political party in a late developing country: it bridged the rural-urban gap by acting as a melting pot in which the peasant and city dweller met. Thus the party unified various strata of the population into one single stream oriented toward the political objective of national liberation and following the leadership of the administrative elite.[24] In addition to party branches in urban areas, the Neo-Destour incorporated the central trade union, the Union Générale de Travailleurs Tunisiens (UGTT), into the party. After World War II, 80 percent of the union members were also members of the Neo-Destour.[25] Other "national organizations" were founded on party directives and controlled by the party including the Union Tunisiens des Artisans et Commercants (UTAC) and the Union Générale des Etudiants Tunisiens (UGET). Although the UGTT exercised some autonomy from the party, the general trend was toward party dominance of the national organizations.

In sum, the Neo-Destour was the first political organization to be truly open to Tunisians of all regions and classes.[26] Bourguiba and the rest of the administrative elite aimed squarely at the peasantry and labor while also courting the bourgeoisie. Rural and urban mobilization occurred as national unity, and the fight for liberation took precedence over social cleavages and structural difficulties in the Tunisian economy.

The Administrative Elite and National Development

With independence in the mid–1950s, the Neo-Destour leadership had to transform its party from national movement to a stable government able to develop political institutions, promote economic growth and equity, and deal with the legacy of colonialism and relative economic backwardness. The administrative elite at independence set out to transform and modernize Tunisian society according to its own agenda while managing a range of constituencies of varying degrees of political power.

As soon as it had been formed in 1956, the Tunisian government was confronted with a series of urgent problems, including increased unemployment in urban and rural areas and an inequitable division of property into small holdings, large land ownership (partly Tunisian, but mainly foreign), communal tribal lands, and *habous.*[27] Traditional Tunisian agriculture suffered from low productivity, and the country depended on French and other foreign agricultural enterprises. The biggest problem, however, was the low standard of living and the inadequate average income in Tunisia as a whole. It has been estimated by the United Nation's Food and Agricultural Organization (FAO) that in 1962 each of 4,000 French families held on average 240 hectares of land and each of 5,000 Tunisian families held 100 hectares. This means that 3 to 4 percent of all farmers possessed about half of the arable land.[28]

Overall, the Neo-Destour faced the challenge common to nearly all recently decolonized countries: the creation of an industrial economy. In the Tunisian case, a scarcity of extractive resources (some oil but nothing like neighboring Algeria and Libya) and fertile land meant that leaders needed foreign aid, which was accompanied by a possible loss of economic independence, in order to accumulate capital for industrialization and to modernize agriculture. In the relative absence of capital for investment, few options remained other than transferring capital from agriculture to industry. This option would pit party leaders against their historical support from large landowners.

In spite of these difficult circumstances, the administrative elite had sufficient power at independence to attempt to meet the challenges of national development. Within the elite, some people preferred planning and state management of economic assets, the trade union elements of the party in particular. Others favored a liberal economic policy. The ideologies and interests of the administrative elites were diverse, but riding the wave of a populist nationalist movement, their political decisions at independence largely reflected the choices of these new gallicized elites from the provinces. Once established as the state party, the Neo-Destour faced few challenges to its call for national unity and development under the auspices of a single political party.

From 1956 to 1961, the Tunisian government practiced a liberal economic policy. Private investment and initiative, however, did not manifest itself. For example, the investment rate decreased from 19.5 percent in 1953 to 7.7 percent in 1957. The economic situation continued to worsen.[29] By 1961, a group of unionists and administrators within the higher ranks of the Neo-Destour convinced President Bourguiba to dismiss the liberal minister and adopt a ten-year plan for development, the Perspectives Decennales (1962–1971). The plan was put forth by a team of economists under the leadership of trade union head Ahmed Ben Salah who became the head of a superministry of planning and finance. The party name was changed to the Socialist Destour Party.

Tunisian Socialism

The era of Tunisian socialism, from 1962 to 1969, when it ended abruptly, illuminates the extent and limitation of the administrative elite's autonomy from vested interests more than any other period. Ben Salah's program challenged the interests of the powerful rural bourgeoisie. It attempted to create support in the countryside through direct interaction with and support from the small peasantry while also attempting to modernize this group in the image of the elites.

A cooperative system was at the center of the ten-year plan, first in agriculture, then in trade and other sectors of the economy. The cooperative system was geared primarily to the modernization of agriculture and to the support of the small peasantry.[30] Planners nationalized European land (on May 12, 1964), and the state retained ownership of it even though it was highly coveted by large landowners. The cooperatives were based on the colonial farms and the surrounding areas of small plots. These cooperatives were designed both to become the center of modern agriculture in Tunisia and to provide minimum sustenance to the small peasantry with inadequate access to land and employment and who utilized traditional and less effective farming methods. Service cooperatives were also initiated. The diversification and intensification of production was an enormous investment for the state and came to constitute a heavy drain on the cooperative budget. Still, Ben Salah's team strived to reach its goal of increasing the annual income per family to a decent level (roughly US $250), balance the budget eventually, and, it was hoped, transfer surplus capital from the agricultural cooperatives to industry:

> A cooperative unit was to be composed, ideally, of the original farm—about 200 hectares—along with 300 hectares of surrounding parcels. Thirty families were to farm this unit, with priority first given to the previous workers of

> the unit under colonialism and then to the peasants. This scheme was adopted to make full use of equipment, fertilizers, and crop rotation, and able also to transcend the bifurcation between modern and traditional agriculture.[31]

The government's capacity to anchor itself in the countryside by dealing directly with the small and medium peasantry through cooperatives failed in one sense: bureaucratic control of small holder property alienated the small peasantry. The power elite ran the program from the top down, and the rural peasantry came to view the cooperative policy as illustrating elite restrictions on their freedom. *Cooperateurs* never felt ownership of the project, many desired their own individual piece of land, and most resented the program when targets were not met and their standard of living hardly improved.[32] Although the *cooperateurs* were represented in the administrative structure, in reality the units were managed through the state hierarchy of organizations and technicians. An official report noted, "The population installed does not really participate in the improvement work, except perhaps as salaried workers."[33]

It is difficult to underestimate the material and symbolic significance of the cooperative movement. This was the first substantial push at national development by the state party. Policy was used for both economic and social development. Party militants aided by governmental technicians launched a vast campaign to convert a major part of the best land into cooperatives and move peasants from traditional to modern agriculture. By the end of 1968, 30 percent of the nation's best land was in cooperatives holding more than 750,000 people and representing 27 percent of the rural population.[34]

For several reasons, the cooperative policy failed. For political reasons, the landless and near landless were included in cooperatives but more as subjects to be modernized than as full decision-making participants. The use of cooperatives to absorb surplus labor lessened the benefits to each member and limited the chances for profitability. Technical success also required that large landowners be included in cooperatives, testing the resolve of the party to challenge its most powerful constituents. While denying large landowners access to colonial lands, the Socialist Destour initially declined to alienate this group further by including their land in the cooperative system. A belated effort to do so in 1969 failed partially because by this time the small and medium peasantry had also turned against the project. Also, modernization of agriculture in the Tunisian context meant the conversion of cereal-producing lands to olive and fruit trees, which have long gestation periods before benefits can be seen. The investments made during the cooperative push came to fruition only after the policy had become unpopular. Eventually, foreign aid sources turned against the project. Confronted with increasing state farm deficits, representatives of the World Bank urged a period of consolidation and some representatives of USAID in Tunis privately urged an abolition of cooperatives.[35]

Eventually, the hostile forces within the country, especially the rural bourgeoisie, urged a policy change. Taking advantage of their historical relationship, the 5,000 or so members of the largest landlord class went directly to President Bourguiba when the cooperatives targeted private large land holdings. They pointed to the inefficiency of the existing state farms, more than half of which were in extensive debt in 1968.[36] In 1969, Ben Salah was ousted and Bourguiba implemented a sweeping reshuffling of government. Economic policy switched to the maintenance of three sectors, private, state, and cooperative, but new emphasis would be placed on the private sector.

During the apex of Tunisian socialism, the administrative elite sought to transform the countryside. Rapid technical and socioeconomic changes were achieved, but the overall policy still failed. Even the small peasantry turned against the cooperative system of which they were to be the primary beneficiaries. The administrative elite placed the goal of maintaining political support behind what it must have viewed as its historic mission to modernize the Tunisian economy and change traditional peasant patterns of life and values—including the central value of land ownership.

Elites were even willing to challenge the rural notables from which they originated, first by denying them access to the fertile colonial farms, and then by attempting to place their land in cooperatives. In the end, the party's overly bureaucratic approach that alienated the rural masses, the need for foreign aid in a resource-poor small country, and the growing political mobilization of large landowners ended the strongest period of the political autonomy of the administrative elite.

Gradual Economic Liberalization

Tunisia's administrative elite broke the hold of the entrenched national elites of the Old Destour by mobilizing the countryside. In building a rural-centered political party to wrest power from urban elites, peasant support was developed through a patron/clientlike relationship between the government and the peasantry. Peasants traded their support in hope of receiving a range of benefits: small amounts of land, credit, and technical and marketing assistance.[37] Their hopes were partially realized during the cooperative movement. A special relationship also developed between landed elites and the party. Once the Neo-Destour captured the nationalist movement, it was able to create a melting pot party that also incorporated the labor movement and the general support of the bourgeoisie.

Inevitably, after independence the interests of the various constituencies in the fold of the Neo-Destour party were pitted against one another. The cooperative movement, which at first appeared to be extending to all sectors of the economy, illustrated the administrative elite's capacity to follow its own social and political program regardless of the vested interests of any social group. Its failure made closer constituency management an imperative for the government party.

From the beginning of economic liberalization in the 1970s, state policy revealed a bias in favor of the landed elite. For example, the general policy toward privatizing land after 1970 has involved distributing the lion's share of land under state control to large-scale farmers while preserving a small percentage of farmland to small peasants to stabilize their families.[38] The law that officially shifted policy toward increasing privatization (the law of September 9, 1969 on the reform of agrarian structures) provided for the cession of land under cooperatives to agricultural workers on these lands.[39] In practice, however, only about 50 cooperatives were distributed to landless laborers and agricultural workers. Many of the 200 agricultural production cooperatives on the largest and best land (300,000 hectares, according to an FAO study) remained cooperatively owned until they were distributed in long-term leasing arrangements exclusively to large landowners in the 1980s and 1990s.[40]

In addition to land policy, credit policy during economic liberalization has also clearly favored large landowners. According to the government's own assessment, fewer than 20 percent of the landowners have been beneficiaries of credit, almost all of these in the category of those holding more than 50 hectares.[41] Most of the credit was in the form of grants; the rate of interest was significantly lower than that paid to banks, and purchases of materials and equipment were subsidized by the government when credit was used to make such purchases. Most importantly, no serious effort was made to ensure proper repayment, so that most loans, in fact, were not repaid. Agricultural credit thus essentially constituted transfer payments to large farmers.[42]

The rural bourgeoisie used its privileged access to the administrative elite to prevent land reform and partially sabotage Ben Salah's overall economic plan of the 1960s. Many of them also used their resources and political contacts to convert themselves into an urban bourgeoisie:

> Ben Salah's policies had favored the growth of a new commercial bourgeoisie in construction, public works, and tourism, and they had accumulated capital during the 1960s while consumer imports were restricted. Not a few of these entrepreneurs had been provincial landowners, and they had accumulated capital in the agricultural sector, buying *habous* properties for example, and increasing their productivity through mechanization. They also diversified their investments beyond commercial agriculture to transport, construction, hotel

> management. Partly because of the continued significance of patronage, they enjoyed easy, often preferential, access to government and private credit. It was they who would profit from economic liberalization, and Bourguiba was to give them the opportunity in the 1970s.[43]

In the 1970s, the rural bourgeoisie and its new urban offshoot began to dominate government policy. A low wage policy was maintained to attract foreign investment and protect the profit margins of the indigenous bourgeoisie. Initially the promotion of the private sector produced a positive economic picture in the aggregate. Between 1970 and 1976 gross domestic product grew 9 percent a year, well over double the rate of the 1960s, while the government's share of total new investment in manufacturing dropped to half of the 85 percent it held in the 1960s.

However, the picture worsened late in the decade. In 1977, growth in GDP dropped by half and unemployment doubled.[44] Discontent with the bias in government policy toward capitalists became evident as student and labor groups backed frequent demonstrations and strikes.[45] The late 1970s was one of the most unstable times in the Tunisian political system since independence. Strikes were numerous and involved both private and public sector workers protesting low wages. Outbreaks of violence during a strike in Ksar-Hellal, birthplace of the Neo-Destour, precipitated the first intervention of the Tunisian army to quell civil disturbances. The national union, the UGTT, became the rallying point for opposition to the regime. In a sense, Huntington's focus on an opposition forming in the cities was born out in the Tunisian case:

> . . . the party which was strong in the countryside normally secured control of the national government and inaugurated a regime characterized by a high degree of political stability. Where no party had a clear base of support in the countryside, some form of instability was the result. In some instances, urban revolts may overturn rural-based governments, but in general governments which are strong in the countryside are able to withstand, if not reduce or eliminate, the continuing opposition they confront in the cities.[46]

Government policy had weakened party support in the countryside while opposition grew in the city. However, by this time Tunisia had likely undergone enough change to reduce the relevance of a peasant base of support for political stability. According to Huntington's analysis, in the course of overall modernization, eventually government stability depends on urban support as urban-rural political power changes:

> If revolution is avoided, in due course the urban middle class changes significantly; it becomes more conservative as it becomes larger. The urban work-

> ing class also begins to participate in politics, but it is either too weak to challenge the urban middle class or too conservative to want to do so. Thus as urbanization proceeds, the city comes to play a more effective role in the politics of the country, and the city itself becomes more conservative. The political system and the government come to depend more upon the support of the city than the countryside.[47]

In sum, the administrative elite faced a substantially different political environment in the late 1970s. Growing urban-based clientele groups became more politically important and exerted increasing influence on internal party politics. Government policy reacted by favoring the urban sector. Government food subsidies benefited the urban working class to the detriment of the rural poor by artificially depressing the prices of agricultural produce. Elites were still favored in the remaining agrarian reform program and, in addition, benefited from the government's interest in extracting resources from the agricultural sector to fund industrial expansion as they diversified their economic activities.[48]

The Socialist Destour appeared to recognize the growing importance of urban areas for its own stability and economic growth. The capitalist sector of the economy was much stronger than in the 1960s, thanks in part to significant foreign involvement, and the government neither needed nor wanted to incur its displeasure.[49] The administrative elite increased its link to capitalists and made some concessions to the urban masses in this period.

The government partially mollified rural masses by maintaining its two-pronged agricultural strategy of using most of the state land to bolster capitalist agriculture while reserving some land to stabilize peasant families. The peasantry had developed a patron/client relationship with the state, and the Socialist Destour remained the only political organization with resources to offer. This reality kept much of the peasantry tied to the party even as its share of state resources dwindled dramatically.

Even with the policy shifts, the polity remained unstable in the early 1980s; strikes and civil disturbances continued. An Islamist movement, which had taken shape in the early 1970s as neglected sectors looked for a political voice, continued to grow.[50] As it became apparent that the single party was leaving too many groups dissatisfied, tension mounted for political liberalization. In 1980 a new prime minister, Mohammed Mzali, was appointed by President Bourguiba. Mzali advocated political liberalization to match the state's general commitment to capitalist development.[51]

Until this point there had never been a strong push for political pluralism within the administrative elite. Modernizing Tunisia socially and economically was a project to be guided by state authorities and party leaders. All Tunisians were considered Destourians under the tutelage of the administrative elite as it led the country toward an industrial economy. However, by the 1980s the party could contain neither the growing cleavages among the elite nor those in larger society within a single party format.

Since independence, party methodology had consisted of choosing an economic policy direction while maintaining a gradualist approach of bargaining with groups disadvantaged by the policy. In fact, Bourguibism, with its long-standing hostility for doctrines, became a synonym for this type of pragmatism.[52] The large landowners kept their land during a policy of socializing agriculture; small peasants were to be stabilized during the promotion of capitalist agriculture. The liberal economic direction undertaken in the 1970s and 1980s eventually led to a break from Bourguibism, from pragmatic bargaining. The party began to align itself more firmly with private capitalists. Dissenters within the party were permitted to leave and form their own political organizations.

Members of the administrative elite themselves joined with social forces to contest state policy when the state permitted November 1981 National Assembly elections to be openly contested. A small communist party was formed by ex-Neo-Destour activists. Supporters of the deposed and exiled Ahmed Ben Salah ran lists as the Mouvement de l'Unité Populaire (MUP) II; former Defense Minister Ahmed Mestiri organized a party called the Social Democrats. Both the MUP II and the Social Democrats favored secular modernization, but were less enthusiastic about private sector capitalism.

Bourguiba hoped that the appearance of pluralism would defuse much of the articulate dissatisfaction with the regime.[53] However, the strongest opposition social force, the Mouvement de Tendance Islamique (MTI), was repressed and outlawed from formal political participation. Bourguiba's increasing persecution of this group and the resulting political upheaval would be a major reason for his ouster in 1987.

The 1981 elections fell far short of political pluralism. The National Front, an alliance of the Neo-Destour and the UGTT, swept the assembly seats; not a single opposition candidate was elected. Apparently the Socialist Destour had second thoughts about political pluralism and arranged that no opposition group receive more than 5 percent of the vote.[54] The election—and the election irregularities—demonstrated that the Socialist Destour remained unchallenged in the countryside in spite of its policies that favored the urban sector. More than anything, this was due to the exclusive access of local party functionaries to state patronage.[55]

The acceleration of economic liberalization since the mid–1980s has been characterized by the state party's increasing abandonment of the rural masses while the ruling elite cements its ties with the rural and urban bourgeoisie and refuses to relinquish its firm control of the state apparatus.

Accelerated Economic Liberalization: The International Dimension

The administrative elite chose a partial attempt at political pluralism to maintain what remained of its capacity to guide the development agenda. It was hoped that political competition would legitimize the regime's economic liberalism.[56] However, the ruling elite had no intention of allowing the formation of any serious competition, something illustrated by the corruption in election results and the persecution of Islamists in the 1981 elections. Continuing authoritarianism meant that electoral rules in the 1980s and 1990s would be manipulated to stifle the development of political competition. The political parties that formed as offshoots of the Socialist Destour continue to suffer from their agreement to play by Destour rules: they are largely unrecognized as independent political forces.

Political competition has yet to be allowed to legitimize economic liberalism in Tunisia. Elections in 1988 and 1994 fell short of open competition. Repression has been effectively used to dismantle opposition. The peasantry views the Destour party as the only hope for access to state resources—a reasonable response of the vulnerable. Some dissenters have joined the clandestine Islamist movement. Many constituencies, like labor, continue to deal with the ruling party as if development strategy were still marked by gradualism and bargaining between the administrative elite and all constituencies in Tunisia. However, the union's demand for worker participation in the policymaking councils of government forming the capitalist strategy were refused in the 1970s.[57]

State policy in Tunisia since the 1970s has reflected an increasing unwillingness of the state to challenge capitalists and an increasing willingness to alienate other constituencies. The power of the rural and urban bourgeoisie within the hegemonic party indicates that political choices by this party over time came to serve the interests and ideologies of these groups rather than the values of a modernizing ruling elite independent of vested interests. Choices in economic policy have also been affected by international pressure for marketization and privatization.

The major political issue in Tunisia in the 1970s and 1980s concerned the degree of economic liberalism: people within and outside of the party fought the development of what they saw as unbridled private-sector capitalism; how much of the state-dominated economy should be privatized was hotly debated. In spite of the general liberal economic direction undertaken in the 1970s, the government's share in total capital investment never dropped below 50 percent throughout the decade.[58] In the early 1980s, the state still seemed somewhat committed to public, cooperative, and private economic sectors.

International forces in this period swung sharply toward private sector capitalism. The collapse of the Soviet Union increased the power and international influence of Western industrialized economies. Access to finance capital from lending institutions began to be tied to market-oriented economic policies. The global context has been another spur for increasing economic liberalization in Tunisia and weakening the power of the administrative elite.

Since the 1980s all late-developing countries (and advanced industrial ones, for that matter) have had to deal with the growing transnationalization of markets, production, and finance in the international economy. Within the global context, local states tend to lose power and initiative if their economies falter. One of the defining features of underdevelopment is that international dynamics press more urgently on economic policy in Third World countries.[59]

Like other late-developing countries, Tunisia confronts these new challenges from a position of relative weakness due to a combination of internal and external economic and political developments: the seeming inadequacy of earlier state-led development strategies (resulting in low growth and balance of payment difficulties), the growing power of the EU, and the international financial institutions upon which Tunisia has increasingly had to depend. With its growing need for imported food and capital, its lack of significant natural resources like oil to produce external rent, Tunisia has little choice but to rely on access to international financial institutions and cooperation agreements with Europe.[60]

The Tunisian state since independence had committed itself to directly or indirectly fostering industrialization, as well as to maintaining social programs such as consumer subsidies. Neither a state-led nor private-sector-led growth strategy was effective in preventing fiscal deficits and inflation while the ruling elites pursued their goals. Even during the period of gradual economic liberalization the Tunisian economy suffered from rising inflation, shortages of food and consumer goods, and the inefficient use of capital—much of it borrowed. In the early 1980s, the country experienced stagnant growth rates. Balance of payment difficulties led to borrowing and debt that reached a near crisis level in the mid-1980s. Like many other countries, Tunisia resorted to a short term macroeconomic stabilization program and mid-term structural adjustment program in 1986 to gain access to finance capital that would relieve the crisis.

International Monetary Fund (IMF) stabilization and World Bank structural adjustment programs prescribe orthodox macroeconomic policy, trade liberalization, some form of privatization, deregulation, a general move toward increased reliance on market forces, and further integration into the world economy. At the core of these prescriptions is the notion that development should be achieved through competitive markets, not centralized planning.[61] The ideology of economic liberalism in a strong form entered Tunisia's economic policy circles more forcefully with agreements with these international financial institutions. The loans were also subject to the principle of conditionality, requiring market reforms for access to the loans. It is difficult to imagine that the debates in Tunisia about the degree of economic liberalism have not been affected by the state's increasing link to transnational capital.

Stalled Democratization

Until the 1980s the variants of the Destour party largely viewed democracy as something that functioned within a single party framework. Party activists were organized in all areas of the country and directed their attention to all social groups. During economic liberalization, the party began to seek a less inclusive set of constituencies; opposition political parties were authorized, and political pluralism established a toehold. The Socialist Destour continued, however, to monopolize the political system and fell far short of removing the association of the Socialist Destour with the state. While the structural adjustment program of 1986 further clarified economic liberalism as state policy, political liberalization proceeded much more fitfully.

One of the most volatile aspects of the Tunisian political system in the 1980s and 1990s is that the state party is shedding constituencies and moving toward unbridled private-sector capitalism while smothering the development of legal credible opposition parties. Liberal economic policies are being imposed by an illiberal political regime that hopes to combine what Clifford Geertz once characterized as a combination of a Smithian way of getting rich with a Hobbesian way of governing.[62]

The strain of authoritarianism and general discontent in Tunisia brought the country to the brink of major civil strife in 1986. The Islamist movement, the MTI, served as the most important voice of the neglected Tunisians during economic liberalization. President Bourguiba personalized the conflict between the MTI and the state and attempted to eradicate the group. Members of the banned MTI and other Islamists were put on trial in the fall of 1986. Some were condemned to death and others given lighter sentences. Bourguiba demanded a retrial of Islamists who had received lesser sentences. Zine Al-Abidine Ben Ali, former national head of security as Interior Minister, who had been recently appointed prime minister, pointed out the illegality of this course of action and its civic danger.

Apparently, there was also a plot by the militant wing of the MTI to assassinate top political figures, including Bourguiba and Ben Ali, if the Islamists' trial was reopened. The brewing conflict and the octogenarian

Bourguiba's failing mental state led to the accession of Ben Ali to power on the night of November 6–7, 1987. Ben Ali assembled seven doctors who declared Bourguiba incapable of governing.[63]

As president, Ben Ali immediately began to halt the destabilizing repression of the Islamists; indeed, his initial platform focused on the need for political pluralism. The hegemonic party name was changed to the Rally for Constitutional Democracy (RCD). On Ben Ali's first anniversary in power, he witnessed the signing of a National Pact by 16 political and social organizations, including the primary Islamist group. Initially, the Ben Ali political reforms were impressive. Clemency was granted to more than 3,000 political prisoners and bans were lifted on many long-term political exiles. Opposition forces were allowed new freedoms, and steps were taken to legalize parties and allow for more press freedom. The presidential term of office was limited after Bourguiba had served as president for life.

The National Pact of November 1988 aimed to move all social forces in Tunisia in the same general direction. The MTI was allowed to participate in exchange for some important concessions: acceptance of the principle of competitive democracy, renunciation of violence, and recognition of the code of the 1957 personal status.[64] Soon after, the MTI formed a political party, al-Nahda (the Renaissance). In the first post-transition election in April 1989, al-Nahda offered the only challenge to RCD hegemony. The "independent candidates" representing al-Nahda (legislative steps were being taken at the time to legalize the party) won nearly 14 percent of the vote nationally and up to 25 percent in some large cities, but in the winner-take-all electoral format, the RCD won every seat.

The RCD victory was the result, among other factors, of the belief by many that the party was the only one capable of delivering patronage resources. At the same time, RCD officials were alarmed by the strength of al-Nahda and quickly moved to make religious parties illegal. The combination of the two events seemed to make it clear that serious confrontations and bargaining remained among social forces before one could see Tunisia implementing liberal, democratic, and pluralistic rule. During this period, the Algerian fundamentalist movement, FIS, gained in strength leading up to electoral victory in municipal elections. A year later the FIS was poised for victory in national legislative elections when the military suspended the vote after the first round. Chilled by the ascent of the FIS and an evolving civil war in Algeria, the Tunisian government instituted implacable repression of al-Nahda. Some political Islamists reacted to repression with violence.

By the time of the legislative and presidential elections in March 1994, only compromised political parties were allowed to participate; the government had charted a new course, which excluded organized religion from participation in formal politics. The hope that the National Pact would be a device for a transition from authoritarian rule seemed lost as the 1994 elections—won by the hegemonic RCD with nearly 98 percent of the vote—ended up being largely an empty exercise. In sum, a period of increasing marketization in Tunisia has coincided with and probably contributed to increasing authoritarianism.

Guilain Denoeux described the electoral campaign run by the RCD in 1994 as a morose exercise in which the regime used the elections to hammer home favorite themes instead of allowing real pluralism. Economic prosperity through liberal economic policies and the fear of Islamic fundamentalism were used to justify a status quo in which the RCD retained hegemonic control of institutions. Power remained concentrated in the hands of the president, and the press remained a simple instrument of the party in power.

> The gap continued to deepen between, on one hand, the democratic rhetoric of a regime incarnated by a "the man of the change," and the reality of a government personalized to the extreme and that tends to smother all competition in the name of stability. Certainly, the stability enjoyed by Tunisia is not only the result of a police system. One should not minimize the accomplishments of the regime, notably in education, the rights of women, economic growth, and the assistance given to the most disadvantaged classes and regions. But, in a country where the middle class is important and aspires to play a real political role, can the regime still legitimize itself exclusively by its engagement in favor of economic growth and its role of barrier against the green threat [of fundamentalism]? Doesn't the absence of a true political opening represent a significant source of instability in a society that continues to change rapidly economically and politically?[65]

A close look at the division of state benefits in the agricultural sectors raises questions about the assistance given to the most disadvantaged by the regime, noted here by Denoeux.

Conclusion: Economic Reform and Continuing Authoritarianism

Tunisia's postindependence political system has always been authoritarian. The issue has been whether or not the dominant political party and the bureaucratic establishment it colonized had autonomy from vested interests. The autonomy of the administrative elite meant that they could use the state to respond to all constituencies while promoting national development. The analysis of a generation of scholars witnessing Tunisia's independence movement and postcolonial years of Tunisian rule was that the Neo-Destour was a mass party, a populist party that stood out in the late developing world for its mobilization of all constituencies. The leadership of the party, in this view, promoted modern values and seemed destined to transform Tunisia gradually into a multiparty democracy, yielding its own power to that of society as a whole.

In the meantime, the administrative elite played the role of a patron state that bargained with and ensured some distribution to all social groups. Patronage, activism, and organization throughout the country, along with repression when necessary, helped to insure the Neo-Destour's monopoly of political power and maintained the perception that the state was for everyone. For a while, well into the 1970s, the administrative elite maintained its umbrella party and continued to play the most powerful role in economic policy making.

From the beginning of the nationalist movement, however, by funding and supplying the Neo-Destour with its early leadership, the rural bourgeoisie has had a special role in the mass party.[66] There were signs in the 1970s that the rural bourgeoisie and its urban offshoot had become powerful enough to dominate state policy. This trend seems to have become a fait accompli during structural adjustment.

A prime illustration of the link between the rural bourgeoisie and the state is the final dispensation of the agricultural production cooperatives that were the centerpiece of Tunisian socialism. Privatization of cooperatives pitted agricultural laborers and small landholders against large landowners who coveted this valuable agricultural land, which had been initially slated for distribution to cooperative workers. Ultimately, the bulk of the land went to large landowners.

The government used an economic and technical efficiency rationale to justify the distribution of cooperatives to wealthy landowners even though evidence suggested that medium-size farms of 10 to 20 hectares are the most efficient in Tunisia.[67] Large landowners have been a major disappointment in terms of increasing productivity and promoting modern, commercial farming through the postindependence era.[68]

A reasonable explanation for state policy favoring the rural bourgeoisie, while disregarding earlier bargaining with all affected groups including the rural poor, is the erosion of the administrative elite's power while the bourgeoisie increasingly made the state its vehicle. Discussions between the World Bank and the Tunisian government reveal the government's efforts to advance the interests of its most powerful allies and abandon other constituencies during economic reform:

> Allocation of state-owned land and collective land to private title holders is occurring, with at best neutral, and probably negative consequences for the poor. The government is pursuing a policy of increasing productivity and promoting modern, commercial farming on the 0.8 million hectares of crop land

> that it owns. In the last several years the government has more aggressively pursued leasing state-owned crop lands to private commercial partnerships for up to 40 years. Although there may be some indirect benefit to the rural poor from this transfer of management through job creation that follows intensification, the government is expressly not distributing these lands to improve the land assets of the rural poor.[69]

Privatizing cooperatives has also increased rural unemployment as new management, i.e., large landowners, attempts to cut labor costs with mechanization and less labor-intensive crops. The net impact on rural employment is the opposite of the expectation of the World Bank. This is acknowledged in some of its documentation of the impact of structural adjustment. "There was almost no net job creation in agriculture; most of the growth in employment was in manufacturing and services."[70] Overall, official unemployment has increased during structural adjustment from 13.1 percent in 1984 to 16.1 percent in 1993.[71]

Agricultural policy during structural adjustment has driven home the reality of the near complete abandonment of the rural masses by the state. The dual strategy of favoring large commercial enterprises and also making a much smaller effort to stabilize family farms through state policy has ended. Peasants have noticed:

> The workers have become beggars. The sun shines on everyone. Normally the state looks after us all. Why give the land to the rich? They already have land. If you give them more they will no longer think of the poor. What are they going to do with more, buy another car? It's no good. You find people with 1,000 hectares while others won't even have one hectare. The poor wanted land. Some farmers before got land and they're doing well. [In the early 1970s, a small amount of state land was distributed to former cooperative workers.] If you have connections you can get land. Those who were fired like me always go to the administration asking for work. We tell them you fired us, so give me something to buy bread. Nothing happens. The cooperative used to employ eighty people, but now only thirty work there. Those thirty are almost always women because they are paid less. They work for twelve hours a day with someone standing over them the whole time. Men require four dinars a day [one dinar is approximately equal to one U.S. dollar] while the women work for three something. You know the ministry tells them to pay us five dinars a day.
>
> The poor will always stay poor around here. The poor lack rain and grass for their animals. The rich won't allow them to graze on their land. Before you could graze your animals and they would also give you money. Now the rich don't give you anything. I went to a rich farmer and asked for a little wheat. He said, "get out, God will help you." Another man, rich with a 404 truck, asked and he gave him the wheat. The rich and the administrators help each other. For example, the Hajj [Islamic term for person who has made the pilgrimage to

> Mecca. Here, he is referring to the man who is the largest landowner in his area] will give 10 or 20 kilos of wheat to the poor, but he'll give a lot more to the rich without them coming by.
>
> If there's assistance from the state the umda [local government administer] will give out fifty per cent of it and give the rest to his friends or keep it. If you complain the umda would create worse problems. To get assistance you go to the délegué. Before the délegué will help you, he asks the umda. [The délegué is the highest government representative in town.] My four-year-old son needed medicine for heart disease, but the umda said I didn't need anything. That I'm doing fine. If you go into my house you'll know how poor I am. I went to the délegué when my son got sicker, he made the umda deliver the money for medicine to my door.[72]

The new market arrangements in Tunisia, which began in the early 1970s, have not been accompanied by democratization, as some analysts suggest.[73] Rather, in Tunisia, economic liberalization has been associated with continuing authoritarianism, growing ties between the bourgeoisie and the state, and the abandonment of many constituencies. There has also been an increasing influence of international financial institutions in economic policymaking circles.

It should also be noted that Tunisia is a typical late-developing country in many regards. It is situated in the semi-arid tropics, a vast zone girdling the world. Mexico, India, and much of the Middle East and Sahelian Africa lie in the same zone. Rain-fed agriculture supplemented with groundwater irrigation predominates, as does village habitation. Land distribution is typically skewed and production varies enormously with rainfall. Many countries in the semi-arid tropics are undergoing structural adjustment, so the lessons one learns in Tunisia may have resonance in other parts of the world.

Economic reform places particular pressures on a dominant party state. While obviously not being even-handed with all social forces, Tunisia and other North African states had developed social contracts with labor, peasants, private investors, the middle class, and many other social groups. But the Tunisian state exchanged state-led economic activities, subsidies, and subventions for fealty; repression was used against those groups who questioned the new social order.[74] Even after the state clearly sought to organize a less inclusive set of constituencies, the expectation remained of a patron state accessible to all. In a political arena in which a hegemonic party insists on monopolizing power, state agents continue to foster an inclusive rhetoric even after state policy has dramatically shifted to favor the true constituents of the party. Party operatives are still organized throughout the country and seek to maintain party hegemony; repression has become an even more important element of the political system.

The state party in Tunisia has responded politically to the social changes accompanying development and economic reform. As Huntington suggested, the political support in urban areas became more important to government stability than the countryside as demographics change over time. The urban middle class grows and becomes more conservative; industrialization expands. The rural masses in Tunisia, who helped the administrative elite from the provinces take power from the traditional urban-based elites in the 1930s, have become the most neglected constituents in state policy. Large landowners reap the benefits of agricultural policy and diversify into urban areas. To an extent, the peasantry adapts to these changes through clientage with rural notables and through the acceptance born of helplessness in the face of the increasingly paltry benefits of state patronage.

Market liberalism stresses export promotion and private investment—both domestic and foreign. The rural and urban bourgeoisie within Tunisia are in the best position to take advantage of such a strategy. Economic adjustment is a process that tends to lead to coalitions that favor commercial agriculture, private industrialists, and export sectors.[75] If the state was afraid to alienate the increasingly powerful capitalist sector in the 1970s,[76] then there is even more reason to assume that state policy reflects the vested interests of this group today.

Labor unions tend to lose much and gain little from economic reform: owners and managers gain greater freedom to hire and fire workers, food subsidies are reduced, and wages become tied to productivity, not cost of living. Organized labor, simply by virtue of being organized, is usually in a better position to protest reform than other social groups.[77] However, there is evidence that the reform-minded state in Tunisia has used negotiations to gain labor acceptance of structural adjustment and the market economy.[78]

Agricultural laborers and small peasants, according to the prevailing literature, are supposed to benefit from economic reform: "[G]overnment changes in producer prices for agricultural goods as part of broad structural reforms leads to demand for labor and improved wages. Thus urban bias is reversed and farm workers and small and large landowners benefit."[79] This proposition is contradicted by the evidence in the Tunisian case, in which there has been a bias toward large landowners in the structural adjustment program. In addition to land policy increasing land concentration and increasing rural unemployment, price reform improved prices for the crops produced by the wealthy and had little or negative impact on the nonirrigated crops produced by the peasantry.[80]

It is likely that the Tunisian state party has created a coalition of commercial agriculture and industrialists from the remains of a once-populist party. Continuing negotiations with elements of labor that accept the state agenda and with private capitalists increase regime stability. Tunisia's recent economic growth rate has excited World Bank and IMF officials who tout the country as an example of successful structural adjustment. Within

Tunisia the regime bases its legitimacy partially on its claims to having guided the country to economic prosperity.

Still, there are significant problems on the horizon. Ordinary Tunisians appear to react more forcefully to a sense of inequity in the economic reform process than a belief in the economic scorecard touted by the state and officials in international financial institutions. The sense of relative losses may be more important politically than aggregate economic growth. The Islamist movement, the only true opposition group, remains strong. Repression has increased during Ben Ali's reign. Organizations such as Amnesty International and the Tunisian League of Human Rights often cite the government for detentions, possible torture, and general harassment of opposition figures, in particular members of organized religious movements.

Continued economic growth, a more efficient distribution of benefits, well-executed repression, and a fear of an Algeria-like situation may keep the Tunisian Islamists at bay. However, ultimate political stability will require real political opening. The RCD will have to be recognized as having abandoned its historical commitments to equity to become a party representing the interests of rural notables, the urban bourgeoisie, and transnational finance. Political parties to represent labor and the peasantry must be allowed to develop and flourish in a truly competitive political system.

Notes

1. Abdelkader Zghal has used the term administrative elite in discussions of Neo-Destour autonomy from the Sahelian Bourgeoisie and the rest of Tunisian Society. The Sahel is an agricultural region on Tunisia's eastern coast. It is known for settled villages and private land ownership that prevented French colonialism from making major inroads into the region. These elites largely originated from the Sahel. Abdelkader Zghal, "L'Elite Administrative Et La Paysannerie en Tunisie," in Charles Debasch, ed., *Pouvoir et Administration Au Maghreb: Etudes Sur Les Elites Maghrébines* (Paris: Editions du Centre National de la Recherche Scientifique, 1970).
2. Rhys Payne makes the point that comparative analyses in the 1970s stressed the distinctions between the political orders of the Maghrib, but all four countries had similar socioeconomic problems in the 1980s and adopted similar structural adjustment programs in the 1990s regardless of regime type or ideology. See "Economic Crisis and Policy Reform in the 1980s," in Habib and Zartman, eds., *Polity and Society in Contemporary North Africa* (Boulder, CO: Westview Press, 1993).
3. According to the World Bank, GDP growth from 1987 until 1993 was 4.7 percent per year. From 1980 to 1986 the figure was 3.65 percent per year. See World Bank, *Republic of Tunisia Growth, Policies, and Poverty Alleviation,* 1995, I.2.

4. Public fear of the "green threat of fundamentalism," partially fanned by Ben Ali's regime, state repression, and a government personalized to the extreme in the identity of "the man of change" are regime tendencies noted by Guilain Denoeux in his analysis of Tunisia's 1994 legislative and presidential elections, "Tunisie: Les Elections Presidentielles et Legislatives 20 Mars 1994," *Monde Arabe: Maghreb Machrek* 145 (July-Sept. 1994).
5. Lisa Anderson, "Policy Making and Theory Building" in Hisham Sharabi, ed., *Theory, Politics and the Arab World* (London: Routledge, 1990), p. 54.
6. C. A. Micaud, ed., *Tunisia: The Politics of Modernization* (New York: Praeger, 1964), p. xii.
7. Ibid.
8. Elements of modernization theory and a focus on elites can be found in Clement Henry Moore, *Tunisia Since Independence: The Dynamics of One Party Government* (Berkeley: University of California, 1965); Elbaki Hermassi, *Leadership and National Development in North Africa* (Berkeley: University of California, 1972); and Leon Carl Brown, "Stages in the Process of Change," in Micaud, ed., *Tunisia: The Politics of Modernization* (New York: Praeger Press, 1964). To varying degrees, all three scholars viewed most of the original leadership of the party as coming from rural areas and as having significant ties with the rural masses.
9. Leon Carl Brown, "Stages in the Process of Change," in Micaud, p. 41.
10. A point made by Henri De Montety, "Old Families and New Elites in Tunisia," in William Zartman, ed., *Man, State and Society in the Contemporary Maghrib* (New York: Praeger, 1973), p. 176.
11. Clement Henry Moore, in Micaud, p. 81.
12. Ibid., p. 81.
13. Samuel Huntington, *Political Order in Changing Societies* (New Haven, CT: Yale University Press, 1968), pp. 433–461.
14. Ibid., p. 435.
15. Ibid., pp. 438–443.
16. Lisa Anderson, *The State and Social Transformation in Tunisia and Libya* (Princeton, NJ: Princeton University Press, 1986), p. 167.
17. Ibid., p. 169.
18. Ibid. Anderson recounts this incident and its significance for the party.
19. Ibid., pp. 170–172.
20. Hermassi, pp. 165, 186.
21. Quoted in Hermassi, pp. 126–127.
22. Hermassi, p. 126.
23. Moore, p. 81.
24. Huntington, pp.433–434.
25. Hermassi, p. 125.
26. Moore, pp. 82–83.
27. *Habous* is the plural form of *Habs.* It refers to religious endowment of land in Muslim tradition. *Habous* was divided into public and private usage. Income derived from public habous is given over to the support of some pub-

lic cause, such as a school, mosque or hospital. Any land committed to private *habous* was designated to support heirs of the owners, so long as the family line might continue. However, should the line of descent cease, the private *habous* would become public *habous.*

28. Cited in Hermassi, p. 186.
29. Ibid., pp. 184–185.
30. Ibid., p. 186.
31. Ibid., pp. 186–187.
32. John Simmons, "Land Reform in Tunisia," *USAID Country Paper,* 1970.
33. Hermassi, p. 187.
34. Ibid.
35. Simmons, p. 62.
36. Ibid., p. 61.
37. John Duncan Powell, "Peasant Society and Clientelist Politics," *American Political Science Review* 64 (June 1970): 422.
38. Mohammed Elloumi, "Politique Agricoles, Stratégies Paysannes et Development Rural," *Bulletin De L'IRMC* (Spring 1994): 2.
39. United Nations, Food and Agricultural Organization, *Etude Multidimensionnelle et Comparative Des Regimes De Tenures Foncieres Communales Et Privées En Afrique: Le Cas de Tunisie,* 1994, 21.
40. Ibid., p. 22.
41. Samir Rawan, Vali Jamal, and Ajit Ghose, *Tunisia Rural Labour and Structural Transformation* (London: Routledge, 1991), p. 38.
42. Ibid., pp. 40–41.
43. Lisa Anderson, *The State and Social Transformation in Tunisia and Libya* (Princeton, NJ: Princeton University Press, 1986), p. 240.
44. Ibid., pp. 241–242.
45. Ibid.
46. Ibid., pp. 242–243.
47. Huntington, p. 77.
48. Anderson, pp. 244–245.
49. Ibid., p. 246.
50. Ibid., p. 245.
51. Ibid., p. 246.
52. Hermassi, p. 163.
53. Anderson, pp. 248–249.
54. Ibid., p. 248.
55. Ibid., p. 249.
56. Ibid., p. 243.
57. Ibid., p. 243.
58. Ibid., p. 240.
59. See Dirk Vandewalle and Karen Pfeifer, introduction and chapter 1, *North Africa: Development and Reform in a Changing Global Economy* (New York: St. Martin's Press, 1996).
60. Ibid., p. 6.

61. Ibid., p. 9.
62. Quoted in Vandewalle and Pfeifer, p. 13.
63. I. William Zartman, "The Conduct of Political Reform: The Path Toward Democracy," in Zartman, ed., *Tunisia: The Political Economy of Reform* (Boulder, CO: Lynne Rienner Publishers, 1991), pp. 12–13.
64. Guilain Denoeux, "Tunisie: Les Elections Preésidentielles et Legislatives 20 Mars 1994," *Monde Arabe: Magreb Machrek* 145 (July-Sept. 1994).
65. Ibid.
66. The analysis of Hermassi and Anderson tended to view the Neo-Destour as linked with large landowners more than most studies.
67. See Samir Rawan, Vali Jamal, and Ajit Ghose, *Tunisia Rural Labour and Structural Transformation* (London: Routledge, 1991).
68. Ibid.
69. World Bank, "Republic of Tunisia Growth, Policies, and Poverty Alleviation," (1995), II.Annex C.3, pp. 5–6.
70. World Bank, *Republic of Tunisia Poverty Alleviation Preserving Progress While Preparing for the Future* (Washington, D.C., 1995), I.6.
71. World Bank, "Republic of Tunisia Growth, Policies, and Poverty Alleviation" (1995), I.ii.
72. Stephen J. King, *The Politics of Market Reform in Rural Tunisia,* Ph.D. Dissertation, Princeton University (1997), p. 183.
73. Scholars who suggest that the processes of economic liberalization are conducive to democratization include Samuel Huntington, *The Third Wave: Democratization in the Late Twentieth Century* (Norman: University of Oklahoma Press, 1991); Larry Diamond, "Economic Development and Democracy Reconsidered," *American Behavioral Scientist* 35:4 (March-June 1992): 450–499; and Carlos Waisman, "Capitalism, the Market, and Democracy," *American Behavioral Scientist* 35:4 (March-June 1992): 500–516.
74. Pfeifer and Vandewalle, p. 26.
75. John Waterbury, "The Political Management of Economic Adjustment and Economic Reform," in *Fragile Coalitions: The Politics of Economic Adjustment,* ed., Joan Nelson (Washington, D.C.: Overseas Development Council, 1989.)
76. Lisa Anderson, p. 246.
77. John Waterbury, p. 46 in Nelson's *Fragile Coalitions.*
78. Chris Alexander, "State, Labor, and the New Global Economy in Tunisia," in Vandewalle and Pfeifer, eds., p. 177.
79. Joan Nelson, "Poverty, Equity, and the Politics of Adjustment," in Haggard and Kaufman, eds., *The Politics of Economic Adjustment* (Princeton, NJ: Princeton University Press, 1992), p. 227.
80. World Bank, *Republic of Tunisia Growth Policies and Poverty Alleviation* (Washington, D.C., 1995), I.20.

Part V

In Search of Pan-Maghribism

Chapter 9

Dreams and Disappointments

Postcolonial Constructions of "The Maghrib"

David Seddon

Introduction

In Arabic *al-Maghrib* means "the west"; in the Arab world, it is divided from *al-Mashriq* (the Middle East) by Egypt; to the west of Algeria, it is *Al Mamlaka al Maghribiya* (the Kingdom of Morocco); while in Morocco, it is the Atlantic coastal plains. For some, the Maghrib is the region once referred to by Europeans as, "Barbary,"—the land of the Berbers. Others refer to it simply as North West Africa, comprising Libya, Tunisia, Algeria, Morocco, the Western Sahara, and Mauritania, "which can be seen as a link joining North West Africa to black Africa south of the Sahara"[1] and is part of the southern Sahara, which "embraces the whole of Mauritania, together with the northern part of Mali, most of Niger and the northern portion of Chad."[2]

If the borders between the Maghrib states are today more or less agreed upon, they have in the recent past been the subject of conflict. Even more difficult have been relations between the North African states and their southern neighbors: Morocco recognized Mauritania only in 1969, nearly a decade after independence; the very existence of the Western Sahara as a distinct political entity has been challenged by both Mauritania and Morocco; Libya has attempted to annex northern Chad; Mauritania has clashed with Senegal; and Morocco is still at war with the Saharawis in the western Sahara. But if definitions of "the Maghrib" as a region or as a set of independent states have been and remain both contingent and contentious, the construction of the Maghrib as an integrated political-economic entity has been even more fraught. For well over half a century, nationalist movements in the Maghrib have struggled, first to achieve emancipation from European rule and then to achieve a degree of autonomous development.[3] In those struggles the idea of a "greater" unified Maghrib has always been a dream, but the reality has proved more of a disappointment.

This chapter examines how visions of a unified postcolonial Maghrib, and attempts to realize it, have been shaped and constrained, both internally by nationalism and the realities of the postcolonial state, and by the external forces of European neocolonialism and Western-dominated globalization. The struggle for national development on the one hand, and the continued domination of the political economies of the Maghrib by Europe on the other, while in some ways contradictory, have actually combined to inhibit a viable process of integrated regional development that might have more effectively promoted and fulfilled the needs and well-being of ordinary Maghribis.

Early Visions of an Independent Maghrib

The colonial experience created the Maghrib as a European periphery. It also gave rise to movements of resistance, rebellion, and revolt that combined a number of distinctive features (nationalism, republicanism, Islamism, Arabism), all of which played a part in the construction of the image of what an independent Maghrib might be.[4] Given the division of the Maghrib into separate colonial territories, it was to be expected that opposition to European rule would be molded to the contours of a colonial reality that emphasized such fragmentation. But the relationship between nationalist struggle and the vision of a Greater Maghrib was not always contradictory; at least, as Fawzi Mellah remarks, "ces deux projets—patriotique et maghrebin—[etaient] contemporains."[5]

The eventual establishment of a North African Republic was considered as early as 1915[6] by a handful of exiles based in Constantinople, Geneva and Lausanne, where the Comite Algero-Tunisien held a conference in 1916.[7] Discussions concerning cultural links between Tunisia, Algeria, and Morocco took place from 1916 onwards in the *Revue du Maghreb,* published in Geneva. But concern for new political freedoms and even independence, as well as for cultural and religious liberation, began to take organizational form only after the First World War. Such early initiatives were shaped by the contours of the colonial state. Thus, in 1919, year of the publication of *Tunisie Martyr,* reference to a supranational republic was suppressed in favor of detailing specifically Tunisian "injustices,"[8] while in Libya, the Tripolitanians first attempted, in 1918, to form their own republic and then agreed in 1921 to join forces with the followers of Said Muhammad Idris as-Sanusi in Cyrenaica to obtain rights as "Libyans" and to accept Idris as amir of Libya.[9] In Morocco, resistance to the Spanish occupation in the north developed into a major rebellion,[10] and in 1922, Abd al Krim declared an Islamic republic in the Rif, which endured until 1926. Abun Nasr claims that "Abdul Karim's defeat initiated his myth as a hero fighting for faith and country. The myth gave a nationalist direction to a movement in the French zone which until 1925 remained one of political and social protest."[11]

A pan-Maghrib dimension was, however, explicit in some political movements of the interwar period, such as the Etoile Nord-Africaine (ENA), founded in 1926 and led by Messali Hadj. Spencer notes that "Messali was one of the few who held out for the vision of an independent federation of North African states (that is, free from association with France), but the immediate impracticality of its realisation led to his eventual marginalisation."[12] The ENA was also based in Paris rather than in the Maghrib, and it was heavily dominated by Algerians, which militated against its capacity to develop a coherent and practical strategy for achieving Maghribi independence. Some influential pan-Arabists, like Shakib Arslan, recognized the distinctiveness of the Maghrib; Arslan devised the concept of "pan-Maghribism" and supported the founding in 1932 of the Moroccan nationalist journal *Maghreb.*[13] Another organization that maintained a pan-Maghrib outlook and membership (although numerically dominated by Tunisians) was the Association of Muslim North African Students (AEMNA), founded in 1927. The AEMNA had an active presence in the Maghrib, holding conferences in Algiers in 1931, Tunis in 1932, and Tlemcen in 1935, and helping orchestrate a solidarity strike in Tunisia in November 1937 after uprisings and arrests in Morocco and Tunisia.[14] Significantly, the demands presented to the French Popular Front government in 1936 were the work of a Maghribi "united front" inspired by the ENA and countersigned by the Committee for the Defence of Freedom in Tunisia and the Committee for the Defence of Moroccan Interests.[15]

But their demands were refused and "the consequences of their collective disappointment had to be faced nationally."[16] In Morocco, the Istiqlal (Independence) Party, formed in 1944, brought together virtually all strands of the nationalist movement; in Tunisia the nationalist movement, dominated by the Neo-Destour, proclaimed itself in favor of independence. In neither case were these movements explicitly linked to those in the other territories. In Algeria, the second version of the Manifesto of 1943 demanded recognition of the Algerian nation but also alluded to a future federation or union with the other states of North Africa; by the time the Friends of the Freedom Manifesto (AML) was formed in 1944, however, there was no longer any emphasis on "pan-Maghribism," even in Algeria. Generally, there were few attempts by the political leadership over the next decade to spread the idea of Maghribi unity more widely.[17]

After the Second World War, a new internationalism gave added impetus to the collective struggle against colonialism. Shortly after the formation of the Arab League in 1945, a North African Congress was held, with the participation of the Front for the Defence of North Africa, formed by exiles from within the French Maghrib who assembled in Cairo to mingle with Egyptian as well as other Arab political activists. In February 1947, the Congress of the Arab Maghrib concluded that the nationalists in Cairo should coordinate their activities for a common struggle, and created the Bureau of the Arab Maghrib.[18] Abd al Krim, exiled leader of the Moroccan Rif Republic, was granted political asylum in Egypt and joined other prominent exiled Maghribis (Bourguiba of Tunisia, Allal al Fassi and Abdelkhalek Torres from Morocco). By the end of 1947, he was head of the Committee for the Liberation of the Arab Maghrib—an extension of the Bureau of the Arab Maghrib. The charter of the new committee was signed by the major nationalist parties from the three French colonies,[19] in which they agreed not to negotiate with France until the independence of all three was recognized. But even in Cairo, national rivalries came to take precedence over internationalism. The dominance of the Moroccan element there was one of the major reasons for Bourguiba's return to Tunisia in 1949, although he was also disillusioned with the Arab League and by the corruption of King Farouk's court.[20] Such attempts as there were—at Chantilly in January 1952[21]—to form a united Maghribi front were to prove abortive, both because the French refused to deal with such an entity and because of the level of organization required.

In Libya, the occupation in 1942 of Cyrenaica and Tripolitania by the British and of Fezzan by the French led to the administration of the territory on a "care and maintenance basis" until well after the war. The Italian occupation had failed to establish a unified national identity, but in October 1951, a new constitution was promulgated, creating a regime based on a federal government under a constitutional monarch—King (formerly Amir) Muhammad Idris. Building national unity in a new country, in which previously loyalty had been to tribe and clan, was the priority, but developing external links with the Arab world was also important. Recognized as an independent state by the United Nations in 1951 four years before Moroccan and Tunisian independence, Libya, not surprisingly, looked toward the Mashriq rather than the Maghrib. It joined the Arab League in 1953 and, in 1956, signed a trade and payments pact with Egypt.

Meanwhile, the Algerians maintained a rhetorical commitment to the struggle for national independence "within a North African framework," and in August 1956, at the Soummam conference, the National Council of the Algerian Revolution (CNAR) called for a North African Federation. But for the Moroccans the vision of an independent Maghrib was dominated by that of a Greater Morocco. Before the colonial period, Morocco had remained outside the control of the Ottoman Empire, unlike other parts of the Maghrib. This historic independence and Morocco's imperial interpretation of its past nourished dreams of a Morocco stretching southward across the western Sahara and Mauritania to the Senegal River, and eastward from the Atlantic to include the Saharan regions of Colomb-Bechar and Tindouf in Algeria. The Istiqlal (Independence) party was explicitly concerned from its formation in 1944 onwards both to reunify Morocco (divided in 1912 between the Spanish and the French) and to "reclaim" the Spanish Sahara and Mauritania. Virtually all Moroccan nationalists shared this vision, and when in 1953 they formed an "alternative government," all were agreed on the goal of a Greater Morocco. During the final years of colonial rule (1955–1956), the Army of Liberation, under the auspices of the Istiqlal, mounted attacks against French and Spanish forces in the Sahara as far afield as Tindouf in southwest Algeria and northern Mauritania.

Early Post-Colonial Maneuvers

After independence, the Istiqlal leader, Allal al Fassi, returning from exile in Cairo, claimed that decolonization was incomplete: "If Morocco is independent, it is not completely unified. The Moroccans will continue the struggle until Tangier, the Sahara from Tindouf to Colomb-Bechar, Touat, Kenadza, Mauritania are liberated and unified. Our independence will only be complete with the Sahara! The frontiers of Morocco end in the south at Saint-Louis-du-Senegal!"[22] In July 1956, the newspaper *Al Alam* published a map of Greater Morocco incorporating a vast portion of the Algerian Sahara, including the oases of Touat, Gourara, and Tidikelt, the Spanish Sahara and Mauritania, and even a corner of northwest Mali.

Al Fassi's espousal of a Greater Morocco as the cornerstone of an independent Maghrib rapidly gained official support in Morocco. The Istiqlal endorsed these territorial demands in August 1956, and in March 1957, al Fassi declared, while touring southern Morocco, that "the battle for the Sahara has just begun."[23] Muhammad V could not allow the principal nationalist party to outdo the monarchy in its nationalist fervor, and the cause of Greater Morocco was officially embraced by the government, under the auspices of the king. In October 1957, Morocco laid claim at the United Nations to Mauritania, Ifni, and Spanish Sahara; in November, al Fassi was named director of Saharan and Frontier Affairs in the Ministry of the Interior and a few days later, "the Voice of the Moroccan Sahara" started broadcasting. For Morocco, clearly, any Greater Maghrib would have to accommodate a Greater Morocco.

President Bourguiba of Tunisia had a different vision. In response to the FLN's call for a North African Federation at the Soummam conference in August 1956, he invited national representatives to Tunis to discuss the resolution of the Algerian conflict within a Franco-Maghribi Confederation.[24] The talks never took place; but in an interview published in *Le Monde* in October 1956, Bourguiba suggested that "au dela de l'independence algerienne, tunisienne, marocaine, pourra a mon sens etre constitue en ensemble nord-africain associe a la France sous des formes qu'il faudra determiner. Une sorte de federation nord-africaine? Je ne veux pas prononcer le mot de federation. Je propose seulement une idee; les modalites resteront a definir au cours d'eventuelles negotiations" ("over and above Algerian, Tunisian and Moroccan independence, as far as I'm concerned, there could be constituted a North-African ensemble associated with France under structures yet to be determined. A kind of North-African federation? I do not want to utter the word federation. I'm only proposing an idea; the modalities will have to be defined in the course of eventual negotiations").[25]

At this point, Bourguiba clearly saw the proposed Maghribi Confederation as linked to France. But in January 1957, he spoke publicly of the "unification of North Africa from Soloum in eastern Libya to Casablanca,"[26] implying a broader conception of the Maghrib. Since leaving Cairo in 1949, Bourguiba had identified a gulf between the Arab east *(mashriq)* including Egypt, and the west *(maghrib)*—a gulf accentuated by divisions between the European colonial powers and after 1954 by the policies of President Nasser. His vision of a unified Maghrib now evidently included Libya. A treaty of friendship between Tunisia and Libya was duly signed, although disputes over the frontier intervened and it was only in 1963 that the treaty was ratified.

Libya was not included when, in March 1958, King Muhammad V of Morocco declared his wish "to see the three countries of north Africa unified through the creation of a Federation called for and justified by geography, history, economics and a common civilization." In May, at a Conference in Tangiers (attended by the Moroccan Istiqlal, the Tunisian Neo-Destour, and the Algerian FLN), the Moroccan king spoke of a union of the countries of the Maghrib that "would reinforce their position in the world and would permit them to play an appropriate role in international politics."[27] The creation of an Algerian government-in-exile was recommended, and a Consultative Assembly, consisting of ten deputies from each state and ten from the National Council of the Algerian Revolution (CNRA), was to be set up. In June 1958, a Permanent Maghrib Secretariat was established. It met twice before the end of 1958 and then fell into oblivion;[28] the Consultative Assembly never materialized.

Despite their evident incapacity to convert the dream of Maghrib unity into reality, the vision of a Greater Maghrib was built into the constitutions of all three ex-French North African states: thus, the Tunisian Constitution of July 1959 refers to the desire of the state to "remain faithful . . . to the unity of the Greater Maghrib"; in the Moroccan Constitution of December 1962 (and March 1972), the Kingdom of Morocco "constitutes a part of the Greater Maghrib"; and the Algerian Constitution of September 1963 declares that "Algeria . . . is a integral part of the Arab Maghrib."[29] This Greater Maghrib, however, failed to include Libya, and Morocco at least continued to regard both Mauritania and the western Sahara as integral parts of Greater Morocco. In February 1958, the king had repeated Morocco's claims to the western Sahara and declared that "we have decided to so orient our activities as to integrate that province into the national territory."[30] Morocco also refused to recognize Mauritania, which joined the United Nations in 1960 and the OAU in 1963 as an independent state; and relations with Tunisia were severed after its swift recognition of Mauritania, to be resumed only after the Arab summit conference in 1964. When King Muhammad died in 1961, his son, Hassan, reiterated Morocco's claim to the Spanish Sahara, to Mauritania and to parts of southwestern Algeria in the name of Greater Morocco.

Tunisia claimed Algerian territory in the southeast Sahara,[31] but it was Morocco's claims that created the sharpest divisions within the region after Algerian independence in 1962. In dispute was the frontier area around Tindouf and the iron-bearing Gara Djebilet. During the final stages of the Algerian war of independence, Morocco had agreed to support the Algerians against French attempts to detach the Sahara from Algeria in return for recognition of this frontier issue. The newly independent Algerian government, however, insisted on the integrity of the existing frontiers. The dispute led to war in 1963, and was not finally resolved until 1970, after a treaty of friendship had been signed and the basis for a settlement agreed to. Other factors also divided Morocco and Algeria during the 1960s, not least the difference between an increasingly conservative monarchy under Hassan II and a radical "socialist" regime, and their very different stances on international relations.

But Libya concluded agreements with Morocco in 1962 and with both Algeria and Tunisia in 1963, and a new initiative to promote greater cooperation within the Maghrib led first to a meeting of foreign ministers in Rabat in 1963, and in October 1964 to the creation of a Permanent Maghrib Consultative Committee with an executive council of ministers. This time, significantly, Libya was involved, and the emphasis was less on political unity than on shared approaches to economic problems. The committee was to meet seven times between 1964 and 1975[32] and to set up a number of commissions to explore various aspects of economic cooperation. Knapp suggests that "over the next few years, the idea of the Greater Maghrib was kept in the air and gained in attractiveness with the discovery of Libyan oil, which some saw as providing the possible resources for the economic development of the region as a whole. But while Libyan ministers sometimes paid lip service to the idea, they obviously set no store by it, and spoke equally often of Libya as the hyphen between the Maghrib and the Mashriq—the Arab east."[33]

In fact, Libya had joined the Arab League in 1953. Morocco and Tunisia both joined at independence in 1956; Algeria joined in 1962; and Mauritania, belatedly, in 1973. All hoped thereby to benefit from closer relations with the Mashriq. The Arab League's principal objectives were to protect the independence and integrity of its member states and to encourage economic and cultural cooperation. The Council of Arab Economic Unity—a separate initiative—met first in 1964 and agreed to establish an Arab common market. This was formally set up the following year. Its members included all of the countries of the Maghrib, including Mauritania and Libya. Customs duties and other taxes on trade between member countries were gradually eliminated between 1965 and 1971. The second stage was to be a full customs union, and ultimately all restrictions on trade between member countries were to be abolished. In practice, however, limited progress was made over the next two decades.

In 1966, Tunisia, dissatisfied with the Arab League, in part because of antagonism between Bourguiba and Nasser, adopted the project of an Islamic Conference. This was condemned in Cairo, Damascus, Baghdad, and Algiers as "American-inspired." Morocco, however, approved and invited the shah of Iran and the kings of Jordan and Saudi Arabia to a conference in Rabat. The Organization of the Islamic Conference (OIC) was eventually established in 1971, with its headquarters in Jeddah. This confirmed a major "fault" within the Arab world that was to prove significant over the next two decades. As Samir Amin remarked at the time, " . . . it would not be misleading to state that Algeria's sympathies lie with France, the USSR and the 'socialist' group of Arab states (the UAR, Libya, Syria, and Iraq), while Tunisia and Morocco are drawn rather towards the United States and the 'moderate' group of Arab states (Saudi Arabia and Jordan)."[34]

If links with the Arab world were seen as a priority in the early years after independence, there was also a clear recognition of the "winds of change" blowing through Africa. In January 1961, representatives of several African countries (including Morocco and Libya) met in Casablanca, where they established the "Casablanca Group." Its object was the creation of a joint military command and an African common market; to this end, it established political, economic, and cultural committees, a supreme command, and a headquarters in Bamako in Mali. The Casablanca Group opposed the independence of Mauritania, largely as a result of pressure from Morocco. The group as a whole was regarded as radical; it advocated a socialist path of development for Africa and a strong role for the state. Despite the fact that its head of state was King Muhammad V, the dominant political force in Morocco was now the Istiqlal, whose radical offshoot (the UNFP) was particularly influential. John Waterbury notes that by 1959, "pretensions to socialism in Morocco had not only become acceptable, they had become politically necessary."[35]

Tunisia joined a different group. At a meeting in Brazzaville in December 1960, twelve francophone states (including Tunisia and Mauritania) agreed to maintain close ties and a special relationship with France. In May 1961, no fewer than twenty African states (including the "Brazzaville Group," a majority of former British territories, and Libya) met in Liberia, to constitute the "Monrovia Group." From this, the Africa and Malagasy Union (AMU) was formed in September 1961. The AMU was largely opposed to the project of the Casablanca Group and favored a looser confederation of independent African states. It aimed to adopt a common stand on international issues, the promotion of economic and cultural cooperation, and the maintenance of a common defense organization; but the member countries were diverse, geographically widespread, and too immersed in their own problems to work effectively together.

In May 1963, a meeting in Addis Ababa established the Organization of African States (OAU) which would orchestrate collective defense, decolonization, and cooperation in economic, social, educational, and scientific matters across Africa. The OAU represented a move away from the strong federal type of structure favored by the Casablanca Group towards the looser association preferred by the Monrovia Group. It stressed the sanctity of existing frontiers and prioritized its role in the peaceful settlement of disputes between African states. Despite its diverse membership and many internal differences, the OAU came to have an increasing influence on African affairs and eventually eclipsed both the Casablanca and the Monrovia groups. Four of the Maghrib states (Algeria, Morocco, Mauritania, and Libya) were founding members.

In 1967, Algeria recognized Mauritania. Mauritania attended the Islamic conference in Casablanca in 1969, and diplomatic relations with Morocco were eventually established at the beginning of 1970 (although the Istiqlal party condemned this and continued to refer to "the Shinqit, known as Mauritania"). Meanwhile, in January 1969, a 20–year treaty of friendship and cooperation was signed by Algeria and Morocco; and in May 1970, the heads of state of Morocco (King Hassan) and Algeria (Boumediene) established a joint commission that, with the assistance of the National Geographical Institute of Paris (which had provided the same service on the Algerian-Tunisian frontier), was able to define the border and open the way for a commitment to the joint exploration of the iron ore reserves of the Gara Djebilet. Morocco formally recognized the border two years later, although the agreement was not ratified.

In 1967, after the Six-day War, Libya—with oil production now rapidly increasing—agreed to make substantial aid payments to the United Arab Republic and Jordan to alleviate the consequences of the war. This eastward orientation was to increase markedly after the coup that overthrew King Idris and brought Col. Muammar Qadhdhafi to power in 1969. The new Libyan head of state immediately proposed an economic union between Libya and Egypt, with Sudan as the third member. In the summer of 1970, Libya withdrew from the Maghrib Permanent Consultative Committee and appeared to be intending to realign itself definitively toward the Mashriq and away from the Maghrib. But the proposed federation with Egypt and Sudan fell into abeyance after Sudan's withdrawal and Nasser's death, and despite involvement in a Federation of Arab Republics (with Egypt and Syria) that came into existence in 1972, this had few practical consequences.

Meanwhile, Libya had forged a new union with Tunisia. This was not welcomed by Tunisia's neighbors. As Knapp remarks, "far from being welcomed as a prelude to the realization, at last, of the Greater Maghrib, it was vigorously resisted by both Algeria and Morocco,"[36] which resented Libya's withdrawal from the Permanent Maghrib Consultative Committee. Libya's relations with Tunisia continued to improve, but relations with Morocco deteriorated rapidly. Formal relations were severed in July 1971 after the Libyan government announced its support of an abortive attempt to overthrow the king. In the same month, Qadhdhafi's regime assisted President Nimeiri of Sudan to regain power after a communist-led coup had ousted him.

At the same time, Mauritania continued to resist Moroccan claims to the whole of the Sahara, and Algeria remained anxious about the extension of Moroccan territory further south. In December 1965, the UN had called on the Spanish government "to liberate Ifni and the Spanish Sahara from colonial domination," and in 1969 required Spain to consult with Morocco and Mauritania in preparation for a referendum. Three meetings of the heads of state of Mauritania, Morocco, and Algeria between 1970 and 1973 produced no agreement. Eventually, in July 1973, a joint communiqué was issued, affirming "the unwavering attachment of the three parties to the principle of self-determination" and their concern to ensure that this principle "be implemented within a framework which guaranteed the free and genuine expression of the will of the Saharawis in conformity with UN resolutions." But the fourth summit of the Non-Aligned Movement held in Algiers in September 1973 revealed clear divisions between the position of Algeria on the one hand and that of Morocco and Mauritania on the other.

In 1974, the Spanish government promised a referendum under the auspices of the UN and a program of gradual withdrawal from the territory involving a period of internal self-government prior to full independence. King Hassan immediately warned that "we will not accept seeing a puppet state erected in any form in the southern part of the country."[37] As to the referendum, he declared that Morocco would reject it. While stating his preference for "a diplomatic, political and peaceful path," he made it clear that "if Morocco ascertains that this path will not lead to the recovery of its territories, it will certainly not hesitate to find other means."[38] Moroccan troops were now deployed in the south of Morocco, and the Istiqlal Party immediately approved this move, as did the other major parties, including those on the left. The king also solicited the view of the International Court of Justice. In 1975, a UN mission concluded that the majority of the Saharawis sought liberation from Spanish rule and supported the POLISARIO Front (created in 1973 to struggle for independence); shortly thereafter, the World Court ruled in favor of self-determination for the Saharawis.

King Hassan, who had hoped the court would legitimize Morocco's claim to the western Sahara, first initiated a peaceful march into the territory and then launched a military assault on the POLISARIO in an attempt to seize the Western Sahara by force. Spain, meanwhile, had concluded a secret agreement with Morocco and Mauritania to withdraw, leaving the western Sahara to be divided between them. In February 1976, the POLISARIO, struggling against the armed forces of the two neighboring states, declared the Saharan Arab Democratic Republic (SADR). Algeria, which recognized the SADR immediately and allowed Saharawi refugees to establish camps near Tindouf in southwest Algeria, provided support; so too, shortly afterward, did Libya. The Moroccan government managed to persuade both the UN General Assembly and the Non-Aligned Movement at its summit in August 1976 from taking positions on the western Sahara, and the OAU equivocated on the issue. In the absence of effective external intervention, the conflict continued for the next 15 years, preventing any major initiative for regional cooperation.

In the face of these internal divisions, the prospect of a unified Greater Maghrib seemed remote.[39] Furthermore, membership of the various Arab and African regional associations and groupings had failed to create any lasting basis for effective economic or other cooperation between the Maghrib states; as Samir Amin observed, after a decade of independence, "all these tentative and fragile groupings had little real impact."[40] The persistence of dependency on Europe, by contrast, seemed inevitable.

Europe and the "Independent" Maghrib

In the early years after independence, the economies of the new Maghrib states failed to achieve the growth and stability that had been hoped for. Amin stresses the extent to which "between 1955 and 1965 production remained stagnant . . . investments fell . . . and exports, with the exception of oil, were in decline."[41] Furthermore, despite their efforts to build links outside the region and to break ties with the former metropolitan powers, the Maghrib states remained critically dependent on Europe (and France in particular). They also faced an emerging European Community (EC) concerned to maintain control over its member states' former colonies through a combination of aid and trade, in a form of "imperialism without colonies."[42]

In effect, the Treaty of Rome—signed in March 1957 shortly after Moroccan and Tunisian independence—established the foundations for new forms of economic dependency in the Maghrib. As one observer noted, "this dependence is further exacerbated by the fact that the economies of these countries, particularly those of northern Africa, specialise in producing a small number of agricultural goods, like citrus fruits, wine and olive oil, which are mainly destined for the markets of western Europe. Because of this specialisation, these countries have to import large amounts of basic foodstuffs. This type of economic structure is mainly the result of their colonial past when production was geared to the needs of the metropolis. They are also dependent on the EEC for foreign investment, tourism, aid and for exporting their surplus labour."[43]

The export of labor from the Maghrib to Europe became a major feature of the dependency relationship during the 1960s: by 1973, workers' remittances amounted to 23 percent of total exports for Morocco and 22 percent for Tunisia.[44] Algerian migrants, mainly in France, were also responsible for a substantial inflow of foreign exchange during the same period, despite efforts by the Algerian government to limit emigration, precisely because of the dangers of dependency. During the late 1960s, the EC concluded a series of trade agreements with Algeria, Morocco and Tunisia.[45] These included two five-year association agreements with Morocco and Tunisia, signed in 1969, the former conferring "partial association" with the EC. By the end of the 1960s, trade exports to Europe from the Maghrib countries accounted for almost 30 percent of their GDP.

In 1972, the European Council declared that the EC would from then onward develop a more coherent and comprehensive Mediterranean policy. The aim was not only to consolidate long-standing economic relations but also to work towards a free trade zone in industrial goods encompassing the EC and the entire Mediterranean area. The EC would reduce tariffs to zero by 1977. Almost full reciprocity would be demanded from the more developed countries of the northern Mediterranean, but for a few "sensitive" products the timetable would be extended to 1985, and for the Maghrib and the Mashriq it would be extended even further.[46] Further cooperation agreements were signed in April 1976 with Morocco, Algeria, and Tunisia; these envisaged free access to the EC market for all industrial goods, with the exception of a few so-called "sensitive" products. A reduction in customs duties was offered for Mediterranean agricultural exports, but quotas applied for olive oil, citrus fruits, and wine exports from the Maghrib. These concessions were always made on the condition that the rules applying to the organization of the EC market were respected and were subject to safeguard clauses. On the other hand, no reciprocity was demanded at least for an initial period of five years. A specified amount of financial assistance was offered to each country, while separate clauses provided for the treatment of immigrant workers from the Maghrib in the EC. In 1977, Tsoukalis wrote: "it remains to be seen whether anything concrete will emerge out of this list of good intentions written into the agreements."[47]

Whatever the intentions, the immediate application of the agreements was effectively constrained by the deteriorating economic climate in Europe during the second half of the 1970s and the early 1980s, and by the increased protection afforded the EC agricultural sector by the strengthening of the Common Agricultural Policy. One consequence was a rapid deflation of the rhetoric regarding the "global Mediterranean policy." At the same time, however, the EC began to move towards the strategic incorporation of the southern European states. From 1975 (when the Greek application was lodged), through 1981 (when Greece became a member state), until 1985 (when the treaty providing for the accession of Spain and Portugal to the EC was signed), the focus of Europe was on "the second enlargement."

The implications were serious for those excluded. As Tsoukalis noted, "the increase in the Community's self-sufficiency in all Mediterranean products will reduce the export possibilities of other Mediterranean countries for which western Europe has traditionally been an extremely important market outlet. The three applicant countries already account for almost half of all agricultural imports to the Community from the Mediterranean area. Their share is bound to increase with accession. What will then happen to Moroccan and Israeli oranges, Tunisian olive oil and Algerian wine?"[48] He predicted that "it is therefore almost inevitable that relations with Mediterranean non-member countries will become even more difficult in the future."

One possible alternative to the peripheralization of the Maghrib was the development of a strong regional association based on increased flows of capital, commodities, and labor between the economies of the Maghrib. But persistent political divisions and conflicting nationalist ambitions made co-operation and integration difficult. As Knapp had observed in the mid-1970s, "their geographic position gives all of them the same interest in the European market for agricultural produce, traditional exports (such as carpets), and, if possible, industrial products; but their approach to the European Economic Community has been marked by historical differences . . . and by national rivalries."[49] Thus, "in spite of the similarity of interest among the several states . . . competition (or simple disregard of the other Maghrib states) has generally prevailed over community of purpose."[50]

Now, in addition to the political divisions between the Maghrib states that militated against a common project of regional development, pressures were growing for structural adjustment and economic liberalization, which were to give rise to popular resistance and political instability and further weaken the capacity of the Maghrib states for concerted international action for development.

Crisis in the Maghrib

While Europe concentrated on the strategic enlargement and effective consolidation of the EC, the Maghrib (like most other parts of the Third World) experienced the profound trauma of "adjustment." The effect of the recession on the Maghrib economies (with the partial exception of Libya) was a deepening economic crisis, associated with a deteriorating balance of payments and growing foreign debt. This led to pressures, both from within and outside, for economic reforms to promote stabilization, structural adjustment, and liberalization. Morocco and Tunisia experienced these pressures first, Mauritania and Algeria somewhat later. Only Libya, with its growing oil revenues, managed to avoid most of these pressures.[51]

Morocco was by the second half of the 1970s in serious economic difficulties. In 1978, a three-year stabilization program was introduced, but austerity measures were met by a wave of strikes throughout the winter and spring of 1978–1979. The government faced pressure from international creditors to implement more far-reaching "adjustment," but when implemented these resulted once again in widespread social unrest: in June 1981, price increases provoked strikes and demonstrations; the resultant clashes between protesters and the security forces left more than 600 people dead in Casablanca alone. The government understandably hesitated to push ahead with more stringent policies but risked the disapproval of the IMF and the World Bank and the withdrawal of their support. By 1982, however, the external public long-term debt was about two-thirds of GDP and more than twice the value of all exported goods and services. In August 1983, a rigorous stabilization program was initiated. The IMF approved and signed a stand-by arrangement for Special Drawing Rights (SDR) 300 million; shortly thereafter, Morocco's creditors initiated a program for debt relief and support for exceptional balance of payments assistance. A second round of cuts in subsidies led to further price rises in December, and the draft budget for 1984 proposed to raise prices again.

At the beginning of January 1984, a wave of strikes, street demonstrations, and clashes between protesters and security forces washed across Morocco's major cities. After two weeks of sustained social unrest, during which around 9,000 people were arrested and some 400 killed, the king was prepared to appease the protesters and rule out price increases in the 1984 budget. But, apparently oblivious to the political repercussions, the international financial institutions pressed for more of the same. The Moroccan government was obliged to implement rigorous austerity measures and embark on a far-reaching structural adjustment program; this brought renewed support from the IMF and the World Bank and from the Paris Club during 1986–87.[52]

In Tunisia, the emphasis on state-led growth in the 1960s was reversed over the next decade or so: in the late 1960s, over 85 percent of investment in manufacturing came from the public sector; by 1976, it was only 40 percent. The dismissal of the Minister of Finance, Economy and Planning in 1969 marked the turn toward economic liberalism; further initiatives in the early 1970s consolidated the trend. A relatively strong economic performance over the next decade or so was, however, insufficient to offset the effects of the deepening international recession and growing European protectionism. Despite the new investment code, foreign investment dropped from $339 million in 1982 to $62 million in 1986,[53] and the external debt rose from $106 million in 1970 to $2.2 billion in 1985. Further reforms, including cuts in subsidies on consumer goods, were introduced, which provoked widespread rioting in January 1984. The government retreated temporarily, but in 1985 accepted the IMF stand-by arrangement it had avoided for so long: "Tunisia adopted the usual recipe: cut the budget, cut investment, reduce subsidies, devalue the currency."[54] Virtually all state controls were removed on investment in industries deemed to sell in competitive markets (covering some 60 percent of industrial production), effectively deregulating prices. The trade deficit fell by about 10 percent, but exports continued to decline and the entire program was overwhelmed in 1986 by the collapse in oil prices.

In Mauritania, severe drought exacerbated a generally dismal economic performance through the 1970s; it also precipitated the overthrow of Ould Daddah's regime in 1978 and the withdrawal of Mauritania from the costly war in the western Sahara. The new military government's Five Year Plan (1981–1985) involved an ambitious investment program to help restore economic growth, but by 1983 the difficulty of achieving plan targets was apparent. Drought struck again and the government declared the whole country a disaster area. Between 1980 and 1984, average annual growth was only 0.2 percent; the balance of payments deficit in 1984 was equivalent to 26 percent of GNP, and the level of foreign debt more than twice GNP. In December 1984, Ould Taya seized power; his government immediately initiated a short-term stabilization program (in agreement with the IMF) in April 1985 and drew up a Program for Economic and Financial Adjustment (PREF). The PREF involved a 16 percent devaluation, cuts in public expenditure, and reductions in subsidies. During the four years of the PREF (1985–1988) economic growth was 3.6 percent a year, inflation was reduced, and the financial situation improved significantly. But the social costs were considerable as cuts in public expenditure hit the more vulnerable sections of the population through higher prices, wage freezes, and job losses (especially in the public sector).[55]

In the case of Algeria, it was not until the mid-1980s that economic liberalization became clear government policy, although there had already been attempts to redress growing economic problems by encouraging the private sector and rationalizing public sector enterprises without abandoning state control. Richards and Waterbury have referred to this strategy, which began in 1982, as "*infitah* with a socialist face."[56] By the mid-1980s, this strategy was replaced by more vigorous economic liberalization. In October 1988, largely as a result of the social impact of the austerity measures introduced, Algeria was rocked by serious unrest. The state responded with unprecedented violence, and several hundred Algerians were killed in clashes between the security forces and protesters. Over the next ten years, Algeria was to slide into a bloody civil war.

Even Libya, which had been effectively insulated from the international recession of 1979–1983 by its oil revenues, was hit by falling oil prices during the 1980s: rates of growth in GDP went into reverse during the first half of the decade as international oil prices slumped to an average –6.1 percent a year. Internal opposition began to mount, and the Libyan regime initiated a series of repressive measures to quell opposition at home and abroad. The latter, combined with a series of "adventurist" foreign initiatives, including active intervention in Chad, were to lead to Libya's international political isolation during the late 1980s and 1990s.

Throughout the rest of the Maghrib, economic liberalization opened up national economies to international market forces while popular protest threatened to destabilize the regimes that had undertaken the reforms. The reform of the economies of the Maghrib failed to promote any significant intraregional flows of capital or commodities—trade with other Maghrib economies had by the mid–1980s rarely risen above 5 percent of any state's external trade, and in some cases had fallen in percentage terms since the late 1950s[57]—but the dependence of the Maghrib economies on Europe and the OECD was increased, if anything, rather than diminished by their liberalization.

In the early 1980s, Italy was still Libya's major trading partner, supplying one fifth of its total imports and purchasing nearly one fifth of its exports. Other EC countries also figured strongly in Libyan trade statistics. Between 1965 and 1985, the share of Algeria's total merchandise exports to the OECD remained at over 90 percent, with the bulk of these exports going to France. Tunisia's economic liberalization was also associated with an increase in the proportion of its total merchandise exports going to the OECD, up from 61 percent in 1965 to 81 percent by 1985. Morocco was in much the same position, with EC countries providing about half of its imports and taking about half of its exports, France alone accounting for roughly one fifth of imports and a quarter of exports. Mauritania's principal trading partners during the 1980s were France and Spain: imports from France and Spain constituted between a third and a quarter of total imports, and exports to those two countries alone accounted for approximately one fifth of all exports.

Recognizing its unavoidably close relations with Europe, Morocco applied to join the EC in 1984; the application was rejected. Morocco expressed concern at the effective protectionism of the EC despite its formal commitment to trade liberalization, and new quota agreements were signed in 1985; it was later agreed that voluntary quotas on manufactured goods should be abandoned, but no agreement was reached regarding agricultural exports. In 1987, Morocco again applied for membership—and was again rejected. Its poor human rights record did not help its case.

International Politics

If Europe still dominated the weakened and divided Maghrib economies while keeping them at arms length, and liberalization increased dependency on Europe and failed to promote closer economic cooperation within the Maghrib, popular unrest at home and political divisions between the Maghrib states also played their part in preventing closer integration during this period. As economic and political crisis at home increasingly preoccupied the governments of the Maghrib during the late 1970s and early 1980s, the issue of the conflict in the western Sahara in particular continued to divide Morocco and Algeria, making effective regional cooperation impossible.

In July 1979, the OAU summit endorsed proposals for an immediate cease-fire and a referendum in the western Sahara. In the same year, Mauritania signed a peace treaty with the POLISARIO and effectively withdrew from the conflict. Through 1979 and 1980, both the Non-Aligned Movement and the UN General Assembly deplored Morocco's occupation of the western Sahara and affirmed the right of the Saharawis to self-determination. In 1980, a narrow majority of OAU members, including Libya, recognized the SADR. In February 1983, pressure from Algeria and other pro-SADR states enabled it to become the fifty-first member state of the OAU. Eighteen other African states supported Morocco, but Morocco, which had now broken off relations with Libya on account of its support for the Saharawis, found itself increasingly isolated within the Maghrib.

In February 1982, despite an incident in 1980 involving a guerrilla raid on the Tunisian mining town of Gafsa, attributed to Libya, Tunisia and Libya signed a mutual cooperation agreement. In March 1983, largely as a means of building a common front against Morocco over the western Sahara issue, Tunisia and Algeria signed a twenty-year-long Treaty of Fraternity and Cooperation, which Mauritania joined in December. The Treaty was dominated by Algeria, which required all adherents to resolve outstanding border problems as a precursor to joining. Libya was not included, despite visits by President Qadhdhafi to both Morocco and Algeria during the second half of 1983. The Libyan regime, embroiled in Chad through the first part of the 1980s, also began to experience increased political opposition both at home and abroad. Attempts to liquidate dissidents abroad led to an incident outside the Libyan People's Bureau in London in 1984, when several people were injured and a British policewoman was killed by shots fired from the bureau.[58] Britain immediately broke off diplomatic relations.

In 1984, Morocco and Libya (both facing increasing international isolation) created an Arab-African Federation, which provided for a confederational structure and economic cooperation. This move, seen apparently by Qadhdhafi as the first step toward the creation of a Greater Maghrib, was very much an attempt by King Hassan to neutralize Libya's support for the POLISARIO in the western Sahara. Mauritania recognized the SADR in February 1984, and Morocco withdrew from the OAU. The SADR finally took its seat, and in July 1985, the president of the SADR was elected as one of the OAU vice-presidents.

The Moroccan-Libyan alliance soon collapsed, following the announcement in 1985 of a treaty between Libya and Iran, and the meeting in 1986 of King Hassan with Israel's Shimon Peres. Libya's relations with the other Maghrib states also deteriorated. In 1985, Egyptians were barred from working in Libya, allegedly in retaliation against a measure preventing Libyans from working in Egypt; about 30,000 Tunisian workers were also deported, Tunisian imports halted, and diplomatic relations between Tunisia and Libya severed. In November 1985, Libya was accused by Egypt of coordinating the hijacking of an Egyptian airliner, and there was increasing tension between the two countries. Egypt later revealed that it had refrained from military action against Libya despite pressure from the United States.

After Britain broke off diplomatic relations with Libya over the incident outside the Libyan People's Bureau in London in April 1984, relations between Libya and the West continued to deteriorate. In November 1985, details of a plan by the CIA to undermine Qadhdhafi's regime were revealed in the American press, and the U.S. government openly accused Libya of harboring and training members of Abu Nidal's Fatah Revolutionary Council and of being "a centre for international terrorism." In January 1986, President Reagan ordered the severing of all economic and commercial relations with Libya and the freezing of Libyan assets in the United States. He was, however, unsuccessful in persuading his European allies to impose economic sanctions. The United States deployed its Sixth Navy to begin maneuvers off the Libyan coast. In March, Libya fired SAM missiles at U.S. fighter planes straying close in-shore; in retaliation U.S. aircraft destroyed Libyan facilities in the town of Sirte and sank four patrol boats. In April 1986, following an explosion in West Berlin, identified by the United States as an act of Libyan terrorism, American military aircraft bombed a range of targets in Tripoli and Benghazi. While the U.S. raids were deplored, there was little support for Libya, even from other members of the Arab League.

At the end of 1988, the crash of PanAm Flight 103 over Lockerbie in Scotland and widespread suspicion that this was the result of the explosion of a bomb planted on the plane by two Libyans heightened U.S. and European hostility towards the Libyan regime. Another plane crash, this time over Niger, in September 1989, was also attributed by the French to the Libyans. Renewed concerns about Libya's role in "international terrorism" were expressed by Western politicians, and in 1992 sanctions were imposed by the United Nations. For the next decade, Libya would be identified as a "pariah state" and barred from normal economic and political relations with the rest of the world.[59]

Growing concern about Libya's role in international terrorism, the threat of a widening regional conflict in the Gulf involving the United States, Iran, and Iraq, and the rising tension between Israel and the Palestinians (the *intifada* began in 1987) involving Lebanon and Syria, all focused attention once again on the Mediterranean as a region of strategic significance for Europe. Ten years before, an evaluation of the EC's so-called global Mediterranean policy, while recognizing the economic significance of trade with the Mediterranean countries and of migrant labor from the region, underlined the strategic and security-related concern as being one of primary importance in any coherent "policy" toward the region.[60]

The enlargement of the EC in 1986 was preceded by an announcement reiterating the importance attached by the EC, despite a period of abeyance in fact of nearly a decade, to a global Mediterranean policy—an importance that "would not be diminished by the accession of Spain and Portugal to the

Community." Once again, Europe directed its attention to its relationship with the countries on its southern periphery, now seeing security as a major issue to be added to that of economic relations.[61]

The United Arab Maghrib

The prospect of a renewed thrust by the EC to define relations with its periphery prompted new efforts by the Maghrib states to develop closer links among themselves. In 1986, Libya proposed a union with Algeria; Algeria, pointing to the existence of the Maghrib Fraternity and Cooperation Treaty of 1983 between Algeria, Mauritania, and Tunisia, suggested Libya join that instead. Links between the two countries continued to develop. In February 1988, the three heads of state of Algeria, Tunisia, and Libya discussed the idea of a regional accord, following which the border between Libya and Tunisia was reopened. In March 1988, Libya and Algeria signed two agreements relating to industrial development, and the following month, Libya and Tunisia signed a cooperation pact encompassing political, economic, cultural, and foreign relations.

During the latter part of the 1980s, despite the continuing disagreement over the future of the western Sahara, the economic and political situation in Algeria deteriorated. The Algerian government reduced its support for the POLISARIO, and the balance of forces in the desert war swung increasingly toward Morocco. At the same time, the prospect of continuing economic liberalization in the face of an enlarged and even more dominant EC prompted a reappraisal of regional economic cooperation. Cautiously, Morocco and Algeria moved slowly toward a closer relationship; in May 1988, they renewed diplomatic relations. The next month, the five heads of state met in Algiers after the Arab summit to discuss prospects for "a Maghrib without frontiers." Shortly afterwards, rail links between Morocco and Algeria were reestablished, the electricity grids joined, and a framework agreed for the further development of transport and communications links; Algeria and Libya discussed the basis for a federation of the two states within a Greater Arab Maghrib; and all of the Maghrib states agreed to send their most senior representatives to regular meetings of the newly established Maghrib Commission. Despite continuing disagreement between Morocco and Algeria over the western Sahara, both countries affirmed their commitment to "a just and final solution" to the conflict based on a referendum for self-determination.

In July 1988, the Maghrib Commission met in Algiers and set up working parties to consider integration in finance and economics, regional security, and education. In August, the Tunisian president visited Libya, signed a series of cooperation agreements, and established a technical commission to accelerate the process of integration. At a second meeting of Maghrib heads of state held in February 1989, the participants concluded a Treaty proclaiming the formation of a Union of the Arab Maghrib (UAM) involving the five Maghrib states, designed to promote and orchestrate improved economic relations within the Maghrib.[62]

The objective was to promote the eventual free movement of capital, goods and services, and labor throughout the countries of the region. Significantly, they sidestepped the issue of the western Sahara—the UAM effectively excluded the SADR from its vision of a united independent Maghrib. A heads-of-state council and foreign-minister council were set up; plans were also made for a parliamentary consultative council, initially of 50 members, but this was doubled in January 1990. Common juridical and financial institutions were also planned. At the second summit meeting of the UAM, held in Algiers in July 1990, it was agreed that Libya would hold the annual presidency in 1991. Plans were drawn up in December 1990 for a staged program of integration—a free trade zone by 1992, a customs union by 1995, and a full common market by the year 2000.

In 1990 and 1991, Iraq's invasion of Kuwait and the subsequent "crisis" diverted attention away from economic issues to those of security in the region. It also tested the capacity of the UAM to develop and sustain a broadly unified position on a crucial yet divisive political issue. When the Arab League met in Cairo in August, Egypt pushed for a resolution supporting a military response involving Western as well as Arab forces. This was opposed by Libya. Mauritania expressed reservations. Algeria abstained. Tunisia boycotted the meeting. Only Morocco supported the proposal and promised 1,500 troops for the multinational force; but King Hassan emphasized that the gesture was purely symbolic and that despite opposing the Iraqi invasion, he recognized the reasons for it and criticized "the greed of our Kuwaiti friends."[63] At the beginning of September 1990, the foreign ministers of the UAM produced a working document setting out a common position, "as a contribution to the search for a solution to the Gulf crisis."

From that time onward, there was a consistent effort on the part of the members of the UAM to develop a coherent approach to a negotiated settlement and "an Arab solution" to the crisis. In October, despite protests from the Maghrib states (including Morocco), the Arab League moved its headquarters from Tunis to Cairo. This, together with the growing commitment of the United States and its allies in the Mashriq to a military build-up and possible war in the Gulf, alarmed the governments of the Maghrib. The Tunisian president, Ben Ali, declared that "Tunisia was re-doubling its diplomatic efforts," and Morocco revised its initial support for the multinational force in the Gulf. King Hassan's call in November for an extraordinary Arab summit to provide "a new and last chance" for a peaceful solution was supported by the other Maghrib states. But the Arab summit never took place. The initiative now moved away from the Maghrib and, indeed, from the Arab world altogether. In the meanwhile, Mauritania had adopted a more positively pro-Iraq stance, at odds with the rest of the Maghrib states. But all of the UAM continued to call for "an Arab solution" right up to (and indeed after) the actual assault on Kuwait and Iraq on January 17, 1991.

In the aftermath of the Gulf War, the divisions within the Arab world were greater than ever. But the Maghrib states had shown a capacity for coordinated diplomatic and political activity during the Gulf crisis; could they maintain that impetus and develop the basis for lasting economic and political cooperation through the UAM? Economic trade and tariff reductions were signed in March 1991; proposals were made for a Maghrib Bank for Foreign Investment and Trade and for a Maghrib International Bank; and plans to move toward standardized exchange rates and the free movement of capital and goods through the UAM were initiated. But, although the UAM heads of state were supposed to meet once every six months, the March 1991 summit was postponed because of disagreements over the UAM's attitude toward U.S. proposals for a Middle East peace conference and because of differences over the Western Sahara. A special summit called in June 1991 (instead of March) was canceled at short notice because of the internal political crisis in Algeria. The next summit, in September 1991, was not attended by Colonel Qadhdhafi, now engaged in an attempt to develop a closer relationship with Egypt. The meeting agreed that the UAM secretariat was to be located in Morocco; the secretary-general was to be a Tunisian; the consultative council was to be located in Algeria, the UAM court in Mauritania, the new financial institutions in Tunisia, and the UAM academy of sciences in Libya.

But UAM activities were faltering. In 1992, Libya effectively withdrew from the organization in reaction to UAM compliance with UN sanctions; Algeria, preoccupied with the rise of the Islamic opposition and deterioration of its internal security situation, had little time for UAM affairs; Mauritania, the weakest of the Maghrib economies, embarked on a new program of structural adjustment under the auspices of the IMF and the World Bank;[64] and Morocco and Tunisia began to concentrate on developing new bilateral relations with the European Union. Joffe argued in 1993 that "the most important and most immediate economic issue facing the five states . . . is that of their relations with the EC in the light of the Single European Market in 1993 and full Spanish and Portuguese membership in 1996. They must anticipate a more difficult trading relationship with Europe as a result of both of these developments and the UAM must, therefore, offer an alternative economic forum for growth."[65] There was little sign, however, that the member states of the UAM were able to constitute "an alternative economic forum for growth." All of the Maghrib governments continued formally to subscribe to the UAM's objectives, but the UAM had been eclipsed and in fact undermined—in part by renewed efforts by Europe to shape its relations with its southern periphery and in part by the preoccupation of the Maghrib states with domestic economic and political concerns.

One of the features that the Maghrib states shared at the beginning of the 1990s was a growing popular challenge to the legitimacy not only of government economic policies but of the regimes themselves. While in Mauritania this led to a cautious but progressive political liberalization, one of the most striking developments in the rest of the Maghrib in the aftermath of the Gulf War was the rise of Islamic militantism. Not confined to the Maghrib—the countries of the Mashriq and Turkey have been importantly affected over the last five years—this proved of major political significance, particularly in Algeria and Tunisia (and Egypt) where the struggle between the state security forces and the paramilitary elements of the Islamic movements has been bitter and bloody.

In Morocco, the government pushed ahead in the late 1980s and early 1990s with economic liberalization and privatization, despite growing concern over the adverse social effects of drastic reductions in public expenditure. The government was able to limit overt opposition to economic reforms and suppress—with effective use of the state security forces—any potential social or political unrest. This gave rise to growing concern in Europe and elsewhere regarding the human rights situation in Morocco. As far as the economy was concerned, however, only the burgeoning foreign debt appeared to worry Morocco's international creditors, and even they were prepared to ignore this problem and to continue to lend heavily to support wholesale economic reform and further liberalization. The EC has supported this program.

In Tunisia, as in Morocco, continuing economic reform gave rise to serious social hardship, and many—the urban poor in particular—suffered from serious deprivation and a decline in living standards. With increasing restrictions on immigrant workers in Europe, employment opportunities, as well as remittances from workers abroad—a major source of foreign exchange since the mid 1960s—fell significantly, as in Morocco. After the Gulf War, Islamic opposition movements began to gain ground, but the government managed to maintain control, largely through heavy state repression of the Islamists. The human rights abuses, although less well known than those of Morocco or Algeria, have given rise to growing international concern.

In Algeria, a degree of political liberalization followed the bloody clashes of 1988. The Islamic Salvation Front (FIS), which had rapidly gathered strength, was officially recognized in September 1989; and in June 1990, it swept to power in the first contested municipal elections since independence, wresting control of all major metropolitan areas from the ruling FLN. The rise of the Islamists as a major political force was confirmed when the FIS proved successful in the first round of the legislative election at the end of 1991. Because of fear that the FIS would come to power through the ballot box, the elections were stopped in January 1992; within a month the FIS was outlawed and thousands of known or suspected supporters arrested and jailed. A state of emergency was declared, and for the next seven years, a virtual civil war tore Algeria apart, with estimates of up to 100,000 dead.[66]

The rise of Islamism during the 1990s is one aspect of a more general determination on the part of the people of the region to express their anger and outrage at what is widely seen as a failure of governments to provide economic policies that safeguard security and welfare and more broadly as a failure to provide the framework for social justice and development. It has emerged out of the groundswell of popular opposition to the austerity measures that accompanied the economic reforms of the 1980s, but it has become increasingly more orchestrated and more ideologically defined.[67]

Increased internal conflict and a growing human rights problem throughout the Maghrib, combined with the concern about Libya's involvement in terrorism, the failure to resolve the conflict in the western Sahara, and continuing political uncertainties of the Middle East in the aftermath of the Gulf War, heightened perceptions in Europe of the entire region of North Africa and the Middle East as a major "security risk." This, in turn, led to renewed efforts by the EC to extend its influence and even control in the Mediterranean.

Europe and the Maghrib in the 1990s

The EC Commissioner for Mediterranean policy congratulated the member states of the new Union of the Arab Maghrib and attempted to calm fears of the possible detrimental effect on EC-UAM trade of the creation of a single European market in 1992, arguing that the new regional grouping would facilitate cooperation between the EC and the Maghrib. President Mitterrand gave the UAM his approval during his visit to Algeria in March 1989 and expressed the hope that it would help reduce tensions and conflict in the region. In December 1989, the European Commission reaffirmed its concern to strengthen ties with all the countries of the Mediterranean; one of the Commission's first initiatives in the context of its "proximity policy" was to present the main points of a "revised Mediterranean policy." This was to go beyond the framework established at the beginning of the 1970s, which was considered "no longer appropriate for the needs of the 1990s." The commission emphasized the importance to Europe of the stability and prosperity of the Mediterranean countries—indeed, the Mediterranean area was seen as "a key element in the stability, prosperity and security" of the Commission itself.[68]

In 1991, the EC announced an aid program that would provide a total of $5.8 billion for eight Mediterranean countries, half of it in the form of concessionary loans. For the three "favored" Maghrib states a rise in aid was envisaged: 46 percent more for Algeria, 31.5 percent for Morocco, and 27 percent for Tunisia. Morocco would receive $543 million, making it the largest beneficiary. But even when the additional structural adjustment aid of 300 million Ecu and funding for regional projects of around 2 billion Ecu was added, the total remained small—less than $1 billion annually. Morocco's aid protocol was also delayed by nine months as a result of a protest by the European Parliament against human rights abuses. Morocco, in return, initially rejected the protocol until appeased by the offer of a free trade agreement.

Despite assurances from Commissioner Abel Matutes and promises of a reevaluation of EC economic policy toward the Maghrib, "the proposals put forward . . . showed little novelty. In essence, they sustained the traditional policies of limited aid but did not offer the economic cooperation that the UAM states so desperately seek and require. Although additional aid was promised, particularly to smooth the path of economic restructuring, there was no bold initiative on economic development or migration, nor, even, on foreign debt."[69] For two of the members of the UAM there was nothing; neither Libya nor Mauritania was included in the EC's vision for "the Maghrib."

Libya, especially since the imposition of UN sanctions in 1992, has been regarded as a virtual pariah by virtue of its distinctive political stance on what have been seen as key security issues in the region. As Jon Marks has observed, Libya "has been reduced by political problems to becoming a white void on the European Commission's increasingly complex map of relations with the so-called Mediterranean Non-Community (MNC) countries."[70] The EC 1992–1996 Fourth Financial Protocol—which produced Cooperation Agreements with Morocco, Tunisia, and Algeria—excluded Libya, despite its membership in the UAM. Only towards the end of the 1990s was there a gradual process of rehabilitation—initiated by members of the OAU (in particular South Africa)—leading eventually in 1999 to the lifting of UN sanctions, the restoration of diplomatic relations with Britain, and the reestablishment of economic and political relations with the wider world.[(71)]

In the case of Mauritania, which was considered to be outside the Mediterranean region on which European policy was now focused, political reforms in 1991 opened up the way for an agreement with the EC under

Lome IV for the period 1992–1994, based on "a very clear and precise program of economic reform."[72] The objectives of the new structural adjustment program were to reduce the country's external debt and improve its balance of payments by devaluation and liberalization, including cuts in public expenditure and reduction of subsidies to help remove "price distortions." Food prices rose immediately by 40 percent and there were riots, leading the government to impose a curfew in the capital, Nouakchott. External "donors," however, approved the austerity measures, and the IMF agreed to a loan to support the economic and financial reform program to September 1995. By 1993 external debt had risen to $2.2 billion, but in May 1994 the "donor" states promised to support the economic reform program to the end of 1996, and in January 1995, the IMF approved a series of loans to run through to 1997. That month, a 25 percent increase in bread prices again provoked serious rioting and clashes in Nouakchott between protesters and security forces, the imposition of a curfew, and a ban on all demonstrations.[73]

Despite this differential treatment by the EC of the UAM member states, "Maghrib unity" has often been presented as complementary to closer and improved relations with the EC. In 1993, for example, George Joffe argued that a formal link between the EC and the UAM "could play a fundamental role in the strengthening and deepening of the UAM process of cooperation and integration."[74] Indeed, he went further and intimated that if Europe did not intervene, the UAM would prove incapable of effective development: "Unless there are bold EC initiatives to help the UAM, this initiative for regional economic integration and development will wither on the vine. Instead, member states will have to deal with their problems separately and will become ever more dependent on an unsympathetic Europe."[75] It has also frequently been argued that economic liberalization in the Maghrib would in itself serve to increase the potential for regional integration. However, in fact, despite a number of bilateral economic links and projects, and a broad commitment to regional economic integration, the UAM has failed to promote a common project of economic and political cooperation.

One reason for this failure is the fact that the UAM member states have undergone more than a decade of reforms designed to further liberalize and "open up" their economies and to reduce the role of the state. This has tended to weaken their capacity for planning, coordination, and collective action. Although some would argue that there is no intrinsic reason why economic liberalization should *not* result in increasing intra-Maghrib capital, commodity, and labor flows, there is little evidence that local regional groupings can alter the dominant north-south direction of such flows without very considerable state and suprastate orchestration. Economic liberalization is inherently inimical to such state intervention.

More significantly still, the failure of the UAM to develop more effective cooperation can be explained in part as a direct result of the initiatives taken by the EC in recent years to "carve up" the Maghrib—thereby directly undermining the UAM—and to integrate favored Maghrib states (Morocco, Tunisia, and Algeria) individually rather than collectively into an unequal partnership in which the enlarged EC (now the EU) is enabled to maintain and deepen its historic dominance and hegemony over individual Maghrib economies.

The advent of the Single European Market after 1992 meant that the Maghrib economies, required to "open up" themselves, increasingly faced serious nontariff barriers (particularly regarding standards and quality restrictions) for their industrial (and even some of their agricultural) exports. Even more strikingly, explicit new controls on the immigration of labor were introduced as a result of the Schengen and Trevi Agreements and the national policies that have been systematically developed by governments in Germany, Britain, France, Spain, and Italy. These informal mechanisms of economic protection and formal (legal) controls on immigration have led to the construction of what some refer to as a "Fortress Europe," to which access by Mediterranean exporters and migrant workers is carefully circumscribed and controlled but from which investment and exports (and tourists) may flow freely into the "adjusted" and "open" economies of the Maghrib and Mediterranean.

There are currently some 2.3 million Maghribi migrants in Europe—representing 8 to 10 percent of the region's labor force. But restrictions imposed on immigrants and on those seeking asylum by governments of the EC member states have increasingly restricted access to employment and residence in Europe; the "free market" does not extend to Maghribi labor. The increasing restrictions on the flow of migrant labor into Europe will have a significant adverse effect within the Maghrib. The rate of demographic increase in the Maghrib is such that Algeria needs to create 90,000 jobs a year to keep pace with demand, while Morocco needs over 70,000 and Tunisia 40,000. To achieve this, national growth rates in GDP would need to be in the order of 2.5 to 3 percent annually. While long-term trends suggest this is feasible (GDP growth over the period from 1960 to 1994 was 4.6 percent for Morocco and 5.3 percent for Tunisia), more recent figures suggest much lower growth. Unemployment is likely, therefore, to rise substantially in the absence of a major expansion of employment opportunities within the region through a substantial growth in the productivity, output, and exports of key sectors of the Maghrib economies. Prospects for such growth are not good, and the social and political implications of large numbers unemployed or on low wages are very serious. The popular unrest that has fueled support for Islamic militancy throughout the Maghrib is closely linked to the failure of economic policies over the last two decades to provide adequate levels of employment at reasonable wages and ensure basic welfare.

The rise of militant Islam in the countries of the southern and eastern Mediterranean littoral during the early part of the 1990s was increasingly seen in Europe to pose a distinct and powerful threat to European security. This, linked to the growing concern regarding immigration from this region, provides a political basis for a renewed effort by Europe to develop a coherent policy toward the region. In fact, it could be argued that "the development of a pro-active European policy towards the MNCs (Mediterranean non-Community Countries) has been founded on a perceived need for Europe to act to defend itself from further instability in the south."[76]

In June 1994, the EU summit at Corfu called for "a new policy" toward eastern Europe and the Mediterranean. One of the key documents produced subsequently proposed that "the objective should be to work towards a Euro-Mediterranean Partnership. This would start with a process of progressive establishment of free trade, supported by substantial financial aid. It would then develop through closer political and economic cooperation, towards a close association, the content of which would be jointly defined at a later stage."[77] In November 1995, a meeting in Barcelona of 27 foreign ministers representing the member states of the EU and 12 Mediterranean "partners"—including Morocco, Algeria, and Tunisia in the Maghrib—unanimously adopted the Barcelona Declaration establishing a Euro-Mediterranean Partnership (EMP).

The declared objective of the EMP was to create, by 2010, a free trade area linking the Mediterranean countries on Europe's southern periphery with the single European market. The EMP had three dimensions: a political and security "partnership," an economic and financial "partnership," and a "partnership" in social, cultural, and human affairs. Each was to be implemented in two separate but complementary ways: via bilateral agreements, and regionally. Priority, however, appears in practice to be accorded to the bilateral economic association agreements; the first two of which were signed in 1995 by Tunisia and Morocco. Others were expected to follow shortly thereafter, including Egypt and Jordan but not Algeria. Turkey and Israel have also concluded trade accords that will draw them into the European Economic Area (EEA). This implies, according to EU officials, a natural extension of the single European market: "The whole Euro-Med idea comes from European history and European construction. From 1958 to Maastricht Europe has been about a body of countries becoming integrated economically and then moving towards political cooperation . . . This implies that there are links of neighbourhood and a steady accumulation of building blocs."[78]

In fact, Lawrence[79] argues that the types of agreements being concluded between the EU and the Mediterranean countries, while having the potential to become "deep integration" arrangements, are perhaps better characterized in fact as simple traditional trade arrangements with an element of support for restructuring and liberalization, but not involving flows of investment, services, or labor. In fact, the contrast between the emphasis on "free trade" into the Maghrib and the growing restrictions on the "free" flow of labor into Europe are striking: "Free trade, Yes (with restrictions); free movement of labour, No!" Also there is little sign of a flow of investment into the Maghrib, while the comparative advantage of the Maghrib with respect to certain agricultural and fish products has been effectively countered by the inclusion of Greece, Spain, and Portugal within the EU. Meanwhile, the European Union (in January 1995) had incorporated Austria, Sweden, and Finland as full members of the EU and was already developing plans for the inclusion of six further full members by 2002–2003, of which only one (Cyprus) was "Mediterranean."

The Maghrib, like the rest of the Mediterranean, has, in effect, been further peripheralized and fragmented. The "partnership" with the Maghrib has focused in practice on two economies out of five. Tunisia and Morocco have both signed comprehensive "integration" agreements with the EU—the first in July 1995 with Tunisia and the second in November with Morocco. One reason given for the prioritization of these was their strong dependence on Europe. In the case of Morocco, France remains overwhelmingly its largest trading partner, accounting for roughly a quarter of Moroccan imports and roughly a third of Moroccan exports. Capital goods comprise about one third of French exports, while consumer goods account for more than one half of imports from Morocco. Spain and then Italy are the two next most important sources of imports and markets for exports. In the first half of the 1990s, approximately half of Morocco's imports came from EC countries, and roughly three-quarters of Morocco's exports went to countries of the EC. A very similar picture obtains in the case of Tunisia, whose international trade is again dominated by France, which accounts for about one third of imports and a quarter of exports, with Germany and Italy as the next most important trading partners. In 1992, Tunisia imported goods worth $4.5 billion from countries of the EC, out of a total of $6.4 billion, and in 1994, $4.4 billion out of $6.5 billion. As regards exports, in 1992, Tunisia exported goods worth $3.1 billion out of a total of $4 billion to countries of the EC, and in 1994, $3.6 billion out of $4.6 billion.

The agreements of the EU with Tunisia and Morocco involve increased aid flows and technical assistance in return for reductions in trade barriers and other impediments to the flow of goods and investment into the Maghrib economies over a period of 12 years. Nearly half of the proposed assistance to the region from the EU's expanded aid program, however, is directed at increased liberalization, which will have the inevitable effect of strengthening existing patterns of comparative advantage. Unfortunately, regarding comparative advantage in a more liberal trading environment, analysts from the World Bank conclude that both Morocco and Tunisia have declining comparative advantage in general, relative to potential trading partners in Europe.[80] Industry-specific estimates tell much the same story; dynamic comparative advantage is also deteriorating at the industry level. Analysis of Morocco and Tunisia's trade patterns suggests a comparative advantage in agriculture and fisheries, but recent agreements regarding access to the European market in agricultural and processed agricultural exports tend to be restrictive—although both allow some scope for expanded agro-industrial exports.[81] Furthermore, Spain and Portugal have now been granted full membership after a ten-year transitional period, and this will severely affect Moroccan and Tunisian agricultural exports.

Analysis of the Tunisian agreement in particular[82] suggests that Tunisia may not have a great deal to gain from entering into this "free trade agreement" with the EU. It will require Tunisia (which already has duty-free access to the EU, except for some agricultural products and certain types of clothing) to eliminate its bilateral tariffs vis-à-vis the EU. The trade diverting effects of such a discriminatory tariff reduction are likely to be harmful, especially in the short run. They conclude that Tunisia will gain little or nothing from the agreement, in the short run at least, and could experience significant adjustment problems stemming from labor and capital movement. Moreover, in the absence of complementary policy actions, no large inflow of foreign direct investment is expected.

Page and Underwood conclude that substantial benefits are unlikely to accrue to either of the two Maghrib countries without additional policies to promote export production and international (global) trade on the one hand; they also argue, interestingly, for the need to promote greater intra-Maghrib trade on the other. The World Bank experts are clearly unprepared to argue that the proposed arrangements with the EU are entirely disadvantageous to the two Maghrib economies involved, but they suggest the need for a parallel agreement that liberalizes trade between the two countries within the overall EU framework and recommend that "both Morocco and Tunisia should begin negotiations for a free trade agreement between themselves."[83]

This is, ironically, precisely what was envisaged, albeit on Maghrib-wide scale, by the UAM, rather than between two states on a bilateral basis. Such moves toward the development of a Maghrib-wide economic union have, however, already been systematically undermined by unequal liberalization under the auspices of the EU. Intra-Maghrib trade remains low, despite the UAM. In the 1990s, less than 5 percent of Morocco's imports came from her Maghrib neighbors and about 7 percent of Moroccan exports went to the three other members of the UAM. Between 4 and 5 percent of Tunisia's imports came from others within the UAM, while between 6 and 7 percent of Tunisian exports went to countries in the UAM.

The undoubted disadvantages to the two Maghrib economies of the arrangements under the EMP could, the World Bank experts suggest, be positively affected by technological upgrading, which depends primarily on foreign direct investment and expansion of exports. They recommend an "export push" strategy combined with policies to attract foreign direct investment to produce an expansion of nontraditional exports for the global market. Policies of this kind, adopted by the governments of the Maghrib states, they suggest, could increase the chances of agreements recently reached with the EU under the Euro-Med integration agreements fulfilling their promise.

But there is little indication that foreign direct investment is growing, while exports face a variety of informal (as well as some formal) barriers. Indeed, Page and Underwood themselves argue, with respect to both Morocco and Tunisia, that "the existing 'hub and spoke' nature of the EU agreements provides no strategic motivation for investors to locate in either economy to serve both markets, nor does it facilitate production sharing arrangements."[84] But the "hub and spoke" nature of the agreements is clearly a crucial feature of the EU strategy and effectively precludes such "complementary" measures by Maghrib governments. The process of liberalization and the terms of the so-called Euro-Med Partnership are limited and highly inequitable; they effectively create a virtual "one-way street" leading from Europe into the Mediterranean partner economies.

Conclusion

During the late 1970s and early 1980s, the project of genuinely independent development for the Maghrib—always a hostage to nationalist dreams and projects and constrained by strong ties to Europe (particularly to France)—was increasingly compromised by mounting debt and growing pressures for economic reform, which led during the 1980s and 1990s to structural adjustment and liberalization. This, while promising access to the benefits of globalization and the "free market," effectively undermined still further the possibilities for independent yet coordinated regional development. It also increased the vulnerability of the individual Maghrib economies to exploitation as separate parts of the periphery of a new Euro-Med region constituted by a hegemonic Europe demanding "free trade" for others while maintaining a strong "fortress" to protect its own strategic interests.

The evidence suggests that the tentative program of the UAM for greater *horizontal* cooperation within the Maghrib has effectively conflicted with the long-standing and now reinforced European policy of *vertical* integration of the Maghrib states into a Europe-dominated regional association. In the first (the UAM), Maghribi solidarity in the face of the prospect of an integrated European common market is emphasized; in the second (the EMP), the links being developed are essentially between the EC/EU and individual Maghrib states in the interests of promoting a closer but fundamentally unequal relationship with Europe. The suggestion of complementarity between the EU's strategy and the development of closer economic integration within the UAM is not borne out by the evidence.

The EMP initiative is undoubtedly one element of a broader European strategy—a "new" regionalism that differs little as far as the Maghrib is concerned from the neocolonialism of the previous 40 years except in the degree and extent to which it is now coordinated and orchestrated under the EU—to forge trade alliances with the open and weakened national economies on Europe's periphery, on terms favorable essentially to the EU. Its benefits to the Mediterranean and Maghrib countries involved are debatable, to say the least; it is my contention that they will prove negligible. Worse still, the new arrangements will further inhibit any effective national or regional development, let alone the establishment of a significant regional "bloc" capable of restoring a degree of balance in what is now a very unequal partnership.

If the declared purpose of the EMP is to create a free trade zone encompassing both flanks of the Mediterranean, it seems that the real objective is to create a safe "backyard" for Europe. But this, as Jon Marks points out, "could prove to be a high-risk strategy. Should Euro-Med policies fail, having left southern economies exposed by the accelerated liberalization necessary to make the Mediterranean free trade zone work, the new EU policy could actually contribute to increasing instability in the region. This would be a bitter irony, considering that one of the main (if not *the* most important) motivations for developing the policy has been to counter fears of instability in North Africa and the Middle East."[85]

Notes

1. Wilfrid Knapp, *North West Africa: A Political and Economic Survey* (Oxford: Oxford University Press, 1977), 1.
2. Knapp 1977, 234.
3. J. Walton and D. Seddon, *Free Markets and Food Riots: The Politics of Global Adjustment* (London: Blackwells, 1994), 175–82.
4. B. Etienne, "Le meilleur ciment de l'unite maghrebine a toujours ete la lutte contre le colonialisme," in R. Le Tourneau, et al., ed. *L'Unite Maghrebine—Dimensions et Perspectives* (Paris: CNRS, 1972).

5. F. Mellah, "Le Maghreb: integration economique et politique," Actes du Colloque "La Construction du Maghreb," Tunis, October 19–24, 1981, Universite of Tunis, Centre 'Etudes et de Recherches Economiques et Socialies, Tunis, Serie Sociologique, no. 9, 1983.
6. Toumi 1982, 39.
7. R. Le Tourneau, ed., *L'Unite Maghrebine—Dimensions et Perspectives* (Paris: CNRS, 1972), 110, cited in Spencer, C. "The Roots of Maghreb Unity—and Disunity," *Morocco—The Journal of the Society for Moroccan Studies,* Occasional Papers 1 (1994): 63–84.
8. Toumi 1982, 40, cited in Spencer 1994, 70.
9. *The Middle East and North Africa, 1989.* Europa Publicaions, London, 1989.
10. Davis S. Woolman, *Rebels in the Rif: Abd El Krim and the Rif Rebellion* (Stanford, CA: Stanford University Press, 1968).
11. J. Abun Nasr, *A History of the Maghrib* (Cambridge: Cambridge University Press, 1971), 366.
12. C. Spencer, "The Roots of Maghreb Unity—and Disunity," *Morocco—The Journal of the Society for Moroccan Studies,* Occasional Papers 1 (1994): 70.
13. J. P. Halstead, *Rebirth of a Nation: The Origins and Rise of Moroccan Nationalism, 1912–1944.* Harvard Middle Eastern Monograph Series (Cambridge, MA: Harvard University Press, 1967), 128. Shakib Arslan's *La Nation Arabe* was widely diffused during the 1930s.
14. Spencer 1994, 72.
15. Toumi 1982, 51.
16. Spencer 1994, 72.
17. Spencer 1994, 76.
18. Spencer 1994, 74.
19. Toumi 1982, cited in Spencer 1994, 82.
20. Charles-Andre Julien, *Le Maroc Face Aux Imperialismes* (Paris: Edition J. A., 1978), 165.
21. Le Tourneau 1972, 375.
22. Tony Hodges, *Western Sahara: The Roots of a Desert War* (Maryland: Scarecrow Press. 1983), 85.
23. D. Seddon, "The politics of 'adjustment' in Morocco," in B. Campbell & J. Loxley, eds., *Structural Adjustment in Africa* (London: Macmillan, 1989), 118.
24. Toumi 1982, 66.
25. Cited in Le Tourneau 1972, 468.
26. Knapp 1977, 11.
27. Documentation Marocaine, *Maghreb Arabe Uni. Conference de Tanger,* April 27–30, 1958, Presidence du Conseil, Information et Tourisme, Documentation Marocaine, Rabat, 1958.
28. Toumi 1982, 67.
29. Spencer 1994, 82.
30. Cited in Seddon 1989, 118.
31. Toumi 1982, 68.

32. Toumi 1982, 70.
33. Knapp 1977, 11.
34. Samir Amin, *The Maghreb in the Modern World: Algeria, Tunisia, Morocco* (London: Penguin Books, 1970), 211.
35. John Waterbury, *Commander of the Faithful* (London: Weidenfeld and Nicolson, 1970), 135.
36. Knapp 1977, 12.
37. Cited in Seddon 1989, 119.
38. Cited in Seddon 1989, 120.
39. Knapp 1977, 12.
40. Amin 1970, 218.
41. Amin 1970, 225.
42. H. Magdoff, "Imperialism without Colonies," in R. Owen and R. Sutcliffe, eds., *Studies in the Theory of Imperialism* (London: Longman, 1972), pp. 144–70.
43. L. Tsoukalis, "The EEC and the Mediterranean: is 'global' policy a misnomer?" *International Affairs* (July 1977): 422–38, 426.
44. A. Richards and J. Waterbury, *A Political Economy of the Middle East: State, Class, and Economic Development* (Boulder, CO: Westview Press, 1990), 390.
45. G. Joffe, "The development of the UMA and integration in the Western Arab world," in G. Nonneman, ed., *The Middle East and Europe: The Search for Stability and Integration* (London: Federal Trust for Education and Research, 1993), 203–218, 200.
46. Tsoukalis 1977, 429.
47. Tsoukalis 1977, 432.
48. Tsoukalis, *The European Community and its Mediterranean Enlargement* (London: George Allen and Unwin, 1981), 228.
49. Knapp 1977, 13.
50. Knapp 1977, 13.
51. Walton & Seddon 1994, chap. 6.
52. Seddon, 1989 passim.
53. Richards and Waterbury 1990, 245–56.
54. Richards and Waterbury 1990, 246.
55. D. Seddon, "The Political Economy of Mauritania: An Introduction," *Review of African Political Economy* 68 (1996): 197–214, 203.
56. Richards and Waterbury 1990, 253.
57. EIU 1984, 28–29.
58. D. Seddon, "Libya on Trial: the making and unmaking of a 'pariah state,'" *Review of African Political Economy,* forthcoming.
59. Seddon 1999.
60. Tsoukalis 1977, 426.
61. Joffe 1993, 1.
62. Seddon 1999.

63. D. Seddon, "Politics and the Gulf crisis: government and popular responses in the Maghrib," School of Development Studies Discussion Paper, no. 219, University of East Anglia, Norwich, 1991; also in H. Bresheeth and N. Yuval Davis, *The Gulf War and the New World Order* (London: Zed Books, 1991), 6.
64. M. Ould Mey, *Global Restructuring and Peripheral States: the Carrot and the Stick in Mauritania* (Maryland: Rowman & Littlefield Publishers, 1996).
65. Joffe 1993, 205.
66. Amnesty International.
67. Walton and Seddon 1994, 211–14.
68. *Europa,* Journal of the European Commission, Brussels, December 1989, p. 1.
69. Joffe 1993, 206.
70. J. Marks, "High Hopes and Low Motives: the New Euro-Mediterranean Partnership Initiative," *Mediterranean Politics* 1:1 (1996): 1.
71. Seddon 1999.
72. *The Courier,* 1993.
73. Seddon 1996 passim.
74. Joffe 1993, 206.
75. Joffe 1993, 205.
76. Marks 1996, 4.
77. European Commission 1994, 2–3.
78. Marks 1996, 3.
79. R. Z Lawrence, *Regionalism, Multilateralism and Deeper Integration* (Washington, D.C.: Brookings Institution, 1996).
80. J. Page and J. Underwood, "Growth, the Maghrib and Free Trade," in A. Galal and B. Hoekman, eds., *Regional Partners in Global Markets: Limits and Possibilities of the Euro-Med Agreements* (London: Centre for Economic Policy Research and Cairo: The Egyptian Center for Economic Studies, 1997), 115.
81. According to Page and Underwood 1997, 111.
82. D. K. Brown, A. V. Deardorff, and R. M. Stern, "Some Economic Effects of the Free Trade Agreement between Tunisia and the European Union," in A. Galal and B. Hoekman, eds., *Regional Partners in Global Markets: Limits and Possibilities of the Euro-Med Agreements* (London: Centre for Economic Policy Research and Cairo: The Egyptian Center for Economic Studies, 1997).
83. Page and Underwood 1997, 122.
84. Marks 1996.

Bibliography

Abd al-Rahman, Majdi. "*Al-Mumiya'* abr thalath tawarikh," *al-Qahira* 159 (February 1996): 220–230.

Abd al-Rahman, Sad. "Rawat al-mur'iyyat fi-l-Mumiya'," *al-Qahira* 159 (February 1996): 194–207.

Abd al-Salam, Shadi. "Counting the Years: Shadi Abd al-Salam's Words," *Discourse* 21:1 (Winter 1999): 127–139.

———"al-Iqa al-Misri al-batí'," *al-Qahira* 159 (February 1996): 244–247.

———"Yawm an tuhsa al-sanin," *al-Qahira* 159 (February 1996): 14–21.

Abrams, Philip. "Notes on the Difficulty of Studying the State." *Journal of Historical Sociology* 1:1 (1988): 58–89.

Abou-El-Hag, Rifaat Ali. *Formation of the Modern State.* Albany: State University of New York Press, 1991.

———. "An Agenda for Research in History: The History of Libya Between the Sixteenth and Nineteenth Centuries." *International Journal of Middle East Studies* 15 (1983).

———. "The Social ?? for the Past: Recent Arab Historiography of Ottoman Rule." *International Journal of Middle East Studies* 14:2 (1982).

Abu-Lughod, Janet. *Before European Hegemony.* Oxford: Oxford University Press, 1989.

Abun Nasr, J. *A History of the Maghrib.* Cambridge: Cambridge University Press, 1971.

Addi, Lhouari. "Religion et Politique dans le Nationalisme Algerien: Le Role des Oulemas." *Revue Mafgrebine d'Etudes Politiques et Religieuses,* Universite d'Oran #1, October 1988.

Adil, Muhammad Ibrahim. "al-Mumiya bayn al-tashkil wa-l-tajsid," *al-Qahira* 159 (February 1996): 186–193.

Ageron, Charles Robert. *Les algériens musulmans et la France, 1871–1919.* 2 vols. Paris: Presses Universitaire de France, 1968.

Aghrout, A., and K. Sutton. "Regional economic union in the Maghrib." *Journal of Modern African Studies,* 28:1, 115–139.

Ahmad, Aijaz. *In Theory: Classes, Nations, Literatures.* New York: Verso, 1992.

Ahmed, Leila. *Women and Gender in Islam: Historical Roots of a Modern Debate.* New Haven, CT: Yale University Press, 1992.

Ahmida, Ali Abdullatif. "Colonialism, State Formation and Civil Society in North Africa: Theoretical and Analytical Problems," *International Journal of Islamic and Arabic Studies* xi:i (1994).

Ahmida, Ali Abdullatif. *The Making of Modern Libya: State Formation, Colonization and Resistance, 1830–1932.* Albany: State University of New York Press, 1994.

Allan, A. J. *Libya: The Experience of Oil.* Boulder, CO: Westview Press, 1981.

———. *Libya Since Independence.* New York: St. Martin's Press, 1982.

Allen, Roger. *The Arabic Novel: An Historical And Critical Introduction.* Syracuse: University of Syracuse Press, 1982.

Alloula, Malek. *Colonial Harem.* Minneapolis: University of Minnesota Press, 1986.

Amin, Samir. *Eurocentrism.* New York: Monthly Review Press, 1989.

———. *Imperialism and Unequal Development.* New York: Monthly Review Press, 1977.

———. *The Maghreb in the Modern World: Algeria, Tunisia, Morocco.* London: Penguin Books, 1970.

Anderson, Benedict. *Imagined Communities: Reflections on the Origin and Spread of Nationalism.* Rev. ed. London: Verso, 1991.

Anderson, Lisa. "Policy-Making and Theory Building: American Political Science and the Islamic Middle East." In *Theory, Politics and the Arab World, Critical Responses.* Ed. Hisham Sharabi. London: Routledge, 1990, 52–80.

———. *The State and Social Transformation in Tunisia and Libya, 1830–1980.* Princeton, NJ: Princeton University Press, 1986.

Asad, Talal. *Genealogies of Religion.* Baltimore, MD: John Hopkins University Press, 1993.

———, ed. *Anthropology and the Colonial Encounter.* Atlantic Highlands, NJ: Humanities Press, 1988.

Ashcroft, Bill, Gareth Griffiths and Helen Tiffin. *The Empire Writes Back: Theory and Practice in Post-Colonial Literatures.* London: Routlege, 1989.

Ashour, Radwa. *Al-Rihla, Yawmiyyat Taliba Masriyya Fi America* (The Trip, Days of an Egyptian Student in America). Beirut: Dar al-Adab, 1983.

Association des Economistes Marocains. *Le Maroc et le monde arabe face a la CEE.* Casablanca: Editions Maghrebines, 1981.

Atiyya, Muhammad Ahmad. *Fi al-Adab al-Libi al-Hadith* (Of Modern Libyan Literature). Tripoli: Dar al-Kitab al-Arabi, 1973.

Avineri, Shlomo, ed. *Marx on Colonialism and Modernization.* Garden City, NY: Doubleday, 1968.

Azan, Paul. *L'armee Indigene Nord-Africaine.* Paris: Charles-Lavauzelle, 1925.

Ayoub, A. "Al-fulkluri al-Arabi fi marhalat ma Baad Al-Istaamar," Dirasat Arabiyya IV, February 1985, 94–110. Also presented at the Conference on Cultural Rights, Representations and Misrepresentations. Berkeley: Interdisciplinary Folklore Alliance, University of California, July 23, 1982.

———. "Al-Tahalil fi al-Mintaqa al-Filahiyya min al-Urdun" ("Lullabies in a Rural Area of Jordan: A Case Study"). *Majallat Rabitat al-Kuttab al-Urduniyyin.* Amman: 1981.

———. "Aspects Evolutifs de la Geste des Bani Hilal en Jordanie." In *Sirat Bani Hilal.* Tunis: MTE, 1985.

———. "Hilali Epic, Material and Memory." *Revue d'Histoire Maghrebine* 34:35 (1985).

———. "Notes a Propos des Revues d'Ethnologie en Tunisie et au Maghreb." *Hesiode* 1 (1991).

Bahloul, Joelle. *The Architecture of Memory.* Cambridge: Cambridge University Press, 1997.

Bakhtin, Mikhail. *The Dialogic Imagination.* Austin: University of Texas Press, 1981.

Bannour, H. "Identity as a Function of Language Choice." *In Identity, Culture and Discourse.* Tunis: l'Or du Temps, 1998.

Barbe, E. "The Barcelona Conference: Launching Pad of a Process." *Mediterranean Politics* 1:1 (1996).

Bazin, Andre. *What is Cinema?* Berkeley: University of California Press, 1967.

Belzoni, Giovanni. *Narrative of the Operations and Recent Discoveries within the Pyramids, Temples, Tombs and Excavations in Egypt and Nubia.* London: John Murray, 1820.

Bennoune, Karima. "S.O.S. Algeria." In *Faith and Freedom: Women's Human Rights in the Muslim World.* Mafnaz Afkhami. Syracuse, NY: Syracuse University Press, 1995.

Bennoune, Mahfoud. "The Origins of the Algerian Proletariat," *Dialectical Anthropology* 1 (May 1976).

———. "Socioeconomic-Economic Changes in Rural Algeria: 1983–1945: A Diachronic Analysis of Peasantry Under Colonialism," *Peasant News Letter* 5 (Jan.-Oct., 1975).

Berger, Monroe. "The Middle Class in the Arab World." In *The Middle East in Transition.* New York: Praeger, 1958.

Berkaoui, Mohamed. *Le Maroc et la Premiere Guere Mondiale.* Unpublished doctoral dissertation, Universite de Provence, 1987.

Berteil, Louis. *Baroud Pour Rome Italie 44.* Paris: Falmmarion, 1966.

Bhabha, Homi. "DissemiNation: Time, Narrative, and the Margins of a Modern Nation." *Nation and Narration.* Ed. Homi Bhabha. New York: Routledge, 1990.

———. "Signs Taken for Wonders." *The Post-Colonial Studies Reader.* Ed. Bill Ashcroft, Gareth Griffiths, and Helen Tiffin. New York: Routledge, 1995.

Binder, Leonard, ed. *The Study of the Middle East.* New York: Wiley Press, 1976.

Blaut, J. M. *The Colonizer Model of the World.* New York: The Guilford Press,1993.

Bodard, Lucien. *The Quicksand War: Prelude to Vietnam.* Boston: Little & Brown, 1967.

Bordeaux, Henry. *Henry de Bournazel.* Paris: Plon, 1935.

Boulata, Issa J. "Encounter between East and West: A Theme in Contemporary Arabic Novels." *Middle East Journal* (1976): 49–62.

Bourguiba, Habib. *La Tunisie et la France.* Paris: Julliard, 1954.

Brennan, Timothy. "The National Longing for Form." *In Nation and Narration.* Ed. Homi K. Bhabha. New York: Routledge, 1990.

Brown, D. K, A. V. Deardorff, and R. M. Stern. "Some Economic Effects of the Free Trade Agreement between Tunisia and the European Union." In *Regional Partners in Global Markets: Limits and Possibilities of the Euro-Med Agreements.* Ed. A. Galal and B. Hoekman. Centre for Economic Policy Research. London: Cairo: The Egyptian Center for Economic Studies, 1997.

Brown, L. Carl. "U.S.-Maghribi Relations: Model or Muddle?" In *Contemporary North Africa: Issues of Development and Integration.* Ed. Halim Barakat. Washington, DC: Georgetown University Center for Contemporary Arab Studies, 1985.

Brunchvig, R. "La Berberie Orientale" and "Etudes Berberes": Proceedings of the Conference of the Group of Berber Studies. Conducted by L. Galand. Paris: Ecole Pratique des Hautes Etudes, Sorbonne IV, 1947.

Brown, L. Carl and Matthew S. Gordon, eds. *Franco-Arab Encounters.* Beirut: American University of Beirut, 1996.

Bulbeck, Chilla. *Re-Orienting Western Feminisms: Women's Diversity in a Postcolonial World.* Cambridge: Cambridge University Press, 1998.

Burke III, Edmund. "The Image of the Moroccan State in French Ethnological Literature: New Light on the Origins of Lyautey's Berber Policy." In *Arabs and Berbers: From Tribe to Nation in North Africa.* Ed. Ernest Gellner and Charles Micaud. London: Duckworth, 1973, 175–199.

———. *Orientalism Observed: France and the Sociology of Islam.* Princeton, NJ: Princeton University Press, forthcoming.

———. "Orientalism and World History: Representing Middle Eastern Nationalism and Islamism in the Twentieth Century." *Theory and Society* 27:4 (August 1998): 489–507.

———. *Prelude to Protectorate in Morocco.* Chicago: University of Chicago Press, 1976.

———. *Struggle and Survival in the Modern Middle East.* Berkeley: University of California Press, 1993.

———. "Towards a History of the Maghrib." *Middle East Studies* 11:3 (October 1975): 306–323.

Burns, Bradford, "The Novel as History: A Reading Guide." In *Latin America.* Englewood Cliffs, NJ: Prentice Hall, 1994, 355–362.

Chatterjee, Partha. *Nationalist Thought in the Colonial World—A Derivative Discourse.* London: Zed Books, 1986.

———. *The Nation and Its Fragments.* Princeton, NJ: Princeton University Press, 1993.

Cherif, S. *L'Idee de l'Unite Maghrebine.* Unpublished memoir. Paris: Faculte de Droit et de Sciences Economiques de Paris, 1964.

Clancy-Smith, Julia. *Rebel and Saint: Muslim Notables, Populist Protest, Colonial Encounters.* (Algeria and Tunisia, 1800–1904). Berkeley: University of California Press, 1996.

Clancy-Smith, Julia, and Frances Gouda, eds. *Domesticating the Empire: Race, Gender and Family Life in French and Dutch Colonialism.* Charlottesville: University Press of Virginia, 1998.

Clifford, James. *The Predicament of Culture.* Cambridge MA: Harvard University Press, 1988.

Combs-Schilling, Elaine. *Sacred Performances: Islam, Sexuality, and Sacrifice.* New York : Columbia University Press, 1989.

Comor, Andre-Paul. *La Legion Etrangere.* Paris: P.U.F., 1992.

Connelly, Bridget. *Arab Folk Epic and Identity.* Berkeley: University of California Press, 1986.

Cooper, Frederick, and Ann Stoler. "Introduction: Tensions of Empire: Colonial Control and Visions of Rule." *American Ethnologist* 16:4 (1989).

Coudry, (Commandant). "L'Armee et la Mise en Valeur du Maroc." *Revue Historique de L'Armee,* Vol. 2, June 1952.

Crubelier, Maurice. *La Memoire des Francais: Recherche d'Histoire Culturelle.* Paris: Henry Veyrier, 1991.

Danziger, Raphael. *Abd al-Qadir and the Algerians.* New York: Holmes & Meier, 1977.

Davis, Eric. *Challenging Colonialism: Bank Misr and Egyptian Industrialization, 1921–1941.* Princeton, NJ: Princeton University Press, 1953.

De Agostini, Enrico. *Le Popolazionie Della Tripolitania.* Trans. Khalifa al-Tilisi. Beiruit: Dar al-Thaqafa, 1975.

De Leone, Enrico. *La Colonizzatione del Africa del Nord.* Padua: Cedam, 1960.

Deleuze, Gilles, and Felix Guattari. *Anti-Oedipus: Capitalism and Schizophrenia,* vol. 1. New York: Viking Press, 1985.

Denon, Vivant. *Travels in Upper and Lower Egypt, During the Campaigns of General Bonaparte.* London: J. Cundee, 1803.

Denoeux, Guilain. "Tunisie: Les Elections Presidentielles et Legislatives 20 Mars 1994." *Monde Arabe: Maghreb Machrek* 145 (July-Sept. 1994).

Diamond, Larry. "Economic Development and Democracy Reconsidered." *American Behavioral Scientist* 35:4 (March-June 1992).

Dirks, Nicholas, Geoff Eley, and Sherry B. Ortner, eds. *Culture/Power/History: A Reader in Contemporary Social Theory.* Princeton, NJ: Princeton University Press, 1994.

Dirks, Nicholas, ed. *Colonialism and Culture.* Ann Arbor: University of Michigan Press, 1994.

Djebar, Assia. *Fantasia: An Algerian Cavalcade.* Trans. Dorothy S. Blair. London: Quartet, 1985.

Documentation Marocaine, *Maghreb Arabe Uni. Conference de Tanger, 27–30 Avril 1958,* Presidence du Conseil, Information et Tourisme, Documentation Marocaine, Rabat, 1958.

Duclos, L-J. "The Berbers and the Rise of Moroccan Nationalism." In *Arabs and Berbers: From Tribe to Nation in North Africa.* Ed. E. A. Gellner and C. Micaud. London: Gerald Duckworth, 1973.

Ducray, Paul. "Les Tirailleurs Marocains, Leur Recrutement." C.H.E.A.M. no. 1143, 1947.

Dunn, John, ed. *Contemporary Crisis of the Nation State?* London: Blackwell, 1995.

Dunn, Ross E. *Resistance in the Desert: Moroccan Responses to French Imperialism, 1881–1912.* Madison: University of Wisconsin Press, 1978.

Eickelman, Dale. *The Middle East: An Anthropological Approach.* Englewood Cliffs, NJ: Prentice Hall, 1981.

Entelis, John P. *Culture and Counterculture in Moroccan Politics.* Boulder, CO: Westview Press, 1989.

Esposito, John L. ed. *Voices of Resurgent Islam.* New York: Oxford University Press, 1983.

Etienne, B. *"L'Unite maghrebine a l'epreuve des politiques etrangeres nationales." L'Unite Maghrebine—Dimensions et Perspectives.* Ed. R. Le Tourneau et al. Paris: CNRS, 1972.

Evans-Prichard, E. E. *The Sanusi of Cyrenaica.* Oxford: Clarendon Press, 1949.

Fagan, Brian M. *The Rape of the Nile: Tomb Robbers, Tourists, and Archaeologists in Egypt.* New York: Charles Scribner's Sons, 1975.

Fanon, Frantz. *The Wretched of the Earth.* New York: Grove Press, 1963.

Al-Faqih, Ahmad Ibrahim. *Al-Wasat* 815 (1995): 60–65.

———. *Al-Sharq al-Awsat.* 5391, September 1, 1993.

———. *Sa Ahibuka Madinatu Akhura* (I Shall Present You with Another City: Trilogy-I). London: Riad al-Rayys Books, 1991, 241 pp. paper.

———. *Hadhihi Tukhum Mamlakati* (These Are the Borders of My Kingdom: Trilogy-II). London: Riad al-Rayys Books, 1991, 166 pp. paper.

———. *Nafaq Tudiuhu Imra Wahida* (A Tunnel is Lit by a Woman: Trilogy-III). London: Riad al-Riyyas Books, 1991, 258 pp. paper.

———. *Al-Qariyya al-Qariyya, al-Ard al-Ard Wa Intihar Raid al-Fada* (The Village the Village, the Land the Land, and the Suicide of an Astronaut). Zawiyya: Mataba al-Wahda al-Arabiyya, 1993.

Al Fassi, A. The Independence Movements in North Africa. Washington D.C.: Octagon, 1954.

Fayad, Mona. "Male Writers Womanize the Nation." In *Aljadid: A Review and Record of Arab Culture and Arts* (Fall 1997).

Al-Faysal, Sammar Ruhi, *Dirasat Fi al-Riwaiya al Libiyya* (Studies in the Libyan Novel). Tripoli: Al-Munsha al-Ama Lil Nashir Wa al-Tawzi Wa Illan, 1983.

First, Ruth. *Libya.* Harmondsworth: Penguin, 1973.

Foucault, Michel. "Governmentality." In *The Foucault Effect: Studies in Governmentality.* Eds. C. Gordon, P. Miller and G. Burchell. Chicago: University of Chicago Press, 1991, 87–104.

France, Peter. *The Rape of Egypt: How the Europeans Stripped Egypt of Its Heritage.* London: Barrie & Jenkins, 1991.

Galal, A., and B. Hoekman. *Regional Partners in Global Markets: Limits and Possibilities of the Euro-Med Agreements.* London: Centre for Economic Policy Research, 1997.

Gauchet, Marcel. *Le Désenchantement du monde: Une historie politique de la religion.* Paris: Gallimard, 1985.

Gellner, Ernest. *Saints of the Atlas.* Chicago: University of Chicago Press, 1969.

Gendzier, Irene L. "Notes Towards a Reading of the Passing of Traditional Society." *Review of Middle East Studies* 5 (1978).

Ghazoul, Ferial J. "Al-Riwaiya al-Sufiyya Fi al-Adab al-Magharibi" ("The Sufi Novel In the Maghrib"). *ALIF* 17 (1997).

Ghoussoub, Mai. "Feminism—or the Eternal Masculine—in the Arab World." *New Left Review* 161 (January-February 1987).

———. "Reply to Hammami and Rieker." *New Left Review* 170 (July-August 1988): 107–109.

Gibb, H. A. R., and Harold Bowen. *Islamic Society and the West.* Oxford: Oxford University Press, 1950.

Gilsenan, Michael. *Recognizing Islam.* New York: Pantheon Books, 1982.

Goldzeiguer, Annie-Rey. *Le royaume arabe.* Algiers: SNED, 1977.

Gordon, David C. *North Africa's French Legacy, 1954–1962.* Cambridge, MA: Harvard University Press, 1964.

———. *Self-Determination and History in the Third World.* Princeton, NJ: Princeton University Press, 1971.

Goumeziane, Smail. *Le Mal Algerian: Economie Politique d'une Transition Inachevee.* Paris: Fayard, 1994.

Gran, Peter. *Islamic Roots of Capitalism: Egypt, 1760–1840.* Syracuse, NY: Syracuse University Press, 1998.

Green, William A. "Periodization in European and World History." *Journal of World History* 3:1 (Spring 1992).

Guha, Ranajit, and Gayatari Chakravorty Spivak, eds. *Selected Subaltern Studies.* New York: Oxford University Press, 1988.

Gunder Frank, André. *Latin America: Underdevelopment or Revolution.* New York: Monthly Review Press, 1970.

Habermas, Jurgen. *Legitimation Crisis.* Boston: Beacon Press, 1973.

Haggard, H. Rider. *She.* New York: Black's Readers Services, 1928.

Hajjar, Lisa, and Steve Niva, "(Re)Made in the USA: Middle East Studies in Global Era." *Middle East Report.* (October-December, 1997).

Halbwach, Maurice, *La Memoire Collective.* Paris: P.U.F., 1950.

Halpern, Manfred. *The Politics of Social Change in the Middle East and North Africa.* Princeton, NJ: Princeton University Press, 1963.

Halstead, J. P. *Rebirth of a Nation: The Origins and Rise of Moroccan Nationalism, 1912–1944.* Harvard Middle Eastern Monograph Series. Cambridge, MA: Harvard University Press, 1967.

Hamdi, Kamel. *Ali Benhadj, Abassi Madani, Mahfoud Nahnah, Abdellah Djaballh: Differents ou Differends?* Alger: Chihab, 1991.

Hamid el-Zien, Abdul. "Beyond Ideology and Theology: The Search For the Anthropology of Islam." *Annual Review of Anthropology* (1977).

Hammami, Reza, and Martina Rieker. "Feminist Orientalism and Orientalist Marxism." *New Left Review,* 93–106.

Hammoudi, Abdallah. *Master and Disciple: The Cultural Foundations of Moroccan Authoritarianism.* Chicago: University of Chicago Press, 1997.

———. *The Victim and Its Masks.* Chicago: University of Chicago Press, 1993.

Harakat, Alal al-Fasi. *AlIstiqlaliyah fi almaghrib al'Arabi.* English trans. H. Z. Nuseibeh. Independence Movements in Arab North Africa. Washington, D.C.: American Council for Learned Societies, 1954.

Harrison, James, "Migrants in the City of Tripoli." *Geographical Journal* 57 (July 1967): 415.

Al-Hashshayshi, Muhammad Bin Uthman. *Al-Adat wa al-Taqalid al-Tunusiyya.* Tunis: CERES, 1994.

Hassan. *Algerie: Histoire d'un Naufrage.* Paris: Le Seuil, 1996.

Hatem, Mervat. "Towards the Development of Post-Islamist and Post-Nationalist Feminist Discourses in the Middle East." In *Arab Women: Old Boundaries, New Frontiers.* Ed. Judith Tucker. Bloomington: Indiana University Press, 1993.

Held, David, et al., ed. *States and Societies.* New York: New York University Press, 1983.

Hennbelle, Guy. "Chadi Abdel Salam une brilliante exception." *Les Cinemas Africains en 1972.* Paris: Societe Africaine d'Edition, 1972.

———. "Hadith an *al-Mumiya*'." *Al-Qahira* 159 (February 1996): 242–243.

Henniker, Frederick. *Notes During a Visit to Egypt, Nubia, the Oasis Boeris, Mount Sinai and Jerusalem.* London: John Murray, 1824.

Hermassi, Elbaki. *Leadership and National Development in North Africa.* Berkeley: University of California, 1972.

Hidson, Michael C. *Arab Politics.* New Haven, CT: Yale University Press, 1927.

Al-Hibri, Azizah. "Islamic Constitutionalism and the Concept of Democracy." *Case Western Reserve Journal of International Law* 24:I (1992).

Hobsbawm, Eric. *Nations and Nationalism Since 1780.* Cambridge: Cambridge University Press, 1990.

Hodges, Tony. *Western Sahara: The Roots of a Desert War.* Maryland: Scarecrow Press, 1983.

Al-Horier, Abdalmolla S. "Social and Economic Transformation in the Libyan Hinterlands During the Second Half of the 19th Century: The Role of Sayyid Ahmad al-Sharif al-Sanusi." Ph.D. dissertation, UCLA, 1981.

Huntington, Samuel. *Political Order in Changing Societies.* New Haven, CT: Yale University Press, 1968.

———. *The Third Wave: Democratization in the Late Twentieth Century.* Norman: University of Oklahoma Press, 1991.

Husayn, Taha. *Mustaqbal al-thaqafa fi-Mis.* Cairo: Dar al-Ma'arif, 1996 [1938].

Ismail, Umar Ali ibn. *Inhiyar Hukim al-Usra alqaramanliyya fi libia, 1790–1835.* Tripoli: Maktabat al-Firjani, 1966.

Jalal al-Azm, Sadiq. "Orientalism and Orientalism in Reverse." *Race and Class* (Autumn 1985).

Jankowski, James, and Israel Gershoni. "Pharaonicism." In *Islam, and the Arabs: The Search for Egyptian Nationhood, 1900–1930.* New York: Oxford University Press, 1986, 164–190.

Jian, Lee Rong. "Mazij Min al-Hulm Wa al-Dhakira" ("A Mixture of Memory and Imagination"). *Adab Wa Naqd* (1992): 110–113.

Joffe, G. "The Development of the UMA and Integration in the Western Arab World." In *The Middle East and Europe: The Search for Stability and Integration.* Ed. G. Nonneman. London: Federal Trust for Education and Research, 1993, 203–218.

———. "The Western Arab World: background assessment." *The Middle East and Europe: The Search for Stability and Integration.* Ed. G. Nonneman. London: Federal Trust for Education and Research, 1993, 197–201.

Johnson, G. Wesley, ed. *Double Impact: France and Africa in the Age of Imperialism.* Westport, CT: Greenwood Press, 1985.

Johnson, Peter, and Judith Tucker. "Middle East Studies Network in the United States." *MERIP Reports* 5 (1975).

Jouin, Yves. "Le Comouflage des Goums Marocains Pendent la Periode d'Armistice." *Revue Historique de l'Armee,* Vol. 2, 1972.

Julien, Charles-Andre, *Le Maroc Face Aux Imperialismes.* Paris: Edition J. A., 1978.

———. "Colons francais et jeunes tunisiens." *Cahiers de Tunisie* (1971).

Kaak, O. *Al-Taqalid al-Shaabiyya.* Tunis: MTE, 1975.

Al-Kabir, Yasin. *Al-Muhajurun Fi Trabulus al-Gharb* (Immigrants to the City of Tripoli). Beirut: Mahad al-Inma al-Arabi, 1982.

Kamal, Ahmad. *Livre des perles enfouies et du mystere precieux au sujet des indications des cachettes, des trouvailles et des tresors.* Le Caire: Imprimerie de l'Institut Francais d'Archeologie Orientale, 1907.

Kaplan, Caren. "Resisting Autobiography: Out-Law Genres and Transnational Feminist Subjects." In *Decolonizing the Subject: The Politics of Gender in Women's Autobiography.* Ed. Sidonie Smith and Julia Watson. Minneapolis: University of Minnesota Press, 1992.

Karoui, Hachemi, and Ali Mahjoubi. *Quand Le vent s'est levé à l'ouest: Tunisie 1881 Impérialisme et Résistance.* Tunis: CERES, 1983.

Kepel, Gilles. "Islamism and the State in Algeria and Egypt." *Daedelus* 24 (Summer 1995).

Khater, Antoine. *Le Regime juridique de fouilles et des antiquites en Egypte.* Le Caire: Imprimerie de L'Institut Francais d'Archeologie Orientale, 1960.

Khatibi, Abdelkebir. *Love in Two Languages.* Trans. Richard Howard. Minneapolis: University of Minnesota Press, 1990.

Khouaja, A. *Al-Tahawwulat al-Ijtimaiyya min khilal al-Ughniya al-Shaabiyya.* Tunis: Alif, 1998.

King, John. "Abd al-Qadir: Nationalist or Theocrat?" *The Journal of Algerian Studies* 2 (1977): 6280.

King, Stephen J. *The Politics of Market Reform in Rural Tunisia.* Ph.D. dissertation, Princeton University, 1997.

Knapp, Wilfrid. *North West Africa: A Political and Economic Survey.* New York: Oxford University Press. 1977: 1.

Lacharef, Mohamed. *Algérie: nation et histoire.* Paris: Maspero, 1965.

Lacoste, Yves. "General Characteristics and Fundamental Structures of Medieval North Africa." *Economy and Society* 3:1 (1974).

Lacoste, Yves, André Noushi, and Jean Prenant. *L'Algérie Passé et Present.* Paris: Editions sociales, 1960.

Lane, Edward William. *An Account of Manners and Customs of the Modern Egyptians.* 1836; reprint. London: J. M. Dent, 1963.

Lanquar, R., et al. "Tourisme et Environnement en Mediterranee, Enjeux et Prospective, Le Plan Blue." *Economia* 8. Paris: 1996.

Laroui, Abdallah. *The History of the Maghrib.* Princeton, NJ: Princeton University Press, 1977.

———. *Les origines sociales et culturelles du nationalisme Marocain.* Paris: Maspero, 1977.

———. *The Crisis of the Arab Intellectual: Traditionalism or Historicism?* Trans. Diarmid Cammel. Berkeley: University of California Press, 1976.

Lawrence, R. Z. *Regionalism, Multilateralism and Deeper Integration.* Washington, D.C.: Brookings Institution, 1996.

Layoun, Mary N. *Travels of A Genre, The Modern Novel and Ideology.* Princeton, NJ: Princeton University Press, 1990.

Lazreg, Marnia. *The Eloquence of Silence: Algerian Women in Question.* New York: Routledge, 1994.

———. *The Emergence of Classes in Algeria: A Study of Colonialism and Socio-Political Change.* Boulder, CO: Westview Press, 1976.

———. "Feminism and Difference: The Perils of Writing as a Woman on Women in Algeria." In *Conflicts in Feminism.* Ed. Mirianne Hirsch and Evelyne Fox Keller. New York: Routledge, 1990.

Lebovics, Herbert. *True France: The Wars Over Cultural Identity, 1900–1945.* Ithaca, NY: Cornell University Press, 1992.

Le Gall, Michel and Kenneth Perkins, eds. *The Maghrib in Question: Essays in History and Historiography.* Austin: University of Texas Press, 1997.

Lerner, Daniel. *The Passing of Traditional Society: Modernizing the Middle East.* New York: Free Press, 1958.

Le Tourneau, R. ed. *L'Unite Maghrebine—Dimensions et Perspectives.* Paris: CNRS, 1972.

Lionnet, Francoise. "'Logiques metisses': Cultural Appropriation and Postcolonial Representations." *College Literature* 19.3–20.1 (October-February 1992–1993): 100–121.

Louis, A. *Bibliographie des Etudes de Sociologie et d'Entnographie en Tunisie.* 1962; reprint. Tunis: IBLA, 1965.

Lugand, (Lt. Col.). "Historique des Tirailleurs Marocains." *Revue Historique de l'Armee* 2 (June 1952).

Lukacs, Georg. *Studies in European Realism.* New York: The Universal Library, 1964.

Magdoff, H. "Imperialism without Colonies." In *Studies in the Theory of Imperialism.* Ed. R. Owen and R. Sutcliffe. London: Longman, 1972.

Makdisi, Saree S. "The Empire Renarrated: *Season of Migration to the North* and the Reinvention of the Present." *Critical Inquiry* 18:4 (Summer 1992): 804–820. Also in *Colonial Discourse and Post-Colonial Theory.* Ed. Patrick Williams and Laura Chrisman. New York: Columbia University Press, 1994.

Malley, Robert. *The Call from Algeria: Third Worldism, Revolution and the Turn to Islam.* Berkeley: University of California Press, 1996.

Marchal, A. "Le Musse au Service du Dialogue Culturel Euromediterraneen." In *Dialogue de Civilisations en Mediterranee.* Ed. M. Hadhri. Tunis: l'Or du Temps, 1997.

Mari, Salah, and Shadi Abd al-Salam. "Al-Bayt wa-l-khayma fi rif Idfu." *Al-Qahira* 159 (February 1996): 90–118.

Mariette-Bey, Auguste. *The Monuments of Upper Egypt.* Alexandria: A. Moures, 1877.

Marks, Jon. "High Hopes and Low Motives: The New Euro-Mediterranean Partnership Initiative." *Mediterranean Politics* 1:1 (1996).

Marx, Karl, and Friedrich Engels. *On Colonialism.* New York: International Publishers, 1972.

Al-Marzouki, Muhammad. *Al-Badwu fi Hillihim wa Tirhalihim.* Tunis: MTE, 1984.

Mayer, Ann Elizabeth. "Legislation in Defense of Arabo-Islamic Sexual Mores." *American Journal of Comparative Law* 27 (1979): 541–559.

———. "In Search of Sacred Law: The Meandering Course of Qadhafi's Legal Policy." In *Qadhafi's Libya, 1969–1994.* Ed. Dirk Vandewalle. New York: St. Martin's Press, 1995.

Mellah, F. "Le Maghreb: integration economique et politique," Actes du Colloque La Construction du Maghreb." Tunis, October 19–24, 1981, Universite de Tunis, Centre Etudes et de Recherches Economiques et Socialies, Tunis, Serie Sociologique, no. 9, 1983.

———. *De L'Unite Arabe—Essai d'Interpreetation Critique.* Paris: L'Harmattan, 1985.

Mernissi, Fatima. *Beyond the Veil: Male-Female Dynamics in Modern Muslim Society.* Bloomingdale: Indiana University Press, 1987.

———. *Dreams of Trespass: Tales of a Harem Girlhood.* Reading. MA: Addison-Wesley, 1994.

Micaud, C. A., ed. *Tunisia: The Politics of Modernization.* New York: Praeger, 1964.

Miliband, Ralph. "Marx and the State." In *Class Power and State Power.* London: Verso, 1983, 3–25.

Miller, Christopher L. "Nationalism as Resistance and Resistance to Nationalism in the Literature of Francophone Africa." Special Issue on Post/Colonial Conditions. *Yale French Studies* 82:1 (1993): 62–85.

Minutoli, Wolfradine Von. *Recollections of Egypt.* Philadelphia: Carey, Lea and Carey, 1827.

Mitchell, Timothy. *Colonizing Egypt.* Cambridge: Cambridge University Press, 1988.

Mohammed, Ellouni. "Politique Agricoles, Strategies Paysannes et Development Rural." *Bulletin De L'IRMC (*Spring 1994).

Mohanty, Chandra Talpade. "Under Western Eyes: Feminist Scholarship and Colonial Discourses." In *Colonial Discourse and Post-Colonial Theory: A Reader.* Ed. Patrick Williams and Laura Chrisman. New York: Columbia University Press, 1994.

Moore, Clement Henry. *Tunisia Since Independence: The Dynamics of One Party Government.* Berkeley, University of California Press, 1965.

Montagne, Robert. *Les Berberes et le Makhzen dans le Sud du Maroc.* Paris: Felix Alcan, 1930.
Morsy, Maghali. "Maghribi Unity in the Context of the Nation State: A Historian's Point of View." *Maghrib Review* 8:3–4 (1983).
———. *North Africa: From the Nile Valley to the Atlantic.* London: Longman, 1987.
Murdoch, H. Adlai. "Rewriting Writing: Identity, Exile and Renewal in Assia Djebar's *L'Amour, la fantasia.*" *Yale French Studies* 83:2 (1993): 71–92.
Mustafa, Ibrahim. *Al-Qawl al-mufid fi-athar al-Said.* Bulaq: Al-Matba a al-Kubra al-Amiriya bi-Bulaq, 1893.
Al-Muwaylihi, Muhammad. *Hadith 'Isa ibn Hisham.* Cairo: Dar al-Shab, n.d.
Al-Nahhas, Muridi. "Shadi Abd al-Salam: Shua min Misr." *Al-Qahira* 159 (February 1996): 7–12.
Najib, Ahmad. *Al-Athr al-jalil li-l-qudama' wadi al-Nil.* Bulaq: al-Matba a al-Kubra al- Amiriya bi-Bulaq, 1895.
Nandy, Ashis. *The Illegitimacy of Nationalism.* New Delhi: Oxford University Press, 1994.
———. *The Intimate Enemy: Loss and Recovery of Self under Colonialism.* New Delhi: Oxford University Press 1983.
Naudou, Jean. "Le Maroc en 1963." C.H.E.A.M. no. 3771.
Norden, Frederick Lewis. *Travels in Egypt and Nubia.* Ed. Peter Templeton. London: Lockyer Davis and Charles Reymers, 1758.
Nora, Pierre. *Les Lieux de Memoire.* Paris: Gallimard, 1986.
Nouschi, André. *Naissance du nationalisme algérien.* Paris: Editions Minuit, 1971.
"Orality." Seminar within the Department of History, University of Tunis. Tunis: UNESCO (Chaire UNESCO d'Archeologie et de Patrimoine), 1997 (annual).
Ould Mey, M. *Global Restructuring and Peripheral States: The Carrot and the Stick in Mauritania.* Maryland: Rowman & Littlefield Publishers, 1996.
Owen, Roger. "The Middle East in Eighteenth Century: An Islamic Society in Decline." *Review of Middle East Studies* 1 (1975): 101–112.
———. *The Middle East in the World Economy 1800–1914.* London: Methuen, 1981.
Page, J., and J. Underwood. "Growth, the Maghrib and Free Trade." In *Regional Partners in Global Markets: Limits and Possibilities of the Euro-Med Agreements.* Eds. A. Galal and B. Hoekman. London: Centre for Economic Policy Research; Cairo: The Egyptian Center for Economic Studies, 1997.
Payne, Rhys. "Economic Crisis of Policy Reform in the 1980s." In *Polity and Society in Contemporary North Africa: State, Culture, and Society in Arab North Africa.* Ed. Habib and Zartman. Boulder, CO: Westview Press, 1993.
Pococke, Richard. *A Description of the East, and Some Other Countries.* London: W. Bowyer, 1743.
Powell, John Duncan. "Peasant Society and Clientelist Politics." *American Political Science Review* 64 (June 1970).
Prakash, Gyan, ed. *After Colonialism: Imperial Histories and Postcolonial Displacements.* Princeton, NJ: Princeton University Press, 1995.

Prakash, Gyan. "Writing Post-Orientalist Histories of the Third World: Perspectives from Indian Historiography." *Comparative Study of Society and History* 32:2 (1990).

Prochaska, David. "History as Literature, Literature as History: Cayagous of Algeria." *American Historical Review* (December 1996).

Al-Qadhdhafi, Muammar. *Al-Qariyya al-Qariyya, al-Ard al-Ard Wa Intihar Raid al-Fada* (The Village the Village, the Land the Land, and the Suicide of an Astronaut). Zawiyya: Mataba al-Wahda al-Arabiyya, 1993.

Al-Qayadi, Sharifa. *Min Awraqi al-Khasa* (*From My Private Papers*). Tripoli: Al Mun sha al-Ama Lil Nashir wa Tawzi Wa Illan, 1986.

Radwan, Samir, Vali Jamal, and Ajit Ghose. *Tunisia: Rural Labour and Structural Transformation.* London: Routledge, 1991.

De Raynaud, Pelissier, et al. *Exploration scientifique de l'Algérie pendant les années 1840, 1841, 1842, publiés par l'ordre du gouvernement.* 39 vols. Paris: Imprimerie nationale, 1844–1867.

Reid, Donald. "Indigenous Egyptology: The Decolonization of a Profession." *Journal of the American Oriental Society* 105:2 (1985): 233–46.

Reid, Donald Malcolm. "Nationalizing the Paranoiac Past: Egyptology, Imperialism, and Egyptian Nationalism, 1922–1952." In *Rethinking Nationalism in the Arab Middle East.* Ed. James Jankowski and Israel Gershoni. New York: Columbia University Press, 1997, 127–149.

Richards, A., and J. Waterbury. *A Political Economy of the Middle East: State, Class and Economic Development.* Boulder, CO: Westview Press, 1990.

Rivet, Daniel. *Lyautey et l'Institution du Protectorat Francais au Maroc,* 1912–1925. Vol. 2. Paris: L'Harmattan, 1988.

Robin, Joseph. *L'insurrection de la Grande Kabylie en 1871.* Paris: Lavauzelle, 1901.

Ross, Kristin. *Fast Cars, Clean Bodies: Decolonization and the Reordering of French Culture.* Cambridge, MA: MIT Press, 1995.

Rousso, Henry. *Le syndrome de Vichy.* Paris: Seuil, 1990.

Saad, Ahmad Sadiq. *Tarikh Misr al-Ijtimai wa al-Iqtisadi, fi dawu al Mamat al-Asyawi lil Intaj* (Egypt's Social and Economic History in Light of the Asiatic Mode of Production). Beirut: Dar Ibn Khaldun, 1979.

Sabbagh, Suha. "The Debate on Arab Women." In *Arab Women: Between Defiance and Restraint.* Ed. Suha Sabbagh. Brooklyn: Olive Branch Press, 1996.

Sahli, Muhammed. *Decoloniser l'Histoire: Introduction a L'Histoire du Maghreb.* Paris: F. Maspero, 1965.

Said, Edward W. *Covering Islam.* London: Routledge and Kegan Paul, 1981.

———. *Culture and Imperialism.* New York: Vintage Books, 1993.

———. *Orientalism.* New York: Pantheon, 1978.

Salkin, Yves. *Histoire des Goums Marocains.* Vol. *2.* Paris: La Koumia, 1989.

Al-Salamuni, Sami. "Hìwar lam yunshir fi hiyat Shadi." *Al-Qahira* 159 (February 1996): 344–352.

Santucci, J. C. "L'unification mghrebine: realisations institutionelles et obstacles politiques." In *L'Unite Maghrebine-Dimensions et Perspectives.* Ed. R. Le Tourneau. Paris: CNRS, 1972.

Seddon, David. "Economic Anthropology or Political Economy: Approaches to the Analysis of Pre-Capitalist Formation in the Maghrib." In *The New Economic Anthropology.* Ed. John Calmer. London: Macmillan Press, 1978.

———. "Libya on Trial: the making and unmaking of a 'pariah state.'" *Review of African Political Economy,* forthcoming.

———. *Moroccan Peasants: A Century of Change in the Eastern Rif 1879–1970.* Kent, England: Dawson, 1981.

———. "The Political Economy of Mauritania: An Introduction." *Review of African Political Economy* 68 (1996): 197–214.

———. "The Politics of 'Adjustment' in Morocco." In *Structural Adjustment in Africa.* Ed. B. Campbell and J. Loxley. London: Macmillan, 1989.

———. "Politics and the Gulf Crisis: Government and Popular Responses in the Maghrib." School of Development Studies Discussion Paper, no. 219. Norwich: University of East Anglia, 1991. Also in *The Gulf War and the New World Order.* Ed. H. Bresheeth and N. Yuval Davis. London: Zed Books, 1991, 104–116.

———. "Unequal Partnership: Europe, the Maghrib and the New Regionalism." In *Regionalism Across the North-South Divide: State Strategies and Globalization.* Ed. J. Grugel and W. Hout. London: Routledge, 1999, 134–51.

Schneider, David. *A Critique of the Concept of Kinship.* Ann Arbor: University of Michigan Press, 1984.

Shafiq, Viola. "Al-Bahth an al-Hawiyya." *Al-Qahira* 159 (February 1996): 118–120.

Sharabi, Hisham, ed. *Theory, Politics, and the Arab World.* New York: Routledge, 1990.

Sherer, Moyle. *Scenes and Impressions in Egypt and in Italy.* London: Longman, Hurst, Rees, Orme, Brown and Green, 1824.

Simmons, John. "Land Reform in Tunisia." *USAID Country Paper,* 1970.

Sivan, Emmanuel. *Communisme et nationalisme en algérie 1920–1962.* Paris: Fondation Nationale de Sciences Politiques, 1976.

Slyomovics, Susan. *The Merchant of Art: An Egyptian Hilali Oral Epic Poet in Performance.* Vol. 120. University of California Publications in Modern Philology, 1987.

Sommer, Doris. *Foundational Fictions: The National Romances of Latin America.* Berkeley: The University of California Press, 1991.

Sonnini, Charles Nicolas Sigisbert Sonnini de Manoncourt. *Travels in Upper and Lower Egypt: Undertaken by Order of the Old Government of France.* London: John Stockdale, 1799.

Spencer, C. "The Roots of Maghrib Unity—and Disunity." *Morocco: The Journal of the Society for Moroccan Studies, Occasional Papers* 1 (1994): 63–84.

Saulay, Jean. *Histoire des Goums Marocains.* Vol. 1. Paris: La Koumia, 1985.

Spillmann, Georges. "Les Goums Mixtes Marocains." *Revue Historique de l'Armee* 2 (June 1952).

Stephens, John Lloyd. *Incidents of Travel in Egypt, Arabia Petraea and the Holy Land.* Norman: University of Oklahoma Press, 1970 [1835].

Stoler, Ann L., and Frederick Cooper, eds. *Tensions of Empire.* Berkeley: University of California Press, 1997.

Taussig, Michael. "Maleficium: State Fetishism." In *Fetishism as Cultural Discourse.* Ed. E. Apter and W. Pietz. Ithaca, NY: Cornell University Press, 1993: 217–247.

Thomas, Paul, and David Lloyd. *Culture and the State.* New York: Routledge, 1998.

Thompson, Scott. *Sir Gardner Wilkinson and His Circle.* Austin: University of Texas Press, 1997.

Thoraval, Yves. *Regards sur le Cinema Ègyptien.* Beirut: Dar el-Machreq Editeurs, 1975.

Tlili, Béchir. *Les rapports culturels et ideologiques entre l'Orient et l'Occident, en Tunisie au XIXeme siecle, (1830–1880).* Tunis: Universite de Tunis, 1974.

Tocqueville, Alexis de. "The European Revolution." In *Correspondence with Gobineau.* Ed. and Trans. John Lukacs. Westport, CT: Greenwood Press, 1974.

———. *Oeuvres complètes.* V, 2:217.

Touaba, Noureddine. *Wajibat Al Mar'a Fi'l Kitab Wal Sunn.* 3rd ed. Qasantina: Daar Al Baath, 1989.

Touati, Amine. *Les Islamistes a L'Assaut du Pouvoir.* Paris: L'Harmattan, 1995.

Tsoukalis, L. "The EEC and the Mediterranean: Is 'Global' Policy a Misnomer?" *International Affairs* (July 1977): 422–438.

———. *The European Community and its Mediterranean Enlargement.* London: George Allen & Unwin, 1981.

Turin, Yvonne. *Affrontements culturels dans Algérie colonial: écoles, medecine, religion.* Paris: Maspero: 1971.

Turner, Bryan S. *Marx and the End of Orientalism.* London: George Allen and Unwin, 1978.

Twain, Mark. *The Innocents Abroad.* Oxford: Oxford University Press, 1996.

Udovitch, Avram, and Lucette Valensi. *Juifs en terre d'Islam: les communautés de Djerba.* Paris: Editions des archives contemporaines, 1984.

United Nations, Food and Agricultural Organization, *Etude Multidimentsionnelle et Comparative Des Regimes De Tenures Foncieres Communales Et Privees En Afrique: Les Cas de Tunisie,* 1994.

Vandewalle, Dirk, and Karen Pfeifer. *North Africa: Development and Reform in a Changing Global Economy.* New York: St. Martin's Press, 1996.

Vandewalle, Dirk, ed. *Qadhafi's Libya, 1969–1994.* New York: St. Martin's Press, 1995.

Vatin, Jean Claude. *L'Algérie: histoire et politique.* Paris: Fondation nationale des sciences politiques, 1978.

———, ed. *Connaissances du Maghrib: sciences sociales et colonisation.* Paris: Editions du CNRS, 1984.

Valensi, Lucette. *Tunisian Peasants in the Eighteenth and Nineteenth Centuries.* Cambridge: Cambridge University Press, 1985.

Waisman, Carlos. "Capitalism, the Market, and Democracy." *American Behavioral Scientist* 35:4 (March-June 1992).

Wallerstein, Immanuel. "Eurocentrism and its Avatars: The Dilemma of Social Science." *New Left Review* 226 (November-December 1997): 2–9.

Wallerstein, Immanuel. *Historical Capitalism.* London: Verso, 1983.

———. "Open the Social Sciences." *Items: Social Science Research Council* 50:1 (March 1996).

Walton, J., and D. Seddon. *Free Markets and Food Riots: The Politics of Global Adjustment.* London: Blackwells, 1994.

Waterbury, Joan. "The Political Management of Economic Adjustment and Economic Reform." In *Fragile Coalitions: The Politics of Economic Adjustment.* Ed. Joan Nelson. Washington, D.C.: Overseas Development Council, 1989.

Waterbury, John. *Commander of the Faithful.* London: Weidenfeld and Nicolson, 1970.

Weygand, Jacques. *Goumier de l'Atlas.* Paris: Flammarion, 1954.

Wolf, Eric. *Europe and The People Without History.* Berkeley: University of California Press, 1982.

Woolman, Davis S. *Rebels in the Rif: Abd El Krim & the Rif Rebellion.* Stanford, CA: Stanford University Press, 1968.

Woodhull, Winifred. "Feminism and Islamic Tradition." *Studies in 20th Century Literature* 17:1 (1993): 27–44.

World Bank. "Republic of Tunisia Growth, Policies, and Poverty Alleviation." 1995, II. Annex C.3.

———. *Republic of Tunisia Poverty Alleviation Preserving Progress While Preparing for the Future.* Washington, D.C.: World Bank, 1995.

Yegenoglu, Meyda. *Colonial Fantasies: Towards a Feminist Reading of Orientalism.* Cambridge: Cambridge University Press, 1998.

Zartman, William. *Man, State and Society in the Contemporary Maghrib.* New York: Praeger, 1973.

———. *The Political Economy of Reform.* Boulder, CO: Lynne Rienner Publishers, 1991.

Zghal, Abdelkader. "Marxist and Weberian Intellectual Traditions and the Social Structures of the Middle East." *International Review of Modern Sociology* 12 (January-June 1982).

Zubaida, Sami. *Islam, The People and The State.* London: Routledge, 1989.

Zuckert, Catherine. "Why Political Scientists Want to Study Literature." *PC: Political Science and Politics* XXVIII:2 (June 1995): 189–190.

Index